PROTECTING CHILDREN AND ADULTS FROM ABUSE AFTER SAVILE

of related interest

Child Sexual Exploitation After Rotherham
Understanding the Consequences and Recommendations for Practice
Adele Gladman and Angie Heal
Forewords by T, Survivor of organised child sexual abuse in Rotherham and Anne Longfield, OBE, Children's Commissioner for England
ISBN 978 1 78592 027 1
eISBN 978 1 78450 276 8

Not My Shame
A Graphic Novel about Child Sexual Exploitation
T.O. Walker
ISBN 978 1 78592 184 1
eISBN 978 0 85701 294 4

Learning from Baby P
The politics of blame, fear and denial
Sharon Shoesmith
ISBN 978 1 78592 003 5
eISBN 978 1 78450 238 6

Working with the Trauma of Rape and Sexual Violence
A Guide for Professionals
Sue J. Daniels
Foreword by Ivan Tyrrell
ISBN 978 1 78592 111 7
eISBN 978 1 78450 375 8

Risk in Child Protection
Assessment Challenges and Frameworks for Practice
Martin C. Calder with Julie Archer
ISBN 978 1 84905 479 9
eISBN 978 0 85700 858 9

Challenging Child Protection
New Directions in Safeguarding Children
Edited by Lorraine Waterhouse and Janice McGhee
ISBN 978 1 84905 395 2
eISBN 978 0 85700 760 5

PROTECTING CHILDREN AND ADULTS FROM ABUSE AFTER SAVILE

What Organisations and Institutions Need to Do

EDITED BY
MARCUS EROOGA

Foreword by Steve Reeves

Jessica Kingsley *Publishers*
London and Philadelphia

First published in 2018
by Jessica Kingsley Publishers
73 Collier Street
London N1 9BE, UK
and
400 Market Street, Suite 400
Philadelphia, PA 19106, USA

www.jkp.com

Library of Congress Cataloging in Publication Data
Names: Erooga, Marcus, 1957- author.
Title: After Savile : child sexual abuse and what institutions and organizations need to learn / edited by Marcus Erooga.
Description: London ; Philadelphia : Jessica Kingsley Publishers, 2018.
Identifiers: LCCN 2017033327 | ISBN 9781785920936
Subjects: LCSH: Savile, Jimmy, 1926-2011. | Child sexual abuse--Great Britain. | Child welfare--Great Britain.
Classification: LCC HV6570.4.G7 A48 2018 | DDC 362.76--dc23
LC record available at https://lccn.loc.gov/2017033327

British Library Cataloguing in Publication Data
A CIP catalogue record for this book is available from the British Library

ISBN 978 1 78592 093 6
eISBN 978 1 78450 356 7

Printed and bound in Great Britain

To Caroline, without whom…

CONTENTS

THE CONTRIBUTORS

Karen Baker, LMSW, has served as the Director of the National Sexual Violence Resource Center (NSVRC) since its inception in 2000. She is also a Managing Partner of Raliance, a collaborative initiative comprised of three leading sexual violence prevention organisations in the United States. Ms Baker is the 2014 President of the National Coalition for the Prevention of Child Sexual Abuse and Exploitation. She served on the Board of Directors of the Association for the Treatment of Sexual Abusers (ATSA) from 2012–2017 and co-chairs the ATSA Prevention Committee.

Jon Brown is a qualified social worker with a Masters in Social Policy from the LSE. During his career as a probation officer and social worker he has been responsible for setting up and managing a range of sexual abuse services, including therapeutic services for child victims, services for children and young people with sexually harmful behaviour and services for adult sex offenders.

Between 2003 and 2007 Jon was Chair of NOTA, the National Organisation for the Treatment of Abusers (www.nota.co.uk); he remains on the Board and is now chair of the Prevention Committee. He is an Expert Advisor to NICE (National Institute for Health and Care Excellence; www.nice.org.uk) and a peer reviewer for the Economic and Social Research Council (www.esrc.ac.uk), the *Journal of Sexual Aggression* and the Australian Royal Commission into Child Sexual Abuse (www.childabuseroyalcommission.gov.au). With the Children's Commissioner for England, he was co-chair for the Office for the Children's Commissioner's Inquiry into Child Sexual Abuse in the Family Environment. He was an expert member of the NICE guideline development committee on work with children and young people with harmful sexual behaviour. Jon is a Board member of the Loudoun Trust, which promotes good practice in the field of treating and preventing the perpetration of child sexual abuse, a member of the International Working Group on best practice in the management of online offending and was a Board member of eNACSO, the European NGO Alliance for Child Safety Online (www.enacso.eu). He has authored a number of book chapters and is co-author of *Preventing Child Sexual Abuse: Towards a National Strategy for England* (NSPCC 2015) and editor of *Online Risk to Children: Impact, Protection and Prevention* (Wiley 2017).

Prior to taking up his current role with the NSPCC, Jon was Operational Director of Children's Services with Action for Children. From April 2010, he was Head of Strategy and Development with the NSPCC, helping to take forward the new organisational strategy in relation to sexual abuse, and since October 2015 he has been Head of Development and Impact. www.twitter.com/jonbrown46

Alice Cave is an Associate at London law firm Farrer and Co. Alice's practice spans employment, education and child protection law. She has advised schools on a number of sensitive child protection cases, as well as on regulatory compliance. Alice was a member of the Farrer and Co. team which acted as solicitors to the Independent Review by Hugh Davies QC into the criminal conduct of teacher William Vahey, with a particular focus on Southbank International School's selection, recruitment and vetting processes. Alice is a governor of a specialist school where she also holds the child protection brief.

Joanne Durkin is a qualified human resources professional with 12 years of experience working within a large acute NHS hospital. For many years Joanne worked predominantly within the recruitment function of the NHS. Joanne then moved to Organisational Development (OD) where she worked collaboratively with the NSPCC and Health Foundation to launch Value Based Interviewing and subsequent OD interventions with measurable success. Joanne also worked as Designated Safeguarding Officer providing training, advice, policy design and investigatory support on safeguarding issues within the NHS. Joanne earned her MA in Human Resource Management and is currently studying towards her PhD at the University of New England in Australia while continuing to work as an independent consultant specialising in safeguarding and organisational development interventions.

Adele Eastman is a Senior Associate at London law firm Farrer and Co. She is widely recognised as one of the leading lawyers in child protection, with expansive knowledge of social policy issues around this area, as well as children's mental health and school exclusion. After qualifying and working for several years at Farrer and Co., Adele spent four years at the Centre for Social Justice (CSJ) as a senior policy specialist. During this time, she gained extensive experience in the state education, child protection and mental health sectors. Adele researched and authored two CSJ policy reports: *No Excuses: A Review of Educational Exclusion* (2011), and *Enough is Enough: A Report on Child Protection and Mental Health Services for Children and Young People* (2014). Having re-joined Farrer and Co. in 2015, Adele specialises in child protection law.

Marcus Erooga is an independent safeguarding consultant and a Visiting Research Fellow at the Centre for Applied Childhood, Youth and Family Research, University of Huddersfield. He spent the majority of his employed career in various roles at the NSPCC as a practitioner, team manager and operational Assistant Director as well as in service, practice and policy development relating to child sexual abuse and sexual offending. He is a past Editor-in-Chief and current Associate Editor of the *Journal of Sexual Aggression* and past Chair of NOTA (the National Organisation for the Treatment of Abusers). Since 2012 he has been an independent Safeguarding Consultant working with a range of organisations including the NSPCC, Save the Children International (SCI), Save the Children UK (SCUK), the Methodist Independent Schools Trust and the Cognita schools organisation. He is an experienced trainer and presenter, having worked across the UK as well as Canada, Italy, Norway, Singapore and the USA. Marcus is the author of some 50 publications on child abuse and sex offender-related issues including four edited books, the most recent being *Creating Safer Organisations: Practical Steps to Prevent the Abuse of Children by Those Working with Them* (2012, Wiley). Marcus recently served as an expert witness on grooming for the Australian Royal Commission into Institutional Responses to Child Sexual Abuse, and was co-principal investigator (with Professor

Keith Kaufman) for a literature review on risk profiles for organisational abuse for the Australian Royal Commission.

Jane Foster is a consultant at the Child Protection Unit of London law firm Farrer and Co. Until July 2016 she was the Tri-Borough (Royal Borough of Kensington and Chelsea, London Borough of Hammersmith and Fulham and City of Westminster) Safe Organisations Manager and Local Authority Designated Officer (LADO). As Tri-Borough LADO and a coordinator of the Pan-London LADO network, Jane played a key role in keeping many of London's children safe and is a well-known figure to many private, public and third sector organisations working with children, including state and independent schools. Jane has considerable experience in delivering training to professionals working with children, having designed and delivered safeguarding training for local safeguarding children boards in both England and Wales. She is an accredited safer recruitment trainer and was a panel member on the 2016 serious case review relating to sexual offending by teacher William Vahey at Southbank International School.

Alyssa Glace is a graduate student in the Department of Psychology's Applied Community Psychology doctoral programme at Portland State University in Portland, Oregon, USA. Her research interests include sexual violence prevention and risk reduction among young adults and specifically on college campuses. Her research pays special attention to vulnerable students, including lesbian, gay, bisexual, transgender and queer students, as well as students with disabilities.

Keith L. Kaufman is a clinical community psychologist and a Professor of Psychology at Portland State University in Portland, Oregon, USA. He has chaired state prevention committees in Ohio and Oregon and co-chaired the committee that created Oregon's first statewide sexual violence prevention plan. Dr Kaufman is a member of the National Sexual Violence Resource Center's advisory board, the National Coalition to Prevent Child Sexual Abuse and Exploitation, Boys & Girls Clubs of America's National Safety Task Force, and Big Brothers Big Sisters' Nation Safety Committee. He is Past President of the Association for the Treatment of Sexual Abusers and recently received that organisation's Significant Lifetime Achievement Award. He is also a past recipient of the US Office of Juvenile Justice and Delinquency Prevention's Gould-Wysinger award for research excellence. Dr Kaufman has provided assessment and treatment to both child sexual abuse victims and juvenile sexual offenders as well as their families. He provides regular training and consultation focused on prevention and enhancing safety in organisational settings, including work with Big Brothers Big Sisters of America, Boys & Girls Clubs of America, the US Olympic Committee, Boy Scouts of America and the Committee for Children. Dr Kaufman has authored two books, a variety of book chapters and numerous research articles addressing sexual violence and sexual violence prevention. His most recent edited book is *Preventing Sexual Violence: A Practitioner's Sourcebook* (2010, NEARI Press). Dr Kaufman co-authored the first prevention chapter to be included in Interpol's member manual and offered their first prevention training. In 2016, he completed (with Marcus Erooga) a comprehensive review of the international literature on risk and protective factors related to child sexual abuse in institutions for the Australian Royal Commission into Institutional Responses to Child Sexual Abuse. Dr Kaufman has recently been awarded a $1 million US Department of Justice grant to develop a Campus Situational Prevention Approach to address campus sexual assault.

Anne-Marie McAlinden is Professor of Law and Criminal Justice and Director of Research in the School of Law at Queen's University Belfast. Her main research interests lie in the areas of the management of violent and sexual offenders, including 'grooming', institutional child abuse and restorative justice, where she has published extensively. Her first book, *The Shaming of Sexual Offenders: Risk, Retribution and Reintegration* (2007, Hart Publishing), was awarded the British Society of Criminology Book Prize 2008 for the best first sole-authored book published in the discipline in the previous year. Her second sole-authored monograph, *'Grooming' and the Sexual Abuse of Children: Institutional, Internet, and Familial Dimensions*, was published in December 2012 by Oxford University Press as part of the prestigious Clarendon Series in Criminology. She is currently working on a third monograph on children who display harmful sexual behaviour, to be published by Cambridge University Press in 2018. In March 2017, Anne-Marie gave evidence as an expert witness on 'grooming and entrapment' to the Australian Royal Commission into Institutional Responses to Child Sexual Abuse.

Erin McConnell is a graduate student in Applied Community Psychology at Portland State University, and holds a BS in Psychology from Purdue University. Her research interests include sexual violence prevention, college campus and community climate and bystander intervention. Erin is currently working as a member of Dr Keith Kaufman's team on the development of the Campus Situational Prevention Approach to improve campus safety.

Ethel Quayle is a Reader in Clinical Psychology, Director of Research in the School of Health in Social Science at the University of Edinburgh and Director of the COPINE research, which until September 2008 was based at University College Cork, Ireland. She is a clinical psychologist and as a practitioner worked with both sex offenders and their victims. For the last 18 years she has been conducting research in the area of technology-mediated crimes, collaborating internationally with government and non-government agencies in the context of research, policy and practice. Recent EU-funded research has focused on the function of coercive and non-coercive self-produced sexual images by adolescents and NSPCC-funded research on deterrence of possession of images. In addition to academic research activities she plays an active role in a number of government and non-government organisations.

Hilary Shaw is the Safeguarding and Child Protection Schools and Education Officer for the London Tri-Borough (Westminster City Council, Hammersmith and Fulham London Borough Council and Kensington and Chelsea London Borough Council) area.

Miranda Sitney is a graduate student at Portland State University's Applied Psychology doctoral programme (Portland, Oregon, USA). Her interests include juvenile sexual offending, juvenile delinquency and criminal recidivism.

David Smellie is a Partner at London law firm Farrer and Co. where he leads the Child Protection Unit and (until recently) Schools Group. He has been heavily involved in advising clients on child protection matters over the last 15 years and, as such, he has witnessed the positive impact of regulatory change over the period. David led the Farrer and Co. team which acted as solicitors to the independent review by Hugh Davies QC into the criminal conduct of William Vahey in 2014. David has also acted as child protection governor at three schools, and is recognised as the UK's top-ranked schools lawyer in Chambers UK.

Peter Spindler retired from the Metropolitan Police Service in 2015 as Commander responsible for murder, rape and child abuse. He had served 30 years in the Met, National Crime Squad and at Her Majesty's Inspectorate of Constabulary. In 2012 he initiated Operational Yewtree, the national investigation into non-current child abuse by high-profile figures. He now works as a senior policing advisor to various organisations both nationally and internationally and chairs the Westminster Abbey Safeguarding Reference Group. He lectures at a number of British universities and is an Honorary Fellow of the Institute of Criminal Justice Studies at the University of Portsmouth.

Kelly Stewart is a graduate student in the Department of Psychology's Applied Psychology doctoral programme at Portland State University (Portland, Oregon, USA). Her interests are in the areas of prevention related to routine activity theory and treatment of juvenile sex offenders.

Maria Strauss is a Senior Associate at London law firm Farrer and Co. She is a disputes resolution lawyer whose particular areas of expertise are child protection and employment law. She works extensively with schools, sports organisations, churches and charities, both on current safeguarding practice as well as non-recent allegations and public inquiry work. Maria is the safeguarding governor of two schools, and recently returned to Farrer and Co. following a five-month assignment with a Premier League football club.

Joan Tabachnick has, over the past 25 years, developed educational materials and innovative programmes for national, state and local organisations. Joan created the programming for Stop It Now! before starting her own consulting practice. Since then she has been the Director of NEARI Press, the executive director of MASOC (Massachusetts Adolescent Sex Offender Coalition) and is currently a fellow with the Department of Justice, SMART (Sex Offender Sentencing, Monitoring,

Apprehending, Registering, and Tracking) Office. Joan is also on the executive committee of the National Coalition to Prevent Child Sexual Abuse and Exploitation, is founding co-chair of ATSA's prevention committee and serves on a number of statewide task forces. Her recent written work includes a National Sexual Violence Resource publication entitled *Engaging Bystanders in Sexual Violence Prevention*, another entitled *Family Reunification after Child Sexual Abuse* and a publication through the Association for the Treatment of Sexual Abusers called *A Reasoned Approach: The Reshaping of Sex Offender Policy to Prevent Child Sexual Abuse.* Visit www.joantabachnick.com for more information.

Jane Wonnacott qualified as a social worker in 1979 and is Director of In-Trac Training and Consultancy and Jane Wonnacott Safeguarding Consultancy Limited. Jane has worked as an independent consultant and trainer for over 20 years with a focus on safeguarding children and has completed in excess of 150 serious case reviews, including Southbank International School and two reviews involving sexual abuse within nurseries. Jane has a particular interest in the impact of staff supervision on safeguarding practice and has published two books on this theme, as well as working with the late Tony Morrison to design and deliver national training programmes commissioned by central government.

Judith Zatkin is a fourth-year graduate student in the Department of Psychology's Applied Psychology doctoral programme at Portland State University (Portland, Oregon, USA). Her research interests include the use of Routine Activity Theory to explain sex offenders' patterns of perpetration as well as to inform primary prevention efforts.

FOREWORD

'That's just Jimmy...' sums up in a single, passing, phrase the grooming prowess of one of the most prolific and predatory sex offenders to come into public consciousness. For those born and brought up in the decades of Jimmy Savile's celebrity the dawn of the new period of his notoriety has been both unsettling and destabilising.

The notion that such a household name, whose fame was so resilient and all encompassing, could have been a notorious predator and sex offender would have seemed fantastical at almost any point prior to 2012. Yet now, as this book is published, it seems so inevitable, so obvious, so proper that we should all have known something sinister was just below the surface of so ubiquitous a figure.

I first met Marcus Erooga in 2009, when he was presenting the findings of his seminal NSPCC safer organisations research (Erooga, 2009). Marcus confessed that he had been unable to satisfy the appetite of some of the senior corporate leaders who had commissioned the research: to find the 'silver bullet' that would keep children safe, the single solution craved by us all. He told us the dynamics were too complex and the body of evidence too narrow to find that 'silver bullet' and more needed to be done to understand and explore the issues.

The irony is that the 'silver bullet' was so elusive back in 2009 because, in our seemingly unending task of keeping children safe, the 'silver bullet' is the work of Marcus and those like him. Our mission to protect children is fuelled by those who do not accept that the challenge is too great or the complexities too overwhelming. Work like this allows us to use evidence to challenge practice, and knowledge to tackle myths. It allows us to maintain a clear focus on the intrinsic value of children and our obligation to protect them.

This book contributes to that by bringing together academics and practitioners, each expert in their field, to help us understand not just what Savile did, but crucially what organisations did not do, that allowed him to offend for so long with such impunity. This is not a book about apportioning blame but rather contributing to solutions, offering perspectives for individuals and organisations on what practical action they can take to minimise risk in the settings in which they work.

Jimmy Savile remains a risk to children; the risk now is that he simply becomes a bogeyman, dismissed as anomalous and so extreme as to never be repeated. We risk allowing Savile's notoriety to exist in the same vacuum of scrutiny as his celebrity. Thanks to the tireless efforts of Marcus and his co-authors, who make the learning from both Savile's life and the events following his death accessible, we have a body of knowledge that transforms a modern-day bogeyman into an actionable agenda for change.

This book, like so much of Marcus's work, illuminates the challenges we face in protecting children and is a testament to the painstaking work and thought that has gone into it. For those of us charged with protecting children, it is books like this that make it possible.

Steve Reeves
Director of Child Safeguarding
Save the Children UK
July 2017

Reference

Erooga, M. (2009) *Towards Safer Organisations: Adults Who Pose a Risk to Children in the Workplace and Implications for Recruitment and Selection.* London: NSPCC. Accessed on 17 August 2017 at www.nspcc.org.uk/globalassets/documents/research-reports/towards-safer-organisations-2009-report.pdf

PREFACE

MARCUS EROOGA

It is difficult to write about Jimmy Savile and what we now know about him without using clichés. However, it seems true to say that his death and the subsequent revelations about his career of sexual abuse and sexual assaults have been catalysts for an extraordinary and largely unexpected series of developments in relation to understanding of, approaches to and attitudes towards sexual abuse in the UK.

These effects have been seen on multiple levels. At an individual level, for those abused by Savile there has been the belated opportunity to come forward and be believed about their experiences, as documented in the joint police/NSPCC report on Operation Yewtree (Gray and Watt, 2013) and the NSPCC's subsequent report (Exton and Thandi, 2013) based on focus groups with a sample of those reporting abuse by Savile. For those abused by other famous people there has been the opportunity not only to speak out but, in some cases, to see their abuser brought to justice, as in the cases of celebrities Stuart Hall, Rolf Harris and Max Clifford.

At the level of investigating sexual abuse cases, there has been fierce public debate about how non-recent cases should be approached, to the extent that a judge-led review was commissioned by the Metropolitan Police (Henriques, 2016) as well as changes in how current sexual abuse allegations should be conducted (CPS, 2013). In practical terms, the national police lead on child protection for the Association of Chief Police Officers, Simon Bailey, has described the Savile case as a 'watershed moment' (BBC, 2015) with police reporting a huge upsurge in reporting of non-recent abuse and of current cases (Laville, 2016) as victims of abuse become increasingly confident that their allegations will be listened to and investigated. Indeed, so far-reaching has been the Savile effect that Mr Bailey said that the rise in the level of investigations has been 'probably the greatest challenge the [police] service, in my view, other than terrorism, has seen in the 21st Century' (BBC, 2015). In addition, police services that had some formal involvement with Savile in relation to allegations during his life, notably West Yorkshire and Surrey police forces (Savell, 2013), and the Crown Prosecution Service (Levitt, 2013), have all been the subject of review and critical appraisal.

In other organisational settings, including the media, health and education, there have been scrutiny and review, with commitment for change in a number of organisations where Savile was believed to have abused including, principally, the BBC (Smith, 2016), Leeds General Hospital (Proctor *et al.*, 2014), Stoke Mandeville Hospital (Johnstone and Dent, 2015) and Broadmoor Special Hospital (Kirkup and Marshall, 2014), as Chapter 1 will outline.

More broadly, the Savile revelations formed the backdrop for the public pressure that has ultimately led to the establishment of the Independent Inquiry into Institutional Child Sexual Abuse (IICSA), established in its final form by then Home Secretary Theresa May in February 2015. Now chaired by Professor Alexis Jay, the Inquiry has powers to compel the attendance of witnesses and the production of evidence by institutions and individuals. Its remit is:

> to consider the extent to which State and non-State institutions have failed in their duty of care to protect children from sexual abuse and exploitation; to consider the extent to which those failings have since been addressed; to identify further action needed to address any failings identified; to consider the steps which it is necessary for State and non-State institutions to take in order to protect children from such abuse in future; and to publish a report with recommendations. (IICSA, 2015)

Described by Mrs May as a 'once-in-a-generation opportunity', the inquiry was established in the context of widespread public concern about Savile and the implications of revelations about his offending. Taken in the context of the truly terrible knowledge we now have about one man's lifetime of sexual offending, the facts are difficult to acknowledge, the implications challenge our view of society and the lessons are not easy to implement. In a newspaper article about the inquiry Mrs May wrote that 'once its work is done, we will never look at society in the same way again' (May, 2015).

It is sincerely to be hoped that she proves to be right and that the learning from Savile and the other cases considered by IICSA will serve to bring about meaningful change in the prevention of sexual violence, the protection of the public and prosecution of offenders – that we make the very best use of the courage it has taken for so many to speak out and maximise the effect of that once-in-a-generation opportunity.

The focus of this book

In total some 75 detailed reviews of practice, process and procedure, both at the time of Savile's abuse and currently, have been undertaken in settings where he was known to have visited, been involved or where it was thought he might have offended. It is those reports (listed in the Appendix) and the learning from them that give an unprecedented opportunity to understand how organisations and their processes work in practice to safeguard their staff and users and which form the starting point of this book.

The first two chapters provide the basis for the book, with the first outlining the facts as they are now known of Savile's offending and the inquiry processes that followed, whilst the second chapter identifies key themes and findings from those reports.

The rest of the book is divided into three further sections with chapters by authors with specific knowledge and expertise in relation to aspects of preventing sexual abuse, reflecting on the learning from the Savile inquiries and crucially identifying what practical steps can be taken to improve organisational safeguarding and minimise the incidence of abuse in the future.

Section 2 considers generalisable aspects of Savile's behaviour, using what we know about his behaviour and the organisational responses to him as the basis for three chapters on wider issues they illustrate.

Section 3 draws on recent thinking about preventing sexual abuse to outline preventive approaches, while Section 4 highlights specific learning for three key agencies which were the subject of reviews – the NHS, the police and education – and one, sport, which was not a setting where Savile is known to have abused but where the implications of the Savile case are all too clear.

Conclusion

In 1994 a report was published of the inquiry into the case of Frank Beck, the officer in charge of several children's homes in Leicestershire and convicted predatory sex offender who was later at the centre of Britain's then biggest investigation into institutional child abuse, between 1989 and 1991. The scale and extent of Beck's abuse seemed, at the time, unthinkable and surely unrepeatable. Presciently the inquiry Chair, Andrew Kirkwood, QC, wrote, 'It would not be wise for anyone to approach this Report on the basis that it all happened a long time ago and that nothing like it could ever happen again' (Kirkwood, 1993, para.1.45). That warning would seem equally applicable to the case of Jimmy Savile – the multiple inquiries into the organisations where Savile abused offer an unprecedented opportunity to learn from his truly terrible career of abuse and consider the key elements of organisational safeguarding. We ignore that learning at the peril of those who are vulnerable and who have a right to expect protection from the organisations that exist to serve them.

References

BBC (2015) 'Norfolk Chief Constable: Child Sex Abuse "Challenge of Century".' *BBC News*, 28 July. Accessed on 26 May 2016 at www.bbc.co.uk/news/uk-england-norfolk-33688374

Crown Prosecution Service (2013) *Guidelines on Prosecuting Cases of Child Sexual Abuse.* London: The Crown Prosecution Service. Accessed on 25 July 2016 at www.cps.gov.uk/legal/a_to_c/child_sexual_abuse

Exton, L. and Thandi, K. (2013) *Would They Actually Have Believed Me? A Focus Group Exploration of the Underreporting of Crimes by Jimmy Savile.* London: NSPCC. Accessed on 15 August 2017 at www.nspcc.org.uk/globalassets/documents/research-reports/would-they-actually-believed-me-savile-report.pdf

Gray, D. and Watt, P. (2013) *Giving Victims a Voice: Joint Report into Sexual Allegations Made against Jimmy Savile.* London: Metropolitan Police and NSPCC. Accessed on 11 August 2017 at www.nspcc.org.uk/globalassets/documents/research-reports/yewtree-report-giving-victims-voice-jimmy-savile.pdf

Henriques, R. (2016) *An Independent Review of the Metropolitan Police Service's Handling of Non-Recent Sexual Offence Investigations Alleged Against Persons of Public Prominence.* London: Metropolitan Police. Accessed on 24 September 2017 at http://news.met.police.uk/documents/report-independent-review-of-metropolitan-police-services-handling-of-non-recent-sexual-offence-investigations-61510

IICSA (2015) *Independent Inquiry into Child Sexual Abuse: Terms of Reference.* Accessed on 25 July 2016 at www.iicsa.org.uk/terms-reference

Johnstone, A. and Dent, C. (2015) *Investigation into the Association of Jimmy Savile with Stoke Mandeville Hospital: A Report for Buckinghamshire Healthcare NHS Trust.* Amersham: Buckinghamshire Healthcare NHS Trust. Accessed on 12 August 2017 at www.speakingoutinvestigation.com/Downloads/Speaking%20out%20investigation/2902210_Investigation%20into%20the%20Association%20of%20Jimmy%20Savile%20with%20Stoke%20Mandeville%20Hospital.pdf

Kirkup, B. and Marshall, P. (2014) *Jimmy Savile Investigation. Broadmoor Hospital: Report to the West London Mental Health NHS Trust and the Department of Health.* London: West London Mental Health NHS Trust. Accessed on 11 August 2017 at www.gov.uk/government/publications/jimmy-savile-investigation-broadmoor-hospital

Kirkwood, A. (1993) *The Leicestershire Inquiry 1992: The Report of the Inquiry into Aspects of the Management of Children's Homes in Leicestershire between 1973 and 1986.* Leicester: Leicestershire County Council.

Laville, S. (2016) 'Police Expect 30,000 New Child Abuse Reports from Goddard Inquiry.' *Guardian*, 19 May. Accessed on 25 July 2016 at www.theguardian.com/uk-news/2016/may/19/child-sex-abuse-police-expect-30000-goddard-inquiry-cases

Levitt, A. (2013) *In the Matter of the Late Jimmy Savile: Report to the Director of Public Prosecutions.* London: Crown Prosecution Service. Accessed on 11 August 2017 at www.cps.gov.uk/news/assets/uploads/files/savile_report.pdf

May, T. (2015) 'Child Abuse in the UK Runs Far Deeper Than You Know.' *Daily Telegraph*, 14 May. Accessed on 17 July 2017 at www.telegraph.co.uk/news/uknews/crime/11471282/Theresa-May-Child-abuse-in-the-UK-runs-far-deeper-than-you-know.html

Proctor, S., Galloway, R., Chaloner, R., Jones, C. and Thompson, D. (2014) *The Report of the Investigation into Matters Relating to Savile at Leeds Teaching Hospitals NHS Trust, Leeds*. Leeds: Leeds Teaching Hospitals NHS Trust. Accessed on 11 August 2017 at www.leedsth.nhs.uk/assets/Uploads/40482-2901955-Libra-Executive-SUMMARY-accessible2.pdf

Savell, J. (2013) *Report into Operation Ornament*. Guildford: Surrey Police.

Smith, J. (2016) *The Independent Review into the BBC's Culture and Practices during the Jimmy Savile and Stuart Hall Years*. London: BBC. Accessed on 11 August 2017 at www.bbc.co.uk/bbctrust/dame_janet_smith

Section 1

WHAT WE NOW KNOW ABOUT SAVILE

1

SAVILE'S SEXUAL OFFENDING

What Do We Know?

MARCUS EROOGA

> A legend and a one off there's no mystery to unravel/
> This miner, DJ, friend to all/ Was simply Jimmy Savile
>
> (Excerpt from Savile's headstone)

Introduction

When he was found dead at his home in Roundhay, Leeds, aged 84, on 29 October 2011, much-loved 'great British eccentric' Jimmy Savile was a national celebrity, fundraiser and for many an icon of their childhoods, having been a ubiquitous presence on British television screens during the 1960s, 1970s and 1980s.

In recognition of his contribution to public causes he was awarded an OBE in 1971, knighted by the Queen in 1990, and the same year was made a Knight Commander of St Gregory the Great by Pope John Paul II. This latter honour is made in recognition of 'an individual's pre-eminent service to their faith, community or the work of the Holy See on a local, national and international level' (Association of Papal Orders in Great Britain, 2013).

Jimmy Savile first came to public prominence as a DJ at a commercial radio station (unique in the UK at that time), Radio Luxembourg, from 1958 to 1967, although his public prominence really began with his BBC career, described below.

From the 1960s onwards, Savile began a parallel career of apparently philanthropic activity, fundraising and volunteering for 'good causes'. As a result, he came into contact with a wide range of hospitals and schools and, it is now known, used his contact with those settings, and his status in them, to abuse.

He wrote two books: his autobiography *As It Happens*, in 1974, reissued in paperback as *Love Is an Uphill Thing* in 1976, and a book about his religious faith, *God'll Fix It* (Savile, 1979). He also features on the front cover and in the introduction of *Benjamin Rabbit and the Stranger Danger* (Keller, 1985), a book for young children about keeping safe from strangers, and on the cover of *Other People's Children: A Handbook for Child Minders* (Jackson, 1976), published by the BBC.

When Jimmy Savile died, no one, even had they been aware of the extent of his lifetime of sexual offending, could have anticipated the extraordinary series of events that would follow. Some 75 inquiries into his activities have been undertaken, a range of other leading public figures have been prosecuted and imprisoned for non-recent sexual abuse as a result of police Operation Yewtree, and a wide-ranging inquiry that goes far beyond Savile, the Independent Inquiry into Institutional Child Sexual Abuse (IICSA, 2015), now chaired by Professor Alexis Jay, has been instituted.

The impact and significance of the revelations about him go far beyond Savile the man, and this is not a book about Jimmy Savile the person. His psychology, his motivation, his inner life are not the subject of this book. It is, to some extent, a book about Savile the sex offender, insofar as it is instructive to understand how his behaviour, his methods and his presentation of himself enabled him to become someone who, what then Metropolitan Police Commander Peter Spindler, author of Chapter 9, described in a phrase that lodged in the national consciousness, 'groomed the nation' (BBC, 2013).

More directly, this book is a consideration of what we can learn from the knowledge that we now have about the way in which a high-profile, trusted and widely respected individual, who lived much of his life in the public eye, could so effectively use his status to facilitate six decades of sexual abuse of girls, boys, men and women. That he did so and not only remained at liberty but, at the time of his death, was considered a 'national treasure', to the extent that the streets of his home city of Leeds were lined by the public to view his funeral cortege on the way to Leeds Cathedral, makes it all the more extraordinary.

This chapter will outline what is now known about relevant key events during Savile's career and developments following his death, and explains the context to the inquiries subsequently conducted into his contact with various organisations, including consideration of why the majority of allegations were not made during Savile's life.

It is a partner to the next chapter, which considers themes from the findings of those inquiries as they relate to institutional abuse, and together form the basis of the remainder of the book, where individual authors draw on the inquiries and other research to identify key learning about the prevention of sexual violence.

This chapter first outlines Savile's contacts with, and alleged offending in, the range of settings where the majority of his abuse is now believed to have been committed: the BBC, Broadmoor, Stoke Mandeville, the Leeds Teaching Hospitals and Duncroft School. Next, it outlines other allegations about Savile's abuse based on the findings of police Operation Yewtree and the handling of allegations made about Savile during his life. The chapter then addresses the issue of what survivors have said were the reasons for not disclosing at the time and what enabled them to do so after his death, and ends with subsequent developments and a conclusion.

Savile's alleged offending across the BBC and various health and education settings

From the various reports published,[1] it is apparent that Savile is believed to have committed sexual offences in a range of settings linked to his TV and radio career and associated philanthropic, fund-raising and volunteering activities. What is now known about the extent of

---

1 As the starting point for this book is the learning from the various inquiries relating to Savile and actions which followed the revelation of his offending, a list of the published inquiries is provided as a resource in the Appendix.

his offending will be considered in relation to the primary settings where he is alleged to have offended: the BBC, Broadmoor, Stoke Mandeville, the Leeds Teaching Hospitals and Duncroft School. All the information below is derived from the inquiries commissioned following his death.

The BBC

In October 2012, following the widespread revelations about Savile's behaviour, the BBC invited Dame Janet Smith DBE – a former High Court Judge who conducted the inquiry published in 2003 into the murders by GP Harold Shipman of his patients – to investigate Savile's sexual misconduct and the BBC's awareness of it. After she was commissioned it was established that another presenter, Stuart Hall, had also committed multiple sexual offences against young people, some at the BBC. Due to a potential conflict of interest for Dame Janet, a freestanding investigation, led by retired High Court Judge Dame Linda Dobbs, addressed Stuart Hall's conduct at the BBC and the report was published as part of the Smith review. The final three-volume report was published in February 2016 (Smith, 2016), publication having been delayed at the request of the police to avoid the possibility of prejudicing ongoing police investigations relating to other suspects.

The report records that, following guest appearances in the late 1950s and early 1960s, Savile's career at the BBC began on 1 January 1964 when he presented the first edition of *Top of the Pops* and continued as a regular presenter of *Top of the Pops* until 1984.

Savile joined BBC Radio 1 in 1968, the year after the station went on air. In 1969, he began to present *Speakeasy*, a joint production between BBC Radio 1 and the BBC's Religious Broadcasting Department. This was a discussion programme for young people about the moral and ethical questions of the time and ran until about 1977. *Jim'll Fix It*, a 'wish fulfilment' programme for young people, was launched in 1975 with Savile as its presenter. This hugely successful Saturday evening family viewing ran until 1994, attracting up to 16.5 million viewers, and brought Savile enormous fame.

In 1977, the National Viewers and Listeners Association, run by social conservative campaigner Mary Whitehouse, presented Savile with an award for 'wholesome family entertainment'. More than any other programme, *Jim'll Fix It* led to Savile being viewed as the 'favourite uncle to the nation's children' (Nikkhah and Malnick, 2011). Savile's role as a regular BBC television presenter ended in 1994 with the demise of *Jim'll Fix It*. In the 1970s he had made a series of public information films on road safety, from which came the tagline 'Clunk Click Every Trip', promoting the use of seatbelts. He was brought back to co-present the final *Top of the Pops* programme on 30 July 2006, an occasion that gave rise to one of the allegations of sexual assault later made to police.

He revelled in his celebrity status, writing in his autobiography of becoming the first DJ presenter of *Top of the Pops* in 1964: 'And so ended the springtime of my pop career. Here then started the 100 degree summer with no clouds to cover the burning brilliance of total recognition by, eventually, nearly all this country's 53 million people' (Savile, 1974, p.74).

In addition to his core work on BBC Television and Radio, Savile made countless guest appearances on a wide variety of popular family viewing programmes, including, famously, *In the Psychiatrist's Chair* with Consultant Psychiatrist Anthony Clare in 1991 and a TV documentary in 2000 presented by Louis Theroux, in which Savile acknowledged the rumours about him being a paedophile, but denied them.

He also regularly featured on news or current affairs programmes, usually in connection with fundraising events such as marathon running or long-distance walks. He was seen with members of the Royal Family at the opening of the new wing of Stoke Mandeville Hospital for which he had raised money and was pictured outside Buckingham Palace after receiving his OBE. In effect, he was almost constantly in the public eye, standing out both by his ubiquity and distinctive presentation in an era before the 'instant celebrity' of recent times (Marshall, 2007).

ALLEGED OFFENDING RELATED TO THE BBC

From her inquiries Dame Janet Smith concludes that 72 people made credible allegations of inappropriate behaviour or offences by Savile. Included are some accounts of what she considers lawful consensual conduct where Savile's conduct was inappropriate because the women concerned were decades younger than him and almost certainly under the influence of his celebrity. They also include six incidents that did not entail any physical contact, but where Savile pestered them or used lewd or insulting words or gestures (Smith, 2016, para.5.337).

Of the 72 victims, 57 are female and 15 are male. Twenty-one of the female victims were aged under 16 years, and 36 victims were aged 16 years and over; 13 of the male victims were under 16 years and two were 16 years and over; eight victims were raped (six female and two male) and one female victim was the subject of an attempted rape; 47 victims were the subject of indecent/sexual assault excluding rape (34 female and 13 male); *Top of the Pops* and *Jim'll Fix It* were the programmes at which victims were most frequently assaulted (with 19 assaults in relation to *Top of the Pops* and 17 in relation to *Jim'll Fix It*). The majority of victims, 44, were assaulted in the 1970s, 10 in the 1960s and 17 in the 1980s (Smith, 2016, para.5.336).

OFFENCE LOCATIONS

All except three of the most serious incidents of rape and attempted rape took place on Savile's own, as opposed to BBC, premises. The exceptions were a 13-year-old girl who was raped in what Smith thinks was probably a disused storeroom at BBC Lime Grove studios in 1959; a 10-year-old boy who was anally raped in Savile's dressing room at BBC Television Centre, London, in 1973; and a 10/11-year-old boy who was orally raped in Savile's dressing room at BBC Television Centre in 1976. Some of the more serious sexual assaults also took place on Savile's own premises – for example, a 14-year-old girl who was seriously sexually assaulted at Savile's London flat in 1975 (Smith, 2016, Appendix 6).

Smith states that Savile would 'gratify himself' whenever the opportunity arose and that the inquiry heard of incidents that took place in virtually every one of the BBC premises at which he worked. There was sexual touching while working on the set of *Top of the Pops* and *Jim'll Fix It* and, on at least one occasion in 1979, when he was actually on camera. She concludes, 'He seems never to have had any fear that any of [his victims] would report him' (Smith, 2016, para.5.338).

Health settings

Once the nature of Savile's contact with a range of health institutions became apparent, in January 2012 the Secretary of State for Health ordered inquiries into Savile's relationship with Leeds General, Stoke Mandeville and Broadmoor Hospitals. As more information emerged this was progressively widened to a total of 44 institutions, with the reports published in two tranches, the first 28 in June 2014 and the remaining 16 in February 2015. The inquiry reports were published on the Department of Health website (DoH, 2015). A report into Guy's and St Thomas' NHS Foundation Trust was published in January 2016.

The picture that emerges led the authors of the NHS inquiries overview report to comment that 'much of the story of Savile and his associations with NHS hospitals is unusual to the point of being scarcely credible' (Lampard and Marsden, 2015, para.4.4). In total, 177 women and men made allegations of abuse by Jimmy Savile, covering a period beginning in 1954 until just before his death in 2011. At least 72 people who gave evidence were children at the time of the abuse, the youngest only five years old. The allegations include rape, assault, indecent assault and inappropriate comments or advances.

Allegations were made in over 41 acute hospitals, almost a quarter of all NHS acute hospitals, as well as in five mental health trusts and two children's hospitals. Further investigations have been undertaken at a children's convalescent home, an ambulance service and a hospice.

This section outlines the findings in relation to Savile's sexual offending in the three health settings where he was most involved: Broadmoor Special Hospital, Stoke Mandeville and Leeds Teaching Hospitals (Leeds General Infirmary; St James's Hospital; Chapel Allerton Hospital; Seacroft Hospital).

BROADMOOR SPECIAL HOSPITAL, BERKSHIRE

Broadmoor is one of three high-security specialist psychiatric hospitals in England, housing mentally disordered people who have either been convicted or are facing prosecution for serious criminal offences. During the relevant period it also provided care and treatment for other men and women who presented significantly less risk.

The prevailing culture was strongly institutional, based on an underlying view that the hospital's principal function was custodial. Residents were 'inmates' rather than patients, regarded as criminals whose mental health happened to be impaired rather than there because their behaviour was the result of their mental health. Patient numbers more than halved in Savile's time from 821 in 1971 to 382 in 2001, while the number of nurses rose from 359 in 1971 to 620 in 2001 (Kirkup and Marshall, 2014).

SAVILE'S RELATIONSHIP WITH BROADMOOR

In 1968, Jimmy Savile made contact with the medical superintendent of the hospital to offer his services, having received fan mail from a number of patients, beginning an association with the hospital that lasted over three decades (Kirkup and Marshall, 2014).

His initial approach was apparently endorsed in order to improve staff and patient morale, and to improve public perception of the hospital. At some point during the next decade he was given accommodation at Broadmoor and use of keys, which allowed him unrestricted access to ward areas within the secure perimeter, described by the Medical Superintendent as 'the highest mark of trust the management can offer' (quoted by Kirkup and Marshall, 2014, para.6.4 from the *Reader's Digest*, November 1978). These enabled his access to ward areas, day rooms and patient rooms. The existence of alternative entrances to some wards and to the female area, and patchy implementation of security procedures by some staff, allowed him not only unsupervised access to some patient areas but to do so without the knowledge of those in charge.

Whilst some staff enforced strict security procedures and Savile had little access to their wards, other staff found him likeable, were more tolerant of his presence in patient areas and failed to enforce strict security and supervision. These staff controlled the wards that he would visit more frequently. His presentation to some staff was charming and persuasive, whilst at the same time he was described by others as grandiose, narcissistic, arrogant, manipulative and lacking in empathy. Many staff were convinced that he had close connections with senior managers and had the power to have them dismissed (Kirkup and Marshall, 2014).

Security systems and adherence to procedures were improved incrementally from 1968 to about 2004. Whilst his right to keys was not formally withdrawn until 2009, the use of personal keys was superseded by new security arrangements in 1998. Following his briefing on how these arrangements operated in 2004 he ceased to visit the hospital (Kirkup and Marshall, 2014).

SAVILE AND GOVERNANCE AT BROADMOOR

During the relevant period Broadmoor was the direct responsibility of the Department of Health and Social Security (DHSS). A Hospital Board was appointed from January 1987, with Savile in a non-executive position. Following continued industrial unrest with the Prison Officers Association (POA) trades union and a governmental restructure, a senior civil servant, Will Graham, took a closer interest in the operation of the three DHSS special hospitals (Broadmoor, Ashworth and Rampton) than his predecessor.

Mr Graham took the opportunity to introduce new management arrangements for the special hospitals, which in the case of Broadmoor included an interim 'Task Force' to manage the hospital in view of the urgent nature of problems there. Government ministers, including Edwina Currie, who briefly had the ministerial lead for mental health services, were briefed on these measures retrospectively. Savile met Mr Graham on his first visit to Broadmoor and they quickly formed a close working relationship. Mr Graham made Savile a leading member of the Broadmoor Task Force, with a direct managerial role in the hospital.

Savile also met Mrs Currie, at his request, when she visited another hospital. He reported having discovered widespread false overtime claims, occupation of staff residences by people not entitled to them and financial irregularities concerning the capital building project. He said he intended to use his knowledge of these to control the POA's activities by threatening to expose them to the press if the union would not cooperate with him.

Mrs Currie did not discourage him in this, although it would have meant tolerating alleged fraud in return for union cooperation. Indeed she said that 'he'd had a look at everything he could use to blackmail the POA… I thought it was a pretty classy piece of operation' (Kirkup and Marshall, 2014, para.7.14), and with her approval Savile ultimately became Chair of the Hospital Advisory Committee. There is little evidence that he did deal with the POA in the way he proposed to Mrs Currie or that there was a significant change in approach after his appointment.

The Hospital Advisory Committee was unusual in combining a range of roles, including a statutory responsibility as 'hospital manager' for certain categories of detained patients. This meant that Savile, a celebrity and fundraiser with no relevant experience, expertise or training, was chairing the body responsible for the discharge of patients detained in Broadmoor. Based on anecdote, the inquiry found that Savile took little interest in the business of the meetings (Kirkup and Marshall, 2014).

ALLEGED OFFENDING AT BROADMOOR

The inquiry states that there is 'no reason to doubt that Savile was an opportunistic sexual predator throughout the time he was associated with Broadmoor' (Kirkup and Marshall, 2014, para.1.14).

It received ten allegations of sexual assault by Savile directly related to Broadmoor and one allegation of indecent exposure to a minor. Six of the allegations of assault involved patients at the time (one male and five female), two involved staff and two involved minors.

On the basis of the detail and consistency of their accounts and the circumstances of the assaults, the inquiry 'conclude[s] with confidence that at least five of the 11 individuals were sexually abused by Savile, and that it is more likely than not that he also sexually abused a sixth. Of these six, two (both patients) were subjected to repeated assault' (Kirkup and Marshall, 2014, para.1.12). The inquiry was unable to speak in detail to the other five.

More generally, until at least the late 1980s, female patients were obliged to undress completely to change into nightwear and to take baths, watched by staff. The inquiry concludes that Savile would sometimes attend wards at these times and watch. He would also look through doorways at female patients bathing and would make inappropriate remarks.

His general behaviour towards women was often flamboyantly inappropriate, including extravagant forms of greeting, inappropriate remarks and physical contact. Many women were uncomfortable with this and found him objectionable, but thought at the time that it was part of his public persona, 'just Jimmy'.

Savile used his Broadmoor accommodation and his caravan to 'entertain' a regular stream of female visitors, none of whom were patients, and some, though not all, female staff regarded him with caution. Department of Health officials were aware of his general reputation for leading a promiscuous lifestyle, but there was no suggestion then that this involved anyone underage and the inquiry found no evidence that his reputation or behaviour caused anyone to question his suitability to access the hospital, or his suitability for the roles which he held.

The inquiry also found no reliable evidence that any staff or patient complaints about Savile at the time were reported to senior staff or investigated, possibly due to the belief that Savile had the power to negatively affect their career and the institutional culture of Broadmoor which discouraged both staff and patients from reporting.

STOKE MANDEVILLE HOSPITAL, BUCKINGHAMSHIRE

Stoke Mandeville Hospital is a large National Health Service (NHS) hospital in Aylesbury, England, and its National Spinal Injuries Centre is one of the largest specialist spinal units in the world.

SAVILE'S RELATIONSHIP WITH STOKE MANDEVILLE

In 1969 Savile went to Stoke Mandeville Hospital as a voluntary porter, appointed with no checks, monitoring or supervision in place. He was given accommodation on the hospital site and had 24-hour, seven day a week access to all parts of the hospital building complex. From an early stage his disruptive behaviour and constant sexual innuendo caused annoyance and distress to the junior staff within the hospital. However, his behaviour was explained away as being part of his eccentric celebrity persona. Savile was feted by senior managers as an important asset to the organisation where he quickly established himself as an integral part of hospital life. It would appear that at no stage were senior managers made aware of his sexual offending, his unsatisfactory portering performance or his 'poor moral behaviour' (Johnstone and Dent, 2015, p.iii).

From 1980 Savile's relationship with Stoke Mandeville Hospital underwent a significant change when he was appointed by government ministers and the Department of Health and Social Security (DHSS) to fundraise for, and lead, the commissioning process for the new National Spinal Injuries Centre (NSIC) (Johnstone and Dent, 2015). What is apparent from the report into Savile's activity at Stoke Mandeville is that a celebrity whose sole qualification was a track record of apparent 'public service' by volunteer portering and fundraising used his relationship with then Prime Minister Margaret Thatcher to become a key figure at Stoke Mandeville. Following private meetings with Mrs Thatcher she decided, against civil service advice, that a significant amount of government money would be contributed to an appeal to fund a new facility (£1m was promised although only £0.5m was actually given) (Johnstone and Dent, 2015, paras.9.75–9.78).

The 'Jimmy Savile Spinal Building Appeal Fund' was launched with Savile as one of four trustees. By the time work began it was noted by the government department responsible, the DHSS (now the Department of Health), that it was too late for them to have any real input into the briefing process by this stage, as arrangements had been made without reference to them (Johnstone and Dent, 2015, para.9.88). Using influence and 'soft power' Savile had once again placed himself in a relatively unassailable position, circumventing usual processes, so, it is now apparent, placing himself in a position which enabled him to abuse with minimal risk to himself.

ALLEGED OFFENDING AT STOKE MANDEVILLE

Two inquiry reports into Stoke Mandeville Hospital were published in February 2015 – the substantive report (Johnstone and Dent, 2015) and a subsequent legacy report into further allegations made by a further six victims after the initial inquiry investigations had been concluded (Vize and Klinck, 2015). The summary below is based on findings from both.

Savile is believed to have abused 63 people, aged from 8 to 40 years, connected to Stoke Mandeville Hospital between 1968 and 1992. Victims were patients, staff, visitors, volunteers and charity fundraisers, almost half aged under 16 years and ten under the age of 12 years. Just over 90 per cent were female. The allegations ranged from inappropriate touching to rape, including the rape of children under the age of 12. The substantive inquiry describes him as 'an opportunistic predator who could also on occasions show a high degree of pre-meditation when planning attacks on his victims' (Johnstone and Dent, 2015, para.2).

Several sex abuse claims were made against him from 1972 to 1985, to different staff members, but only one was a 'formal complaint', which was in 1977 by the father of an 11-year-old female patient and 'should have led to Savile's suspension from the hospital and a formal police report being made' (Johnstone and Dent, 2015, para.13.54).

The detail of that incident is indicative of a number of factors that seem likely to have enabled Savile to act with such apparent impunity. The 11-year-old was a patient in the hospital for some four months and required a skin graft following an operation for skin cancer. The incident occurred when she was in a treatment room with a young student nurse who was cleaning her wound. Savile heard her crying and came into the room despite the girl being naked from the waist down.

When the nurse had to leave the room and closed the door, leaving Savile alone with the girl, she described that he gripped her tightly so she could not move and rubbed his penis against her arm. He then tried to penetrate her vagina digitally. The girl screamed in pain and the nurse returned, finding the girl hysterical and crying. Savile left swiftly. A hospital sister came in and told the girl to be quiet, that Savile would not do such a dreadful thing and that he had raised a great deal of money for the hospital. The girl told her father when he came to visit that evening and heard angry voices raised between her father and the sister. Her father took the matter to the 'registrar'. Savile did not come near her again. The victim recounted that her father 'decided that due to my ill health, age and not wishing to distress me further, not to pursue the complaint to its conclusion' (Johnstone and Dent, 2015, para.6.80).

The inquiry found no evidence that the complaint was ever escalated to a more senior level of staff and that most complaints at the time were dealt with at ward level. The implicit trust in Savile, the scepticism that he could do wrong, particularly at such a gross level, and the absence of a coherent complaints procedure described in this account all appear to be factors which illuminate the broader context of Savile's offending career.

OFFENCE LOCATIONS

The report found that Savile had 'virtually unrestricted access' to clinical areas and patients during the 1970s and 1980s, and incidents were reported in a wide range of settings in the hospital: child and adult wards, side rooms, a patient's TV lounge, a waiting room, a corridor, a toilet, the gymnasium, a restaurant, a cafeteria, the chapel, the porter's room, staff accommodation, Savile's office, Savile's accommodation, Savile's caravan located on the hospital grounds and Savile's car off-site during a fundraising event.

LEEDS TEACHING HOSPITALS

The Leeds Teaching Hospitals include Leeds General Infirmary, St James's Hospital, Chapel Allerton Hospital and Seacroft Hospital. Leeds Infirmary, originally the city's teaching hospital, dates back to the 1700s. It is one of the largest teaching hospitals in Europe, with an annual turnover of £1 billion. It employs over 15,000 staff and each year treats almost 1.5 million patients in its wards and departments (Proctor *et al.*, 2014).

SAVILE'S RELATIONSHIP WITH LEEDS TEACHING HOSPITALS

In 1960, Savile became involved in the Leeds hospital radio service. This was managed by the hospital Head Porter who was a childhood friend of Savile's. In 1968, he was a leading figure in a national campaign to encourage the public to volunteer for 'good causes' and, with the approval of the hospital Board of Governors, he started at Leeds as a volunteer porter.

He continued in this role, and as a celebrity visitor and fundraiser, throughout his 50-year association with the Infirmary. His celebrity status and familiarity with many staff in the Infirmary contributed to him having unchallenged access throughout the hospital (Proctor *et al.*, 2014).

His relationship with the hospital senior management seems to have been relatively close in the 1960s and 1970s and considerably less so subsequently. However, a perception remained amongst staff that he was well regarded at senior levels in the hospital, and this, combined with his celebrity status, appears to have given him freedom to behave in ways that would not have been tolerated in other people. It also appears to have served to discourage disclosure by his victims.

ALLEGED OFFENDING AT LEEDS GENERAL INFIRMARY

The Leeds inquiry (Proctor *et al.*, 2014) states that 64 people gave accounts of abuse or inappropriate behaviour by Savile. Sixty of these accounts concerned abuse in premises run by the Trust or its predecessors, and four related to other healthcare organisations in either Leeds or other parts of West Yorkshire.

Victims from the Leeds Teaching Hospitals NHS Trust or its predecessor bodies ranged in age from 5 to 75 years. Nineteen children and 14 adults were patients at the time of their abuse. In addition, 19 members of staff reported abusive or inappropriate behaviour by Savile. Eight further accounts were from victims who were external to the Infirmary, but whose abusive encounters had a connection with it, for example when they were visiting the hospital.

The majority of Savile's victims were in their late teens or early twenties at the time of his abusive or inappropriate behaviour. The earliest case was in 1962, when Savile was 36 years old, the most recent in 2009, when he was 82. In respect of patient victims specifically, the earliest case was in 1962 and the most recent in 1999. His assaults were mostly opportunistic and many took place in public areas such as wards and corridors. However, eight cases suggest an element of premeditation: in some instances this included grooming victims and their families over a period of months. Usually Savile worked alone, but on occasion others facilitated his abusive behaviour. The behaviour ranged from lewd remarks and inappropriate touching to sexual assault and rape.

OFFENCE LOCATIONS

Incidents took place on wards, in lifts, in corridors and in offices, and off site in a local café, in Savile's mother's house in Leeds and in his camper van. Only four children and five adults reported their experiences at the time to staff or a colleague.

Education settings

In March 2014, the Secretary of State for Education ordered inquiries to be undertaken in relation to 21 children's homes and schools in England, relating to possible offences in the 1960s, 1970s and 1980s. Those reports were published in February 2015 and can be found on the DfE website (DfE, 2015).

During that process and a simultaneous police investigation it became apparent that Savile cultivated a relationship with one particular establishment, Duncroft Approved School for Girls in Staines, Surrey.

DUNCROFT APPROVED SCHOOL

Note: There was no official inquiry ordered into Duncroft School and the information here is derived primarily from a 2015 police review of a Surrey police investigation into allegations about Savile made in 1979 (Savell, 2015).

Duncroft School was opened in 1949 by the National Association for Mental Health (NAMH), now known as Mind, at the request of the Home Office. At that time it was a school for 24 girls and was a 'pioneer experiment designed to take in girls of above average intelligence who were emotionally disturbed'. In October 1973 the school became an Assisted Community Home with MIND as the governing body and the London Borough of Hounslow as the specified local authority. Barnardo's took over the management of Duncroft in 1976 and closed the school in March 1980.

During the period of Savile's involvement, the school accommodated up to 30 girls aged 14 to 16 years who were of 'average and above average intelligence' and who had 'problems of adjustment occasioned by emotional, educational and/or social difficulties' and were in need of residential care. In the grounds was also a separate unit, Norman Lodge, a hostel used as a place of transition for girls who had gained employment.

SAVILE'S RELATIONSHIP WITH DUNCROFT

Savile apparently first visited Duncroft in 1974, introduced, according to his account, by Princess Alexandra, cousin of Queen Elizabeth II, whom he described as a patron of the school (Savile, 1974). He ceased visiting when the school closed in 1979. Written records indicate that he visited Duncroft at least 16 times between 1974 and 1979, although there is evidence from victim and witness accounts that in fact he visited the school more frequently (Savell, 2015).

Written records also show that Jimmy Savile stayed overnight at Duncroft School on two occasions, though again there is evidence from victim and witness accounts that he stayed overnight more frequently, whether in his own camper van or in staff quarters. He is recorded in school logbooks as having taken pupils out, on three occasions with a strong indication that they were unaccompanied by staff. Overall it is evident that Savile was given significant access to Duncroft's grounds and buildings, and that this access was unrestricted and largely unsupervised (Savell, 2015).

POLICE INVESTIGATIONS

Duncroft is unusual in the context of Savile's offending in that allegations were made about his behaviour during his life and led to him being formally interviewed on one occasion. After his death Surrey Police undertook two reviews, both conducted by Detective Superintendent Jon Savell. The first, published in 2013, was a review of Surrey Police's investigation undertaken between May 2007 and October 2009 into allegations of sexual offences against girls at Duncroft, Operation Ornament (Savell, 2013). The second (Savell, 2015) reviews Operation Outreach, the investigation into allegations made after Savile's death about his offending by 23 former Duncroft residents. These women made contact with police directly, contacted the Operation Yewtree helpline or responded to contact made by the police during the Operation Outreach investigation into abuse at Duncroft.

ALLEGED OFFENDING AT DUNCROFT

Of the 23 victims, 10 alleged abuse by Savile on a single occasion and 13 on at least two occasions (five women each alleged seven assaults). The nature of the alleged offending ranged from non-consensual kissing, touching of breasts over clothing, touching of breasts under clothing, vaginal touching, vaginal penetration with hand, forced masturbation, forced oral sex and other sexual touching. Savell (2015) states that under the legislation in force at the time (Sexual Offences Act 1956) the 46 offences of abuse on Duncroft pupils were all offences contrary to Section 14(1) Indecent assault on a woman. If those same offences were considered under current legislation, the Sexual Offences Act 2003, they would be described as:

- One offence contrary to Section 1(1) Rape
- Five offences contrary to Section 2(1) Assault by penetration
- Two offences contrary to Section 4(1) Causing a person to engage in sexual activity without consent
- Thirty-eight offences contrary to Section 3(1) Sexual assault.

OFFENCE LOCATIONS

As with other settings discussed above, it appears that the assaults took place in public spaces and in privacy, including his vehicles. A single offence of abuse is alleged to have taken in each of the dining room, the kitchen, the corridor outside the Principal's office, the Principal's office, the entrance, the TV Room and the ICU/bedroom (the victim was unable to specify). Three offences are described as occurring in the common room, two offences in the music room, four offences in a downstairs corridor and five offences in unspecified 'communal areas'.

In Norman Lodge, a hostel in the grounds used as a place of transition for girls who had gained employment, two offences of abuse occurred in an office, two in the living room, one in the dining room and one in a bedroom.

Within the grounds of Duncroft, four alleged offences took place inside vehicles brought to the school by Jimmy Savile – that is, the vehicle was located within the school grounds at the time of the abuse. Of the abuse that took place off-site 13 offences took place inside vehicles brought to the school by Savile. The remaining two offences took place inside another vehicle.

POLICE ACTION AGAINST STAFF AT DUNCROFT DURING THE RELEVANT PERIOD

Police Operation Outreach noted that there was the potential for staff to have known abuse was occurring but either deliberately ignored what was happening or were aware of it and actively aided the abuse by continuing to allow Savile to visit and have access to the girls (Savell, 2015, para.1.6). On completion of their inquiries Surrey Police submitted a file to the Crown Prosecution Service (CPS) in May 2014 in relation to two members of staff employed at Duncroft during the relevant time period for consideration of prosecution. In November 2014 advice provided by senior Treasury counsel (who prosecute the most serious criminal cases in the country) and considered by the Chief Crown Prosecutor was that, based on all the evidence, there was not a realistic prospect of conviction by a jury. No action was therefore taken (Savell, 2015).

Other allegations of sexual offending after Savile's death – Operation Yewtree

This section considers the allegations made about Savile following his death, primarily through police Operation Yewtree. The terminology adopted in the Operation Yewtree report, and in much other press coverage, is similar to that used in relation to offences committed by convicted offenders. It is important to bear in mind that what is being described here are allegations, not proven offences, although the accounts of those who came forward are compelling. Police state that the information on which the allegations are based has not been corroborated, as the resources required would be considered disproportionate because criminal proceedings cannot now be brought as Savile was dead by that point. However, 'Accounts from victims have left police and NSPCC staff with the unambiguous view that Savile's behaviour was that of a predatory sex offender who opportunely abused people' (Gray and Watt, 2013, para.9.5). Sadly, whatever we may believe about Savile's offending, it will now never be proven.

OVERVIEW OF SAVILE'S ALLEGED OFFENDING FROM OPERATION YEWTREE

Operation Yewtree was a wide-ranging Metropolitan Police investigation launched on 5 October 2012 to address allegations made as a result of the initial Savile revelations. Approximately 600 people provided information to the investigative team. The primary method of contact was a helpline established in conjunction with the NSPCC and the results were published in a joint Metropolitan Police and NSPCC report *Giving Victims a Voice* (Gray and Watt, 2013).

As well as allegations about Savile, Operation Yewtree received allegations about other public figures, some of whom were subsequently convicted – for example, entertainer Rolf Harris, who was convicted of indecent assaults involving four girls aged between 8 and 19 years and sentenced to five years and nine months' imprisonment. Celebrity presenter Stuart Hall, whose offending was considered as part of the Smith BBC inquiry, was already being prosecuted by Greater Manchester Police when Operation Yewtree was launched, but about whom further allegations were made to Yewtree. He was found guilty of indecent assaults involving 15 girls aged between 9 and 17 years and sentenced to a total of five years' imprisonment. A feature of Hall's case was that the judge cited the vociferous protestations of innocence which Hall made to the press during the criminal justice process, effectively suggesting that those he had abused were lying, as an aggravating factor in determining his sentence (Russell, 2013).

The total number of allegations relating to Savile from Operation Yewtree is estimated to be about 450, leading to 214 formal crimes (i.e. police would investigate them if he were alive) being recorded across 28 police force areas. The earliest recorded incident was in 1955 in Manchester. The final recorded offence was in 2009. The peak offending period was between 1966 and 1976 when Savile was between 40 and 50 years old.

The location of reported offending was predominantly in Leeds, Savile's hometown, and London, his main work location. Fifty-seven allegations related to hospital (including hospice) premises, 33 to television or radio studios and 14 to schools.

Seventy-three per cent of the allegations were about those under 18 years old, the total victim age range reported being between 8 and 74 years old at the time of abuse. Eighty-two per cent were female, with the majority aged between 13 and 16 years.

Victim accounts indicate offences were normally opportunistic sexual assaults, but there were others where an element of grooming is said to have occurred. Within the recorded crimes there were 126 indecent acts and 34 rape/penetration offences. Of the rape/penetration offences 26 victims were female and eight were male (Gray and Watt, 2013).

Examples of his offences cited by the Operation Yewtree report (with Savile's age added to provide context) are:

- 1960 (Savile was 34): A 10-year-old boy saw Savile outside a hotel and asked for his autograph. They went into the hotel reception where he was seriously sexually assaulted – classified as assault by penetration.

- 1965 (Savile was 39): A 14-year-old girl met Savile in a nightclub. She later visited his home and was raped – classified as rape.

- 1972 (Savile was 46): A 12-year-old boy and two female friends attended a recording of *Top of the Pops*. During a break in filming Savile groped the boy's genitals and the breasts of his two friends – classified as sexual assault.

- 1973 (Savile was 47): A 16-year-old female hospital patient was befriended by Savile. He led her to an office where he kissed her, touched her inappropriately and then subjected her to a sexual assault – classified as sexual assault.
- 1974 (Savile was 48): Savile took a 14-year-old schoolgirl for a drive in his car and seriously sexually assaulted her – classified as assault by penetration.
- 2009 (Savile was 83): A 43-year-old woman was talking to Savile on a train journey between Leeds and London when he put his hand up her skirt – classified as sexual assault.

(Gray and Watt, 2013, para.7.16)

ALLEGATIONS OF SEXUAL OFFENDING DURING SAVILE'S LIFE

The overwhelming majority of allegations relating to Savile's sexual offending were made after his death. However, during a review by Her Majesty's Inspectorate of Constabulary (HMIC) of responses by police to allegations about Savile reported during his lifetime, seven incidents were identified (HMIC, 2013). HMIC expressed concern about the extent to which victims may have tried to report their allegations to the police during Savile's life that may not have been responded to appropriately. Two were based solely on intelligence records and five based on direct complaints:

- In 1963, in Cheshire, a male victim reported an allegation of rape by Savile to a local police officer the day after it had occurred but had been told to 'forget about it' and 'move on'. The officer had not made a report of the allegation and, consequently, an investigation had not been undertaken.
- There was an entry on an intelligence ledger held by the Metropolitan Police Service (MPS) Paedophile Unit from approximately 1964. HMIC state that it is difficult to assess the significance of the ledger given that little is known of its provenance. However, its existence suggests that by 1964

Savile was known to MPS officers investigating sexual offences against children. No evidence was found to suggest that any investigation was carried out as a result of that intelligence.

- On an unknown date a man reported at a central London police station that his girlfriend had been assaulted at a recording of the BBC television programme *Top of the Pops*. He had been told that he 'could be arrested for making such allegations' and sent away.

- A computerised record of an anonymous letter was received by the MPS in 1998 alleging that Savile was a paedophile who used 'rent boys', one of whom had tried to blackmail him. The letter warned, 'When Jimmy Savile fails, and sooner or later he will, a lot of well-known personalities and past politicians are going to fall with him' (HMIC, 2013, para.5.9).

- A 2003 MPS crime report was based on the complaint of a victim who stated that Savile had indecently assaulted her when she was 15 at a recording of the BBC television programme *Top of the Pops*. No further action was taken.

- A 2007 Surrey crime report was based on the complaints of three victims who stated that Savile had indecently assaulted them in the 1970s and 1980s, two at Duncroft School and one at Stoke Mandeville Hospital. Savile was interviewed in relation to the Duncroft complaints by Surrey Police on 1 October 2009. Transcripts of this interview were subsequently released by Surrey Police as the result of a Freedom of Information request.[2] The Crown Prosecution Service (CPS) advised that there was insufficient evidence to take any further action and no charges were brought. A commentary on that interview transcript was published in *NOTA News* (Erooga, 2014).

- A 2008 Sussex crime report was based on the complaint of a victim who stated that Savile had indecently assaulted her in

2 Freedom of Information request reference no: 165-13-198.

> 1970 when she was 22. A Sussex Detective Chief Inspector concluded that without the support of the victim, who did not want the matter pursued, and her unwillingness to attend court, there was no prospect of a conviction and therefore further police activity was not required. (This allegation became the basis of Operation Baseball, the subject of the unpublished 'Report into the 2008 allegation of sexual assault made against James Vincent Savile, Sussex Police'.)[3]

HMIC concluded that because of the shortcomings in records in these instances, and presumably an unknown number of others, the number of victims who tried to report Savile to the police during his life will never be known. However, based on the ratio of known allegations made to the police compared to the number of alleged offences reported in the police inquiry which followed his death, Operation Yewtree, HMIC estimated that over 96 per cent of victims whose allegations would have been recorded as crimes did not go to the police at the time they were a victim of Savile's abuse. This estimate is borne out by statistics on reporting sexual offences in the UK generally, where only 15 per cent of female victims of the most serious sexual offences state that they reported the incident to the police, although 57 per cent indicate that they had told someone else about what had happened to them (Home Office and Ministry of Justice, 2013, p.17).

Why victims did not speak out at the time

An issue that seems to be particularly challenging to those in the public 'audience' who have not been subjected to a sexual offence is why it took so long for allegations to be made and why so many were then made over a relatively short period. Presenting the Health

---

3 The *Daily Star Sunday* newspaper (Corke, 2013) reported on 17 March 2013 that a four-page summary of this report had been released, but no further information was located on the Internet. A request by this author to Sussex Police resulted in disclosure of a press statement and an internal management review report. These were summarised in *NOTA News 72*, March/April 2014.

inquiry reports, the Health Secretary Jeremy Hunt told the House of Commons, 'People were either too dazzled or too intimidated to confront the evil predator we now know he was' (Hansard HC, 26 February 2015).

Whilst that encapsulates some of the key reasons, this chapter concludes by considering the accounts of those survivors about what stopped them reporting the offences at the time, drawn from two sources. The first is from the Stoke Mandeville Inquiry (Johnstone and Dent, 2015), the second from focus groups with volunteers from amongst those who had contacted the NSPCC Operation Yewtree helpline (Exton and Thandi, 2013).

The Stoke Mandeville Inquiry (Johnstone and Dent, 2015, para.13.19) recorded that the reasons victims gave for not reporting the sexual abuse at the time it occurred were diverse and included:

- they were so young at the time that they did not have the words to explain what had happened to them;
- the abuse took place so quickly, and often in a public place, leaving the victim confused and disorientated as to exactly what had taken place;
- many thought that they were to blame, as they had allowed themselves to get into Savile's space and had been eager to meet him;
- many victims thought that they were to blame for Savile's advances because during the 1970s and 1980s it was often thought that young women aggravated any assault by dressing 'provocatively' (for example wearing short skirts or tight jeans);
- Savile told several of the victims to say nothing as no one would believe them;
- many victims could not themselves understand what had occurred, and decided that no one else would either, so remained silent;

- several victims told parents and other responsible adults outside the Hospital, but were not believed, some were laughed at and dismissed;
- several victims felt embarrassed and degraded and did not want anyone to know, especially not husbands or parents;
- several victims were vulnerable patients who were fearful of some kind of retribution if they spoke out about Savile;
- each victim thought that their encounter with Savile was a unique event, and had no idea that he was regularly sexually abusing other people.

Elements of the list are strikingly similar to those reported by the 26 participants in the NSPCC focus groups, four of whom were adults when Savile's alleged offences occurred.

Delayed disclosure

It emerges from the focus group participants that a range of factors came together to make reporting their abuse at the time feel impossible. These included their perceptions about the likely police response, with participants feeling that the police would not have been understanding at the time and would not have managed allegations effectively. Other factors included their own family circumstances, their uncertainty about what had happened to them (e.g. was it abuse and who was to 'blame'?), and societal values about sexual abuse at the time. Participants felt that there was, and to some degree still is, a stigma attached to being a victim of abuse, and that society will at times 'blame victims', making the prospect of disclosing abuse particularly daunting. This was exacerbated by Savile's status as a high-profile celebrity, a figure respected by the public.

Timing of disclosure

An important finding was that although none of this sample would have been likely to come forward had it not been for the media focus on the allegations against Savile, it was not the media that had encouraged their disclosures but the realisation that they were 'not the only one'. Had other allegations been public at the time of their abuse these participants indicated they would have been significantly more likely to report theirs. They reported that this was closely connected to the prospect of being believed. Whilst they were concerned they would not individually have been believed, they felt they would be more likely to be believed as part of a group, and that this could add weight and corroboration to each other's stories.

Subsequent developments

As noted at the start of this chapter, the revelations about Savile have had multiple consequences, not all of which can be addressed here. Two, though, are of particular relevance. The first relates to a review for the Director of Public Prosecutions of whether criminal justice procedures were followed in investigations into allegations made about Savile at Duncroft (Levitt, 2013). The result of that review was that a new policy was issued for the investigation and prosecution of sexual offences, as part of which it is now permissible for the police to advise witnesses that they are not the only person to have made an allegation (CPS, 2013).

The second is increased debate about how best to address allegations of non-recent abuse. On the one hand there has been increased concern about non-prosecution of other alleged historical offenders, the best known example of which was the case of Greville Janner. Lord Janner died whilst consideration of prosecution was ongoing, a matter complicated by his deteriorating mental state at that time. This led to the Henriques Inquiry (Henriques, 2016) into previous decisions not to prosecute Lord Janner. At the same time cases such as those of pop star Cliff Richard and DJ Paul Gambaccini, both of whom were investigated in relation to allegations which were not proceeded with, has led to vigorous debate about whether there should be a right of confidentiality whilst police investigations are ongoing (Hansard HL, 19 April 2016).

Conclusion

Even at this distance, reviewing the totality of Savile's offending is still deeply shocking and it is apparent that it has had wide-ranging implications which go beyond the traumatic consequences for his many victims. Over 70 organisations have undertaken reviews of their contact with Savile and in many cases of their safeguarding processes and procedures; Peter Spindler, the ex-Metropolitan Police Commander who was the strategic lead for Operation Yewtree, describes it as a 'watershed moment'; and the number of high-profile figures who have been convicted of sexual offences and the level of other allegations about non-recent cases have risen dramatically. In January 2017 police Operation Hydrant, which coordinates the national database of non-recent sexual abuse, had 3535 people registered as offenders/suspects on the database, of which 3118 are recorded as having offended within institutional settings (Sheriff, 2017). Finally, as well as arguably setting the context in which the IICSA was established, as addressed in Chapter 12 revelations about widespread abuse in sport are now emerging.

In contrast to the outpouring of affection which marked Savile's lavish funeral he is now a reviled figure, but more importantly the expectation by the public of all organisations that there is no excuse for safeguarding failings has rarely been more apparent.

The next chapter considers themes and recommendations from the key inquiries into Savile and highlights key learning which might help to minimise the possibility of a future offender as prolific and apparently unfettered as Savile is now known to have been.

References

Association of Papal Orders in Great Britain (2013) Home page. Accessed on 1 June 2016 at www.papalknights.org.uk/index.htm

BBC (2013) 'Jimmy Savile Scandal: Report Reveals Decades of Abuse.' *BBC News*, 11 January. Accessed on 18 July 2017 at www.bbc.co.uk/news/uk-20081021

Corke, J. (2013) 'Jimmy Savile Cops in "Cover-Up" over Probe Sussex Force Blasted.' *Daily Star Sunday*, 17 March 2017. Accessed on 1 August 2013 at www.dailystar.co.uk/news/latest-news/304014/Jimmy-Savile-cops-in-cover-up-over-probe-Sussex-force-blasted

Crown Prosecution Service (CPS) (2013) *Guidelines on Prosecuting Cases of Child Sexual Abuse*. Accessed on 18 July 2017 at www.cps.gov.uk/legal/a_to_c/child_sexual_abuse

Department for Education (DfE) (2015) 'Statement regarding investigations relating to Jimmy Savile and a number of children's homes and schools in England.' Written statement to Parliament. Accessed on 1 June 2016 at www.gov.uk/government/speeches/investigations-into-abuse-in-childrens-homes-and-schools

Department of Health (DoH) (2015) *NHS and Department of Health Investigations into Jimmy Savile*. Accessed on 1 June 2016 at www.gov.uk/government/collections/nhs-and-department-of-health-investigations-into-jimmy-savile

Erooga, M. (2014) 'Commentary on a Police Interview with Jimmy Savile on October 1st, 2009 as Part of Operation Ornament.' *NOTA News 73*, July/August. Accessed on 15 August 2017 at www.nota.co.uk/Content/Media/c292aa945c1d4393a512f738ae84e23a/73NOTANewsAugust2014.pdf

Exton, L. and Thandi, K. (2013) *Would They Actually Have Believed Me? A Focus Group Exploration of the Underreporting of Crimes by Jimmy Savile*. London: NSPCC. Accessed on 15 August 2017 at www.nspcc.org.uk/globalassets/documents/research-reports/would-they-actually-believed-me-savile-report.pdf

Gray, P. and Watt, P. (2013) *Giving Victims a Voice: A Joint Report into Sexual Allegations against Jimmy Savile*. London: Metropolitan Police. Accessed on 11 August 2017 at www.nspcc.org.uk/globalassets/documents/research-reports/yewtree-report-giving-victims-voice-jimmy-savile.pdf

Hansard HC Deb., vol. 593, col. 483 (26 February 2015) Accessed on 24 August 2017 at http://hansard.parliament.uk/Commons/2015-02-26/debates/15022647000002/JimmySavile(NHSInvestigations)

Hansard HL Deb., vol. 771, cols 538–539 (19 April 2016). Accessed on 25 July 2016 at https://hansard.parliament.uk/Lords/2016-04-19/debates/16041939000476/CrimeHistoricSexAbuseAllegations

Henriques, R. (2016) *An Independent Inquiry into Allegations Made against Lord Greville Jenner*. London: MPS. Accessed on 15 August 2017 at www.cps.gov.uk/publications/reports/henriques_report_190116.pdf

Her Majesty's Inspectorate of Constabulary (HMIC) (2013) *'Mistakes Were Made': HMIC's Review into Allegations and Intelligence Material Concerning Jimmy Savile between 1964 and 2012*. London: HMIC. Accessed on 11 August 2017 at www.justiceinspectorates.gov.uk/hmicfrs/media/review-into-allegations-and-intelligence-material-concerning-jimmy-savile.pdf

Home Office and Ministry of Justice (2013) *An Overview of Sexual Offending in England and Wales*. Accessed on 18 July 2017 at www.gov.uk/government/statistics/an-overview-of-sexual-offending-in-england-and-wales

Independent Inquiry into Child Sexual Abuse (IICSA) (2015) *Terms of Reference*. Accessed on 25 July 2016 at www.iicsa.org.uk/terms-reference

Jackson, S. (1976) *Other People's Children: A Handbook for Child Minders*. London: BBC.

Johnstone, A. and Dent, C. (2015) *Investigation into the Association of Jimmy Savile with Stoke Mandeville Hospital: A Report for Buckinghamshire Healthcare NHS Trust*. Amersham: Buckinghamshire Healthcare NHS Trust. Accessed on 12 August 2017 at www.speakingoutinvestigation.com/Downloads/Speaking%20out%20investigation/2902210_Investigation%20into%20the%20Association%20of%20Jimmy%20Savile%20with%20Stoke%20Mandeville%20Hospital.pdf

Keller, I. (1985) *Benjamin Rabbit and the Stranger Danger*. Littlehampton: Littlehampton Book Services.

Kirkup, B. and Marshall, P. (2014) *Jimmy Savile Investigation. Broadmoor Hospital: Report to the West London Mental Health NHS Trust and the Department of Health*. London: West London Mental Health NHS Trust. Accessed on 11 August 2017 at www.gov.uk/government/publications/jimmy-savile-investigation-broadmoor-hospital

Lampard, K. and Marsden, E. (2015) *Themes and Lessons Learnt from NHS Investigations into Matters Relating to Jimmy Savile: Independent Report for the Secretary of State for Health*. London: Department of Health. Accessed on 24 August 2017 at www.gov.uk/government/publications/jimmy-savile-nhs-investigations-lessons-learned

Levitt, A. (2013) *In the Matter of the Late Jimmy Savile: Report to the Director of Public Prosecutions*. London: Crown Prosecution Service. Accessed on 24 August 2017 at www.cps.gov.uk/news/assets/uploads/files/savile_report.pdf

Marshall, P. (2007) *Celebrity and Power: Fame in Contemporary Culture*. Minneapolis, MN: University of Minnesota Press.

Nikkhah, R. and Malnick, E. (2011) 'Sir Jimmy Savile Dies Aged 84.' *Telegraph*, 29 October 2011. Accessed on 12 June 2016 at www.telegraph.co.uk/culture/tvandradio/bbc/8857400/Sir-Jimmy-Savile-dies-aged-84.html

Proctor, S., Galloway, R., Chaloner, R., Jones, C. and Thompson, D. (2014) *The Report of the Investigation into Matters Relating to Savile at Leeds Teaching Hospitals NHS Trust*. Leeds: Leeds Teaching Hospitals NHS Trust. Accessed on 11 August 2017 at www.leedsth.nhs.uk/assets/Uploads/40482-2901955-Libra-Executive-SUMMARY-accessible2.pdf

Russell, A. (2013) *R-v-Stuart Hall, Sentencing Remarks of His Honour Judge Anthony Russell QC, Recorder of Preston*. Accessed on 15 September 2017 at www.judiciary.gov.uk/judgments/stuart-hall-sentencing-remarks-17062013

Savell, J. (2013) *Report into Operation Ornament*. Guildford: Surrey Police.

Savell, J. (2015) *Operation Outreach Report*. Guildford: Surrey Police. Accessed on 11 August 2017 at http://mandatenow.org.uk/wp-content/uploads/2015/04/Operation-Outreach-29-4-2015-11186-link.pdf

Savile, J. (1974) *As It Happens*. London: Barrie and Jenkins.

Savile, J. (1979) *God'll Fix It*. London: Mowbray.

Sheriff, R. (2017) *Operation Hydrant: Latest Statistics and Reporting from the Front Line*. Accessed on 18 April 2017 at www.boltburdonkemp.co.uk/news-blogs/child-abuse-blog/operation-hydrant-latest-statistics-reporting-coal-front

Smith, J. (2016) *The Independent Review into the BBC's Culture and Practices during the Jimmy Savile and Stuart Hall Years*. London: BBC. Accessed on 11 August 2017 at www.bbc.co.uk/bbctrust/dame_janet_smith

Vize, C. and Klinck, B. (2015) *Legacy Report – Further Investigation into the Association of Jimmy Savile with Stoke Mandeville Hospital: A Report for Buckinghamshire Healthcare NHS Trust*. Amersham: Buckinghamshire Healthcare NHS Trust. Accessed on 12 August 2017 at www.speakingoutinvestigation.com/Downloads/Speaking%20out%20investigation/2903580_Legacy%20Report%20Accessible%20v2.pdf

2

SAVILE AND LEARNING FROM THE INQUIRIES

MARCUS EROOGA

Introduction

As outlined in the previous chapter, the revelations of Savile's sexual offending after his death prompted an unprecedented series of inquiries and reviews. To paraphrase Lampard and Marsden (2015) who were quoted in the previous chapter, much of the story of Savile and his offending in various organisations is unusual to the point of being scarcely credible. Whilst the detail is 'unusual', the common themes are far from unique to Savile and offer important contemporary lessons for organisations.

The purpose of this chapter is to summarise what appear to be common themes in unrelated organisations that allowed, or failed to prevent, this predatorial sex offender from preying with such apparent impunity on those he came into contact with.

Few organisations are subject to such detailed scrutiny of their functioning over such an extended period. Using them as examples here is not intended to focus attention on their individual shortcomings but to provide real-life examples of issues that can potentially be identified in current organisations and from which learning can hopefully be derived.

To do so the recommendations from the inquiries, important though they are, will not be summarised. Rather, common themes about organisational functioning and culture and the influence of celebrity will be identified. What is striking about these issues is the diverse range of organisations in which they can be identified and yet the similarly serious effects on their ability to safeguard effectively, and it is this that warrants making them the focus of a chapter.

Organisational functioning and culture

Dame Janet Smith (2016) devotes a considerable portion of the three-volume report into Savile and Stuart Hall to the organisational culture at the BBC during the relevant period. Each of the other key inquiries into the locations where Savile offended most prolifically – Broadmoor (Kirkup and Marshall, 2014); Leeds Teaching Hospitals (Proctor *et al.*, 2014); and Stoke Mandeville Hospital (Johnstone and Dent, 2015) – also consider the organisational functioning and culture at the time and their effect on Savile's ability to behave as he did.

The themes that emerge are organised here in categories, illustrated with examples from inquiry reports. The categories are not discrete, and the dynamics of what is described often interacted with each other within an individual organisation.

Clarity about expectations of staff behaviour

Without the clarity of organisational aims and objectives, and the framework of good practice which they reinforce, 'too much depends on the attitudes and judgments of fallible individuals' (Wardaugh and Wilding, 1993, p.18). Colton (2002) also suggests that without effective management and accountability structures staff can become a law unto themselves, and in this situation an individual organisational culture develops.

From the point of induction onwards, well-regulated organisations make clear their expectations regarding the conduct of staff and volunteers (Erooga, 2009), usually by way of an explicit code of conduct (see, for example, Safer Recruitment Consortium, 2015). A notable feature of organisations where abuse occurs is that frequently such expectations are either not explicit or not consistently followed (Erooga, 2009). That appears to have been the case with some of the settings where Savile abused. Whilst this may be considered to be something which happened in the past but wouldn't occur now, the Broadmoor report indicates that, 'On the basis of the evidence we heard, we believe there was, *until relatively recently*, a culture at ward level in Broadmoor that tolerated boundary violations, including those of a sexual nature, and discouraged reporting – "keep your eyes and ears open and your mouth shut"' (Kirkup and Marshall, 2014, para.9.17; emphasis added).

Absence of procedure

Where such expectations existed it would be expected that they would be communicated in writing, expressed as formal policy, as well as manifested in everyday conduct. However, at Leeds Infirmary the culture of the organisation at the time and attitudes to what was deemed appropriate to report to more senior staff appear to have had a major influence on behaviours, resulting in concerns going largely unreported (Proctor *et al.*, 2014). During most of the time that Savile was associated with Broadmoor there was a notable absence of written policies and procedures. The inquiry indicates that inappropriate behaviour seems to have been deterred mainly by custom and practice, and by the disapproval of the medical superintendent and senior nurses. If there was written guidance (albeit not archived, so not available to the inquiry) they indicate that it was not well known to the staff who would have had to put it into practice (Kirkup and Marshall, 2014).

Actual or anticipated response to inappropriate behaviour

At Stoke Mandeville Hospital, whilst the complaints policy did evolve over the period that Savile was involved with the hospital, the inquiry (Johnstone and Dent, 2015) found that concerns or complaints were mostly dealt with by nurse managers and ward sisters and were not always escalated to the Hospital Administrator. Because of this the overall hospital 'system' would not be aware of a body of concern, an issue returned to below in the section on 'silo management'.

The inquiry notes that the shortcomings of the complaints process were compounded by the 'patient gratitude barrier' (assumed to refer to the inherent gratitude towards staff of dependent patients) and the fear of reprisals felt by staff and patients alike. The inquiry found that whilst on occasion senior managers found Savile's behaviour inappropriate for a hospital setting, this did not prompt action.

At Broadmoor complaints were inhibited by the belief of both employed staff and custodial patients that Savile was in a position of power and authority and so could make their lives much worse. The institutional culture of Broadmoor at the time is described as having strongly discouraged both groups from reporting.

Similarly, at Leeds Infirmary, the organisational culture and attitudes to what was considered appropriate to notify to more senior staff influenced reporting behaviour. Both patient and staff victims reported a strongly held belief that they would not be taken seriously if they reported their encounters with Savile, and that even if they did and were believed, no action would be taken because of their perception that 'senior people' at the Infirmary believed that he did much good for the organisation and this should not be compromised. To use a concept from the BBC inquiry (Smith 2016), they believed that managers viewed him as 'more valuable than the values'.

At the BBC, complaining was seen as damaging to the interests of the complainant – the inquiry found evidence that people who were thinking of making a complaint decided, or were persuaded, not to do so because it would damage their careers. This may have been related to a culture of not complaining about a member of 'the talent', who were effectively protected from complaint.

Absent management and ineffective structures

At Stoke Mandeville Hospital arrangements for the management, monitoring and supervision of Savile in his capacity as voluntary porter and celebrity fundraiser were absent. The inquiry considered that had they been in place those arrangements would have restricted Savile's opportunity for sexual offending at the hospital and that the absence of any monitoring processes, in conjunction with his unrestricted access, created the circumstances in which he was able to offend undetected for two decades.

At the BBC, an impeding factor to preventive action was reported as the lack of any suitable route through which to make complaints, with a hierarchical management structure that did not facilitate making complaints or raising concerns.

Closed culture

Beyer, Higgins and Bromfield (2005) suggest that organisations managed along hierarchical lines can become so highly controlled that it is not possible to challenge their practices. The abuser in this type of organisation is protected, albeit unwittingly, by the hierarchical systems in place. This certainly seems to have been the case in Broadmoor where the institutional culture at the relevant time was closed and introspective, encouraging a custodial approach to 'inmates' and 'permitting instances of harsh treatment' (Kirkup and Marshall, 2014, para.9.17), suggesting that Savile's abuse was an extreme example of a range of what would now certainly be considered inappropriate behaviour. The inquiry indicates that staff showed hostility to colleagues who questioned this approach or attempted to report specific incidents. At the same time, it is instructive to note that the closed culture brought camaraderie, pride in the job and a low rate of sickness absence.

Such attitudes may not be common to the whole organisation but exist in a discrete part of it. In an echo of the team loyalty described at Broadmoor, the BBC report comments on a strong sense of loyalty by staff towards the particular programme on which they were working. This was manifested as pride in the programme, a strong desire that it should succeed, a strong sense of competitiveness with other programmes and a strong disincentive to do anything that might compromise that success.

'Silo management' and consequent 'disconnected senior management'

'Silo management' is used here to refer to different parts of the organisation not communicating with each other, and consequently lack of communication between low- and middle-rank staff. This serves to inhibit an overview of key issues by the senior managers who have the power to take action and initiate change. This seems to have been a feature of some of the organisations where Savile abused and which enabled him to continue doing so largely undetected by the people with the authority to prevent him.

The BBC inquiry (Smith, 2016) comments on a 'silo mentality', which meant that a concern that arose in one part of the BBC was not transmitted to, or discussed with, another part of the organisation. This separation seemed to have the potential for preventing anyone in management from seeing the bigger picture.

The Leeds inquiry (Proctor *et al.*, 2014) reported repeated evidence that the culture in the Infirmary from the 1960s to the 1980s was formal, hierarchical and structured in rigid professional lines of accountability. Generally, the staff who witnessed or who heard disclosures from staff about Savile were closer to the 'front line' of the clinical areas and remote from the management structure. This meant that concerns about Savile were expressed as gossip and rumour, and not formally actioned.

As a result, the inquiry found no evidence to suggest that those in leadership positions knew that Savile was sexually assaulting patients and staff, symptomatic of a broader disconnection between senior managers and the rest of the organisation.

At Stoke Mandeville Hospital, the inquiry (Johnstone and Dent, 2015) considered it beyond doubt that in the 1970s and 1980s Savile was known internally as a 'sex pest', with numerous examples of his behaviour being managed on a ward or at departmental level without concerns being escalated. Most of the witnesses reflected that this was probably because they did not understand how the organisation functioned beyond their individual spheres of work.

More broadly the culture during that period was described as being open and friendly, but also disorganised, diverse and silo-based: 'Leadership did not follow a linear pattern of accountability and this led to informal leadership structures operating for most day-to-day issues' (Johnstone and Dent, 2015, para.1.6).

Savile's sexual offending on the Stoke Mandeville Hospital site went largely unreported. The hospital had complaints policies and procedures in place during the 1970s and 1980s when ten victim reports were made. However, the inquiry described the management infrastructure as disorganised and weak, leading to silo-based management of the complaints process. This prevented complaints being resolved appropriately or coming to the attention of the senior administrative tier. It comments that 'where informal cultures exist in conjunction with invisible and confused leadership delineations, circumstances are created in which complaints, incidents and safeguarding breaches remain undetected by the organisation at large and go unmanaged. This made a significant contribution to Savile's sexual abuse behaviours going undetected over time' (Johnstone and Dent, 2015, para.13.31).

The effect of celebrity

Celebrity may appear to be a rather discrete and context-specific category to focus on. Most child sexual abuse in an organisational (or any other) setting is not committed by 'celebrities', and whilst when it does occur it attracts considerable press attention both in the UK (Jimmy Savile, Stuart Hall, Rolf Harris) and in the US (Jerry Sandusky [Freeh, 2012]), on the face of it celebrity would seem a remote facet of cases of organisational abuse. However, what the Savile inquiries illustrate is the way in which the personal factors of, and perceptions about, an abuser can influence colleagues and organisational responses in ways that impede what might otherwise have been protective factors for potential victims.

Savile, and convicted celebrity sex offender contemporary Stuart Hall (Smith, 2016), are examples of classic 'celebrity', but the phenomenon can also be seen in what Doran and Brannan (1996) suggest is one of the principal archetypes of institutional abusers, the 'charismatic, articulate, well-networked, caring professional' (p.158). A recent example might be seen in the case of William Vahey, the teacher who drugged and sexually assaulted over 50 pupils in the London school where he was teaching (Davies, 2014). Voted the second most popular teacher in the school (Wonnacott and Carmi, 2016), he could be regarded as a school 'celebrity'. An independent review of the case describes him having 'manufactured popularity and approval where he needed it, and traded to criminal advantage off the trust placed by decision-makers in others, including that placed in other decision-makers and him' (Davies, 2014, para.1.12). Similarly, in the case of Australian dance studio owner and dance teacher Grant Davies, convicted in September 2015 of 47 offences relating to various acts of sexual misconduct with children aged between 9 and 14 years over a period of 13 years (RCIRCSA, 2016), one witness said, 'In or around 2005, Grant was treated like a Hollywood star by the students' parents. He would walk out of the studio and have mothers surround him and swoon all over him.'

What is common to all of them is the effect their status had on the way they were regarded by bystanders and on organisational processes, which they were then able to exploit, consciously or otherwise, to behave as they wished.

As this book has a primary focus on Savile, examples of that effect explored here relate to Savile, but they are intended to be used as examples of a phenomenon which can be identified in other settings in relation to 'lesser celebrities'.

The first category of examples relates to the way in which he came to be involved with various organisations. At high-security psychiatric hospital Broadmoor, as outlined in Chapter 1, he began by offering his services in an undefined role in order to improve staff and patient morale and to improve public perception of the hospital. Through what appears to have been a gradual but undefined process, he ended up having unrestricted access to ward areas within the secure perimeter and ultimately taking a senior management role as Chair of the Hospital Advisory Committee (Kirkup and Marshall, 2014).

In Leeds, he initially became involved in the hospital radio service, and subsequently, having been a leading figure in a national campaign to encourage the public to volunteer for 'good causes', with the approval of the hospital Board of Governors he became a volunteer porter. His celebrity status and familiarity with many staff in the Infirmary contributed to him having unchallenged access throughout the hospital (Proctor *et al.*, 2014).

At Stoke Mandeville Hospital – as a voluntary porter, with no checks, monitoring or supervision in place, as well as being provided with accommodation on site – he had 24-hour, seven-day-a-week access to all parts of the hospital complex. As reported in Chapter 1, from an early stage his constant sexual innuendo caused annoyance and distress to hospital junior staff, with the behaviour explained away as being part of his 'eccentric celebrity persona' (Johnstone and Dent, 2015, p.iii). This was no doubt influenced by him being feted by senior managers as an important asset to the organisation.

This effect was seen when he was – as with his appointment as Chair of the Broadmoor Advisory Committee without apparent qualification – appointed by the government to lead the commissioning process of the new National Spinal Injuries Centre. He then used his relationship with Prime Minister Margaret Thatcher to secure, against civil service advice, a government contribution of £0.5m to the cause (Johnstone and Dent, 2015, paras.9.75–9.78).

Finally, at Duncroft Approved School, he was introduced, by his account, to the school by patron of the school Princess Alexandra, cousin of Queen Elizabeth II (Savile, 1974), and was a frequent visitor given significant unrestricted and largely unsupervised access to the grounds and buildings and, it seems, contact with the adolescent female residents (Savell, 2015).

There is no suggestion in any of the inquiries, and it is not intended to suggest here, that any organisation was aware of Savile's abusive behaviour or actively colluded with him. However, it seems manifestly apparent with hindsight that celebrity changed the way in which those organisations would usually expect to behave, with consequent detrimental effects on staff and service users.

Conclusion

McAlinden (2006) suggests that offenders may have a nuanced grasp of what Douglas (1986) terms 'how institutions think'. Whether that grasp is conscious or intuitive, the way 'institutions think' and the consequent ways that they behave are crucial mediators in the possibility of them being settings where abuse may occur. This review of themes indicates what many of those involved with Savile had in common and gives some pointers to what needs to be addressed to minimise that possibility.

The remainder of this book will address those in more detail and by sector, but one issue stands out above all others.

Most organisations consider themselves to have systems for reporting concerns that are as robust as they can be, having a culture that welcomes and nurtures staff and users of its services to feel empowered to raise concerns. That assertion needs to be regularly tested by management, not solely by reference to policies and procedures being in existence by checking the experience of those who are invited to use the policies. This will be a feature of a leadership that fosters what the Leeds report describes as 'a culture of curiosity, scrutiny and constructive challenge, with processes to underpin these behaviours' (Proctor *et al.*, 2014, p.206).

Publicised whistle-blowing policies and procedures, when they are followed, are one element of ensuring appropriate responses to issues of concern and communicate to service users and staff the organisational commitment to openness and addressing difficult issues when necessary. The Huston Inquiry (Social Services Inspectorate, 1994) recommends that agencies providing services to children or vulnerable adults should ensure that a culture of openness and trust is fostered within the organisation, in which staff can share any concerns about the conduct of colleagues and be assured that these will be received in a sensitive manner. Staff should also be encouraged, through formal and informal channels of communication, to question, express concerns or pass on significant information to management regarding the protection of children or vulnerable adults.

Finally, it is tempting to view Savile's offending as a feature of outdated systems and that something similar could never occur now. It is possibly worth reflecting that in 2010, prior to Savile's death, the suggestion that anyone could have behaved as he did would have been met with a similarly incredulous response. However, some of the inquiries discussed here note that organisational culture change has been relatively recent or is ongoing. That is possibly indicative of how challenging it can be to change an organisational culture once established and the danger of assuming that changes in policy equal changes in behaviour. Only a truly engaged management which demonstrates a commitment to the values they espouse on behalf of their organisations can hope to succeed.

References

Beyer, L., Higgins, D. and Bromfield, L. (2005) *Understanding Organisational Risk Factors for Child Maltreatment: A Review of Literature*. Melbourne, VIC: National Child Protection Clearinghouse, Australian Institute of Family Studies. Accessed on 15 August 2017 at https://aifs.gov.au/cfca/sites/default/files/publication-documents/organisations.pdf

Colton, M. (2002) 'Factors associated with abuse in residential child care institutions.' *Children and Society 16*, 1, 33–44.

Davies, H. (2014) *Southbank International School Independent Review Arising from the Criminal Conduct of William Vahey: Final Report.* London: Farrer and Co. Accessed on 18 August 2017 at http://news.bbc.co.uk/1/shared/bsp/hi/pdfs/27_11_14_vahey.pdf

Doran, C. and Brannan, C. (1996) 'Institutional Abuse.' In P.C. Bibby (ed.) *Organised Abuse: The Current Debate*. London: Ashgate Publishing.

Douglas, M. (1986) *How Institutions Think*. New York: Syracuse University Press.

Erooga, M. (2009) *Towards Safer Organisations: Adults Who Pose a Risk to Children in the Workplace and Implications for Recruitment and Selection*. London: NSPCC. Accessed on 17 August 2017 at www.nspcc.org.uk/globalassets/documents/research-reports/towards-safer-organisations-2009-report.pdf

Freeh, L. (2012) *Report of the Special Investigative Council Regarding the Actions of the Pennsylvania State University Related to Child Sexual Abuse Committed by Gerald A. Sandusky*. Washington, DC: Freeh, Sporkin and Sullivan, LLP. Accessed on 17 August 2017 at http://media.pennlive.com/midstate_impact/other/REPORT_FINAL_071212.pdf

Johnstone, A. and Dent, C. (2015) *Investigation into the Association of Jimmy Savile with Stoke Mandeville Hospital: A Report for Buckinghamshire Healthcare NHS Trust.* Amersham: Buckinghamshire Healthcare NHS Trust. Accessed on 12 August 2017 at www.speakingoutinvestigation.com/Downloads/Speaking%20out%20investigation/2902210_Investigation%20into%20the%20Association%20of%20Jimmy%20Savile%20with%20Stoke%20Mandeville%20Hospital.pdf

Kirkup, B. and Marshall, P. (2014) *Jimmy Savile Investigation. Broadmoor Hospital: Report to the West London Mental Health NHS Trust and the Department of Health.* London: West London Mental Health NHS Trust. Accessed on 11 August 2017 at www.gov.uk/government/publications/jimmy-savile-investigation-broadmoor-hospital

Lampard, K. and Marsden, E. (2015) *Themes and Lessons Learnt from NHS Investigations into Matters Relating to Jimmy Savile: Independent Report for the Secretary of State for Health.* London: Department of Health. Accessed on 11 August 2017 at www.gov.uk/government/uploads/system/uploads/attachment_data/file/407209/KL_lessons_learned_report_FINAL.pdf

McAlinden, A-M. (2006) 'Managing risk: from regulation to the reintegration of sexual offenders.' *Criminology and Criminal Justice 6*, 2, 197–218.

Proctor, S., Galloway, R., Chaloner, R., Jones, C. and Thompson, D. (2014) *The Report of the Investigation into Matters Relating to Savile at Leeds Teaching Hospitals NHS Trust.* Leeds: Leeds Teaching Hospitals NHS Trust. Accessed on 11 August 2017 at www.leedsth.nhs.uk/assets/Uploads/40482-2901955-Libra-Executive-SUMMARY-accessible2.pdf

Royal Commission into Institutional Responses to Child Sexual Abuse (RCIRCSA) (2016) *Case Study 37, March 2016, Sydney.* Accessed on 18 April 2017 at www.childabuseroyalcommission.gov.au/case-study/b9cde3b6-9343-4660-b273-235c57f714e4/case-study-37,-march-2016,-sydney

Safer Recruitment Consortium (2015) *Guidance for Safer Working Practice for Those Working with Children and Young People in Education Settings.* Accessed on 7 February 2016 at www.safeguardinginschools.co.uk/wp-content/uploads/2015/10/Guidance-for-Safer-Working-Practices-2015-final1.pdf

Savell, J. (2015) *Operation Outreach Report.* Guildford: Surrey Police. Accessed on 11 August 2017 at http://mandatenow.org.uk/wp-content/uploads/2015/04/Operation-Outreach-29-4-2015-11186-link.pdf

Savile, J. (1974) *As It Happens.* London: Barrie and Jenkins.

Smith, J. (2016) *The Independent Review into the BBC's Culture and Practices during the Jimmy Savile and Stuart Hall Years.* London: BBC. Accessed on 11 August 2017 at www.bbc.co.uk/bbctrust/dame_janet_smith

Social Services Inspectorate (1994) *An Abuse of Trust: The Report of the Social Services Inspectorate Investigation into the Case of Martin Huston.* Belfast: DHSSNI.

Wardaugh, J. and Wilding, P. (1993) 'Towards an explanation of the corruption of social care.' *Critical Social Policy 13*, 37, 4–31.

Wonnacott, J. and Carmi, E. (2016) *Serious Case Review: Southbank International School.* Hammersmith & Fulham, Kensington and Chelsea and Westminster LSCB. Accessed on 15 August 2017 at www.rbkc.gov.uk/pdf/Southbank%20SCR%20REPORT%2012%201%2016.pdf

Section 2

GENERALISABLE ASPECTS OF BEHAVIOUR

3

ORGANISATIONAL SEX OFFENDERS AND 'INSTITUTIONAL GROOMING'

Lessons from the Savile and Other Inquiries

ANNE-MARIE MCALINDEN

This chapter provides a critical overview of a range of high-profile public inquiries and official reviews into allegations of institutional child sexual abuse in England and Wales and elsewhere, including those relating to Jimmy Savile, and some of the key themes arising from them. Those themes relate in particular to the dynamics of institutional sex offending as well as the nature of organisational responses and governance frameworks that can hinder early detection and prevention. Following on from this, it also highlights the dynamics of what I have previously termed 'institutional grooming' (McAlinden, 2006) and the features of the organisational environment that both facilitate institutional child sexual abuse and help mask its discovery or disclosure.

In doing this, the analysis examines the tension between what others have termed 'preferential' and 'situational' or 'opportunistic' sexual offending (Sullivan and Beech, 2004; Wortley and Smallbone, 2006) – that is, whether sex offenders deliberately set out to infiltrate organisations in order to gain access and increase the opportunities to abuse children or whether the motivation to sexually offend only emerges after they become established in an institutional environment. While the behaviour of Savile as a 'predatory' sex offender can be more clearly related to the former, the latter is also significant in terms of the lessons relating to the development of protective environments which reduce the opportunities for abuse to occur.

Following this, the chapter reflects on the learning from some of the key themes arising from the inquiries. It considers what policy and practical steps need to be taken to improve organisational culture around safeguarding and minimise the future incidence of institutional child sexual abuse. This includes changing the policy agenda from reactive 'risk' management to a proactive focus on 'safety' and, within this, balancing the competing needs and interests of potential victims and suspected perpetrators.

Key themes from the inquiries

Public inquiries into institutional child sexual abuse

Over the last two decades, high-profile cases of historical or non-recent institutional child sexual abuse have resounded in a number of jurisdictions worldwide, including the United States (John Jay College, 2004, 2011), Canada (Law Commission of Canada, 2000), the Netherlands (Commission of Inquiry, 2011), England and Wales (Waterhouse, 2000) and the Republic of Ireland. At the time of writing, the Historical Institutional Abuse Inquiry in Northern Ireland has just reported (HIA Inquiry, 2017) and there is an ongoing Royal Commission into Institutional Responses to Child Sexual Abuse in Australia[1] (see generally, McAlinden and Naylor, 2016). The Republic of Ireland has been one of the most prolific jurisdictions in responding to allegations of institutional child sexual abuse within the Catholic Church with four high-profile inquiries within six years (Murphy, Buckley and Joyce, 2005; Commission to Inquire into Child Abuse, 2009; Commission of Investigation, 2009, 2011). The five-volume 'Ryan Report' highlighted the fact that the abuse of children (physical, sexual, emotional and neglect), and the failure of Church and State authorities to adequately respond to the problem, had been systemic in Irish child care institutions for

1 See http://childabuseroyalcommission.gov.au

decades (Commission to Inquire into Child Abuse, 2009, vol. IV, paras.6.09–6.18).

In England and Wales, a number of inquiries have stemmed from predominantly secular organisations in both residential and non-residential settings, including care homes, nurseries and schools (see Reder, Duncan and Gray, 1993; Corby, Doig and Roberts, 2001; and Parton, 2004, for an overview). The inquiries have included the Pindown Inquiry into implementation of an excessively punitive regime in Staffordshire children's homes (Levy and Kahan, 1991); the Ty Mawr Inquiry following allegations of misconduct in Gwent children's homes (Williams and McCreadie, 1992); the Leicestershire Inquiry into sexual abuse by management and staff in children's homes (Kirkwood, 1993); and the Waterhouse Report (2000) into the abuse of children in care homes in North Wales, as well as the Savile-related inquiries discussed below. There have also been a number of related policy reviews (see, for example, the Warner Report (1992) on the selection, development and management of staff in children's homes; the Utting Report (1997) on the safeguards for children living away from home; and the Nolan Committee Report (2001) on child protection policies in the Catholic Church in England and Wales).

This body of inquiries has highlighted a range of recurring themes relating to the occurrence and dynamics of institutional child sexual abuse:

- the abuse normally took place over a number of years and its extent went unrecognised for some time;
- usually more than one victim was involved, and often multiple perpetrators;
- there was often a culture of acceptance or disbelief where other staff either ignored signs of abuse or were afraid to challenge inappropriate behaviour or act on initial concerns;
- many complaints were not formally reported, and victims were afraid to disclose the abuse;

- or when they did no action was taken, either because there was a conspiracy to keep allegations quiet or an acceptance of the denial by the alleged perpetrator in order to protect institutional reputation;
- there were poor internal and external management frameworks in place including the absence of an effective system for complaints.

(see McAlinden, 2006, 2012, p.157)

These factors are confirmed by the literature on institutional child sexual abuse which suggests primarily that the complaints are of a sexual nature, involving both boys and girls, and that the majority have not been reported (Barter, 1999; Gallagher, 2000). As Parton (2004) notes, many of these inquiries made similar recommendations to enhance organisational policies and cultures around safeguarding which were not followed through, raising questions not only about the speed and process of organisational change but also, more worryingly, whether any lessons were actually learned (see Sullivan and Beech, 2002). Indeed, many of these themes, including delays in disclosure, a culture of silence and denial and minimisation of allegations, also arise from an examination of the major Savile inquiries. Moreover, they also relate directly to the process of 'institutional grooming' (McAlinden, 2006, 2012, ch.5) and will be returned to below.

The Savile inquiries

While Savile offended on a prolific and unprecedented scale across a range of entertainment, health, education and child care contexts (with more than 75 inquiries or reviews conducted or ongoing), the principal inquiries or investigations relate to those concerning the BBC (Smith, 2016), Broadmoor Special Hospital (Kirkup and Marshall, 2014), Stoke Mandeville Hospital (Johnstone and Dent, 2015; Vize and Klinck, 2015), the Leeds Teaching Hospitals (Leeds General Infirmary; St James's Hospital; Chapel Allerton Hospital;

Seacroft Hospital) (Proctor *et al.*, 2014) and Duncroft School,[2] all of which were convened posthumously. It is important to note that in tandem with many of the high-level public inquiries into institutional child abuse, such as those involving the State and the Catholic Church in the Republic of Ireland, the remit of most of these inquiries was not only about the nature and scale of Savile's behaviour but also the level of institutional awareness and the failures to respond adequately to the problem. Crucially, as discussed further below, it is both of these elements – sexual offending behaviour combined with the failure to challenge inappropriate or abusive behaviour – which makes institutional grooming and sustained abuse possible.

The sexual behaviour displayed by Savile ranged from abusive behaviour at the very serious end of the spectrum, such as rape and sexual assault, to sexual touching and inappropriate non-contact behaviours involving indecent exposure, or lewd words or gestures against male but predominantly female victims. The victims were also vulnerable to a lesser or greater extent. Many, in addition to the inherent vulnerability of children, were vulnerable by virtue of their status as patients with complex needs, as looked after children or as vulnerable adults. Others had a range of vulnerabilities including mental health issues and social, emotional or educational difficulties. In addition, however, Savile also abused adolescents, adult staff, child and adult visitors, volunteers and charity fundraisers (e.g. at Stoke Mandeville Hospital: Johnstone and Dent, 2015, ch.6). Although Savile procured his victims through these various institutions, the offences took place at a range of locations including within the institutional premises and without, including in his car, camper van and his London flat.

In tandem with the body of general inquiries into institutional child sexual abuse within both England and Wales and elsewhere,

---

2 While there was no official inquiry into Duncroft School, there were two reviews – one in 2013 of Surrey Police's investigation (Operation Ornament) between May 2007 and October 2009 into allegations of sexual offences against girls at Duncroft (Savell, 2013); and the second a review of Operation Outreach, the investigation into allegations made after Savile's death about his offending by 23 former Duncroft residents (Savell, 2015).

there were typically long delays in victim disclosure. The majority of the allegations of abuse were not made during Savile's lifetime as the overwhelming majority of victims disclosed after his death. For those victims who did make a complaint, allegations were either not taken seriously or not followed up by the police or relevant authorities (HMIC, 2013). In organisations where the abuse took place, typically there were flawed internal management frameworks with lax procedures for staff supervision and the absence of a coherent system for complaints. Indeed, during his lifetime, and certainly the peak of his offending during the mid-1960s to mid-1970s, when Savile was 40–50 years old, he appeared to operate with complete impunity and with minimal risk or fear of the consequences that victims would report him. Although Savile typically acted alone, there were instances of both passive and active complicity by front-line institutional staff by either deliberately ignoring suspicions of abuse or actively aiding the abuse by allowing Savile to have unhindered access to victims (see, e.g., Savell, 2015, para.1.6, in the context of Duncroft School).

As Dame Janet Smith noted in the BBC Inquiry: 'He seems never to have had any fear that any of [his victims] would report him' (Smith, 2016, para.5.338). His public persona and self-styled status as a charitable public figure, the use of his circle of contacts and the influence of 'celebrity' served to both deflect the concerns of staff and discourage reporting by victims (Exton and Thandi, 2013). Indeed, the fact that Savile made use of his persona and sphere of influence to gain, in some cases, virtually unrestricted and unchallenged access to victims speaks directly to the dynamics, behaviour and methods underpinning 'institutional grooming' (McAlinden, 2006, 2012).

Institutional grooming

Grooming is a term generally used to describe the preparatory behaviours which precede actual abuse and which is directed at either the victim (usually children), the environment or significant others (Craven, Brown and Gilchrist, 2006; see also Salter, 1995, 2003). As others have put it, it is about gaining *access* to the child; ensuring the child's *compliance*; and maintaining the child's *secrecy* to avoid disclosure (Craven *et al.*, 2006, p.297). Its broad purpose is thought to be twofold: to set up opportunities to abuse and subsequently to prevent disclosure by the victim or discovery by others. To this end, I have previously proposed a definition of grooming which captures its nature and purpose:

> (1) the use of a variety of manipulative and controlling techniques (2) with a vulnerable subject (3) in a range of inter-personal and social settings (4) in order to establish trust or normalise sexually harmful behaviour (5) with the overall aim of facilitating exploitation and/or prohibiting exposure. (McAlinden, 2012, p.11)

This section of the chapter draws on my previous empirical work on grooming in the form of over 50 interviews with criminal justice and other professionals across the United Kingdom and the Republic of Ireland (McAlinden, 2012).

Some of the Savile inquiries have pinpointed the process of grooming children or their families over a period of months (see, for example, the eight cases within the context of Leeds Teaching Hospitals: Proctor *et al.*, 2014; see also the allegations of sexual offending made during Operation Yewtree: Gray and Watt, 2013). Further, evidence from the Stoke Mandeville Inquiry (Johnstone and Dent, 2015, para.13.19) demonstrates that reasons for non-disclosure by victims include, among others, the fact that Savile told victims not to say anything as no one would believe them. This factor was also amplified by Savile's status as a high-profile and, at the time, well-respected celebrity. Indeed, the inquiries surveyed above highlight that Savile often chose the most vulnerable of victims, which simultaneously made them easier to abuse and less likely to disclose. However, since he exhibited an ongoing pattern of sexual offending against multiple victims, there was less need for him to engage in the grooming of particular victims in order to maintain their ongoing compliance and prevent them disclosing. Rather, the scale and scope of Savile's offending was ultimately made possible by a broader and more ingrained process of institutional grooming in which the surrounding environment, as well as the staff who worked within it, might be 'groomed' as part of a pattern of preparatory and ongoing abusive behaviours.

Grooming within organisational environments

While institutional abuse is a sub-category of extra-familial abuse, there are also clear elements of institutional grooming and abuse that closely resemble the dynamics of intra-familial abuse – that is, the particular features of the institutional environment which sex offenders may use to facilitate abuse and prevent disclosure by children and other professionals include features such as trust, opportunity, anonymity, secrecy and power. It is these unique facets of 'vulnerable organisations' (Erooga, 2009b, p.38), or what Hall terms 'the institutional syndrome' (Hall, 2000, cited in Erooga, 2009b, p.38), which enables offenders to manipulate perceptions, create opportunities and prevent suspicion.

The gaining of trust, or 'emotional seduction' (Salter, 1995, p.74), plays a pivotal role in the grooming process with respect to children, protective adults and the surrounding environment. Within the institutional setting, the intimate and social relationships created with the victim and others who might protect them are also based on the creation of loyalty and implicit trust (see generally Ben-Yehuda, 2001). Moreover, as discussed further below, institutions can create multiple opportunities for manipulation and abuse and can allow the offender to take on a different persona and remain anonymous in terms of their deviant sexual tendencies. The organisational culture itself may be conducive to abuse of power, the 'corruption of care' (Erooga, 2009b, pp.39–40) and erosion of the primary functions of care and protection. The fact that Savile was afforded high status as a celebrity enhanced his power and authority and helped to discourage victim reporting for fear of the consequences.

Child care institutions appear to be 'especially self-protective, secretive and closed by nature' (McAlinden, 2006, p.353). As such they discourage the drawing of attention to any deficiencies in policies and procedures and the signs of abuse, out of fear of damaging the reputation or credibility of the institution. The Savile inquiries have established that staff either ignored signs of abuse or failed to act upon disclosures by children as an attempt to preserve the reputation of the institution or disguise the lack of proper procedures in place. Furthermore, if organisations or individuals are held in high esteem by local agencies or parents, as Savile generally was, children may experience added difficulties in both resisting and disclosing the abuse (Gallagher, 2000, p.810).

Indeed, the particular role which these offenders play within certain institutions may also make the environment more facilitative of abuse. Savile had free rein over most of the institutions he was involved with, with few checks and balances on his behaviour and no clear hierarchies of accountability. It is this status or authority that may give abusers the necessary control over the organisational culture, or 'the power to betray' (Ben-Yehuda, 2001, p.28) – it may provide an opportunity for those minded to abuse children to do so in a way that exposes them to less risk, thus reducing the likelihood of detection and potentially leading to an increase in abuse.

The literature establishes that looked after children in residential care, such as those at Duncroft School, are more susceptible to abuse than those within the community (Dawson, 1983; Siskind, 1986). While not all of the settings in which Savile abused were necessarily residential ones, he often had his own quarters or took the opportunity to stay overnight in the various institutions (Broadmoor, Stoke Mandeville). In such contexts, the imbalance of power between adult perpetrators and child victims is exaggerated by the offender's 'caring role and the children's traumatic or abusive histories' (Erooga, Allnock and Telford, 2012, p.62). The specific context of a local authority secure or residential facility where some children may have emotional or learning difficulties, behavioural or psychiatric problems, or drug or alcohol addiction can provide a captive vulnerable population for abusers (Utting, 1997, p.5; Powell, 2007, p.39). Furthermore, vulnerable or challenging children may also be regarded as having little or no credibility if allegations of abusive or inappropriate behaviour are made (Powell, 2007, p.39).

'Staff seductions'

The grooming of colleagues or other staff within an institutional environment may be in addition to, or completely replace, the grooming of the victim. What Salter terms 'staff seductions' (2003, pp.139–156), and Robben 'emotional allurement' (1995, p.83), may be 'particularly acute' in residential settings 'where offenders and staff/volunteers may spend long periods of time together' (Salter, 2003, p.140). Several interviewees in the previous in-depth study of grooming (McAlinden, 2012), referred to above, explained that the purpose of such grooming would be to avert the suspicion or attention of those who would otherwise provide a source of safety or support for the victim. One interviewee stated:

> I've had cases where there was a residential social worker and it was more the grooming of the colleagues as opposed to the grooming of the child…so sometimes the grooming can be around creating with others, who should be calling into question what are you doing, that the grooming is ensuring…that's who I need to work on and not necessarily any grooming of the victim… It's more, why did nobody else come and that's the grooming of others.[3]

Other interviewees pointed out these individuals were often the most popular with the staff and the children (see also Bithell, 1991; Erooga *et al.*, 2012, pp.10, 27). As one professional stated, reflecting on previous cases:

> They were seen as just very positive…two of them were actually the child protection officers, so they took on the mantle of protecting children and were seen in that light, and therefore in a way become inviolable…if they are doing something it

3 Interview, independent social work consultant, Northern Ireland, 23 May 2011.

> must be okay…because they have the responsibility and they are so caring.[4]

Savile's pursuit of charitable works across the myriad institutions he was involved with helped to cement the perception of the benign, inviolable and caring nature of his character. However, the notion of 'institutions as individuals' (Douglas, 1986) – whereby offenders seek to navigate or exploit system weaknesses or personal relationships in order to abuse – is also evidenced in high-profile cases of institutional sexual offending by non-celebrities.

The popularity of an individual member of staff may disempower other staff and make them reluctant or less willing to challenge suspicious or inappropriate behaviour for fear of undermining their own position within the organisation. By way of example, the serious case review into sexual abuse at Little Ted's Nursery in England and Wales in 2010[5] concluded in relation to the behaviour of Vanessa George that her 'power base within the setting and her capacity to draw other members of the staff team into her world…effectively silenc[ed] them' (Plymouth Safeguarding Children Board, 2010, para.5.73). Moreover, by failing to challenge the inappropriateness of certain behaviours, this 'made challenge even less likely and [she] may have interpreted the behaviour as implicit support' (Plymouth Safeguarding Board, 2010, para.5.4). The insidious nature of grooming within this context, however, is often extremely difficult to detect ahead of the discovery of actual harm or abuse. One respondent in the grooming research used the phrase 'system grooming'[6] to explain this process:

> He's grooming the staff, he's grooming the environment, he's grooming for example the rota system. He's doing all of that, but you wouldn't have spotted it because…he didn't show any

4 Interview, senior voluntary sector interviewee, England and Wales, 22 September 2011.

5 Nursery worker Vanessa George had been abusing children in her care and sharing images of the abuse with Colin Blanchard whom she had met via the Internet.

6 Interview, independent social work consultant, Northern Ireland, 23 May 2011.

> specific interest in the victim, so teaching about that wouldn't have rang any bells with anybody because his grooming efforts were through a different system.[7]

This illustrates that practised sex offenders such as Savile are able to negotiate their way around protective individuals as well as organisational procedures.

Within this broader context, Savile also adopted what has been termed a 'blocking manipulation style' (Sullivan and Quayle, 2012) where the offender 'jests' with others in order to promote a view of themselves as fun and risqué while also normalising their inappropriate behaviour. A key component of Savile's mode of 'grooming' was to adopt overtly sexualised behaviour and language to ultimately deflect concerns about potential risk. As Marcus Erooga notes in the opening chapter (page 36), 'His general behaviour towards women was often flamboyantly inappropriate, including extravagant forms of greeting, inappropriate remarks and physical contact.' As the inquiries convey, while many recipients and bystanders of this eccentric behaviour may have found this uncomfortable or objectionable, it was often dismissed as part of his public persona – 'Just Jimmy' (see, for example, the Stoke Mandeville Hospital Inquiry: Johnstone and Dent, 2015, p.iii).

The latter argument also has resonance in relation to the wider processes of social denial (Cohen, 2001) concerning allegations of institutional child sexual abuse. This culture of disbelief was evidenced, for example, by the historical reluctance of Irish society to acknowledge clerical sexual abuse in the Republic of Ireland for decades (McAlinden, 2013). As noted above, the collective failures of the authorities, organisations and the public to act on suspicions of sexual abuse by Savile and to challenge his behaviour were attributed to his celebrity status and his charitable works (Burns and Somaiya, 2012; Boffey, 2014). In the much-quoted words of contributing author to this book and then Scotland Yard Commander responsible for Operation Yewtree Peter Spindler, 'he groomed a nation'.

---

7 Ibid.

Professional grooming

A further manifestation of 'institutional grooming' is how this may appear in interactions between suspect perpetrators and professionals such as the police. Within the context of the small number of police investigations that were undertaken during Savile's lifetime, there is also evidence of what can be termed 'professional grooming' (McAlinden, 2012, ch.5). A review by Her Majesty's Inspectorate of Constabulary (HMIC) of police responses to allegations about Savile made when he was alive highlights that allegations reported to the police may not have been adequately responded to (HMIC, 2013) – complaints tended to be dealt with in a dismissive manner and proper investigations were not carried out. The literature also establishes that within the context of police interviews with suspect offenders (Durkin and Bryant, 1999; Lippert *et al.*, 2010), there may be 'interactional difficulties' in 'negotiat[ing] an account of what actually happened' (Benneworth, 2009, pp.555–556). As Sullivan and Quayle (2012, p.90) have noted, offenders will 'typically attempt to influence how people interpret their behaviour, generating potentially self-serving testimonies'.

An alternative presentation by the offender in this context is that of a 'joker' or a 'clown' (see McAlinden, 2012, pp.190–191). During my research, a police officer explained how one older offender 'did just essentially through the interview play the…I've been a silly old buffoon… And clearly what he had been saying, backwards and forwards online, was not the thinking of a silly old man, but… an attempt to portray himself in one way to everybody else.'[8] This also accords with what Sullivan and Quayle (2012) have identified as a 'blocking manipulation' style, referred to above – where the offender 'jests' with others in order to promote a view of themselves as fun and risqué while also normalising their inappropriate behaviour. As part of this process, many interviewees also explained how offenders can play professionals off against each other, which can result in 'the

8 Interview, senior police officer, Scotland, 22 August 2011.

watering down of the evidence'[9] or in professionals 'los[ing] sight of the risk that someone poses'.[10]

Preferential vs situational/opportunistic sexual offending

In tandem with sexual offending more broadly (Wortley and Smallbone, 2006), there is a dichotomous debate as to whether institutional sexual offending is predatory in nature or situationally derived (Sullivan and Beech, 2004; Erooga *et al.*, 2012, p.52). In reality, it seems more likely that as offenders are not homogenous, both are true. That is, while some offenders may deliberately choose paid work or a voluntary position which provides contact with potential victims, for others, the institutional environment may provide the opportunity to offend once they have become installed in their position (John Jay College, 2011). The opportunistic nature of sexual offending against children means that, for many 'professional offenders', 'the key factor is not the particular sexual attraction but rather the availability and vulnerability of the children' (Erooga, 2009b, p.65), which is often enhanced within an institutional environment.

This broad dichotomy between preferential and situational offending was also reflected in the views of some professionals (McAlinden, 2012, pp.176–178). A treatment professional, for example, commented that 'all of the offenders, bar none, that I've worked with have all got themselves into situations that definitely are a back door, or a side door...into having access to children'.[11] This pattern of offending was related to an 'approach explicit' pathway (Ward and Hudson, 1998) – in which an individual intentionally plans to offend and puts in place clear strategies to achieve this goal – and more ingrained and predatory forms of sexual offending against children. An independent interviewee in England and Wales explained further:

9 Interview, senior social worker, Northern Ireland, 27 July 2011.

10 Interview, forensic psychiatrist, Scotland, 24 August 2011.

11 Interview, treatment professional, Republic of Ireland, 16 May 2011.

> The entrenched child sex offender, i.e. somebody whose needs, so emotionally, socially, sexually, are only met by children, is more likely...to be involved in institutional [sexual] abuse, just simply because they will seek an environment where there is the ability to access victims.[12]

For other interviewees, however, institutional child sexual abuse was 'very situation specific' and linked to organisational risk factors. According to this view, sex offenders may be installed in a position of trust with children prior to the emergence of any motivation to sexually offend. Situational risk factors were succinctly attributed by one interviewee to 'a pressured environment...the element of solo working...[and] the lack of physical boundaries'[13] between children and the staff responsible for their care. It is this blurring of organisational roles and physical boundaries which may serve to normalise the onset of physical and later sexualised contact with children. As discussed below, this divergence in views underlines the importance of developing both external and internal controls on the behaviour of potential sex offenders in institutional settings.

In relation to Savile, while there is some evidence of premeditation in terms of the use of grooming strategies with children and their families as noted above, this distinction between situational/opportunistic and predatory sexual offending is not immediately clear-cut. Within the framework of predatory or preferential sexual offending, for example, Savile does not appear to have had a strong victim preference. As outlined above, the inquiries establish that Savile abused young children and adolescents, as well as adults, across a range of contexts that encompassed both male and female victims. This tends to go against the grain of the literature which establishes that many sex offenders have a strong victim preference, particularly

12 Interview, voluntary sector professional, England and Wales, 19 September 2011.

13 Interview, voluntary sector professional, Scotland, 21 August 2011.

along gendered lines,[14] although those sex offenders with no fixed victim preference, as might be expected, tend to exhibit a greater range of grooming and abusive behaviours.[15]

Moreover, much of Savile's offending was opportunistic yet also had distinct and overriding predatory elements. That is, while Savile undoubtedly made use of the unique institutional opportunities and uncontrolled access to potential victims, the scale and scope of his offending also underlines the insidious and predatory nature of his behaviour. As the inquiry into the circumstances surrounding his offending at Broadmoor Special Hospital notes, delineating this crossover, there is 'no reason to doubt that Savile was an opportunistic sexual predator throughout the time he was associated with Broadmoor' (Kirkup and Marshall, 2014, para.1.14). A similar conclusion was reached in the substantive inquiry into Stoke Mandeville Hospital, which describes him as 'an opportunistic predator who could also on occasions show a high degree of pre-meditation when planning attacks on his victims' (Johnstone and Dent, 2015, para.2). It may even be argued, therefore, that manifold opportunities to offend, such as within institutional contexts, which go unchallenged, may facilitate the development and entrenchment of predatory sexual behaviour.

Learning from the inquiries

The learning identified above in relation to the grooming strategies displayed by Savile within an organisational context, which ultimately

---

14 See, for example, large-scale research by Elliott and colleagues that demonstrated that 58 per cent of offenders targeted girls and 14 per cent targeted boys, while the remaining 28 per cent targeted both boys and girls (Elliott, Browne and Kilcoyne, 1995, p.583). Similarly, Grubin (1998) found that 60 per cent of child molesters target only girls, about 20 to 33 per cent boys, and about 10 per cent children of either sex. Earlier research by Baker and Duncan (1985), on the other hand, reported that 44 per cent of the males in their survey reported being a victim of extra-familial abuse compared to 30 per cent of the girls, which may be indicative of under-reporting by boys.

15 See, for example, Tallon and Terry (2008) in relation to institutional clerical sexual abuse.

allowed him to offend to a prolific extent for decades, has highlighted a number of key themes. These relate, amongst others, to the closed nature of organisational cultures and the dynamics of institutional grooming; the lack of clear governance frameworks; and the absence of protective policies which prize protection of the vulnerable. In the case of Savile, these features were undoubtedly compounded by the influence of the deferential culture of celebrity in that boundary violations were tolerated and not confronted. There are broader lessons to be drawn out, however, for organisations and indeed society as a whole.

A culture of 'safety'

Given the difficulties concerning non-disclosure or significant delays in disclosure by victims which is evidenced in cases of non-recent child sexual abuse, a reactive legal approach which relies on self-identification by victims has enormous limitations. Current organisational responses to the risk posed by potential sex offenders are heavily premised on known and assessed 'risk' (Kemshall, 2001) – that is, where the offender has a clear record of offending or, at the very least, where there is an established history of concerns. Risk-based measures, such as pre-employment vetting and barring, give the 'allure of protection' (Hebenton and Seddon, 2009, p.12) and can, therefore, never hope to adequately safeguard children or other potential victims within an organisational setting (McAlinden, 2010). They are limited inherently to clear, identifiable and preventable risks and not the unknown, hidden and therefore the most dangerous ones.

Part of the difficulty with early detection of potential risks of sexual harm to children within an institutional environment stems from the fact that emotional congruence with children may be indicative of a potential risk to children as well as a desirable characteristic of those most effective in working with children (Sullivan *et al.*, 2011, p.70). Since sex offenders 'share many relevant characteristics with the "general population"' (Erooga, 2009a, p.4), and there is no typical or 'full-proof' profile (Elliott *et al.*, 1995, p.109), it is difficult to identify or predict who is likely to be a risk to children prior to the occurrence of actual harm. It becomes vitally important, therefore, to supplement the risk-based paradigm with effective internal supervision and controls on institutional culture and individual working practices in settings which involve 'close and constant interaction' with children and the vulnerable (Erooga, 2009b, p.65).

This 'new' discourse could be framed around what feminist commentators refer to as a 'politics' (Stanko, 1990) or 'culture of safety' (Busch, 2002) rather than simply around 'risk', incorporating proactive as well as reactive approaches to risk management. One practical means of achieving this is the adoption of broader public health approaches to sexualised violence and abuse (Laws, 2000) that emphasise the protection of children and the vulnerable as everyone's responsibility within wider society as well as organisational contexts specifically. Institutional child sexual abuse, much like intra-familial sexual abuse, emerges as the confluence of three factors – a motivated offender, a suitable victim, and the lack of an appropriate and capable guardian (McAlinden, 2012, p.195). As Erooga (2009b, p.28) contends, therefore, 'without an appropriate organisational culture of safeguarding, any setting…is vulnerable to the corruption of the ethic of care'.

Developing an organisational culture of safeguarding

In practice, as I have argued elsewhere (McAlinden, 2012, p.276), this broad aspiration of safeguarding could be furthered by enhancing staff training around issues specific to sexual offending behaviour, and strengthening external and particularly internal management systems which would maximise 'the features that make organisations safer for children' (Beyer, Higgins and Bromfield, 2005, p.106). This would include at a minimum two key components: (1) systems of staff support and monitoring to facilitate the early identification and effective challenge of inappropriate or potentially harmful sexual behaviour (Sullivan *et al.*, 2011, p.70); and (2) an organisational 'culture of awareness and vigilance' (Erooga, 2009a, p.6) among staff which fosters 'open and constructive questioning of practice and relationships' (Shaw, 2007, p.150). A multi-layered approach to institutional child sexual abuse would offer a more viable means of protecting children and the vulnerable by enhancing children's safety while simultaneously reducing the offender's opportunity to abuse.

Such a culture offers a means of proactively addressing harms to children within intra-familial as well as extra-familial contexts primarily by encouraging a culture of openness and accountability concerning child sexual abuse. It would be orientated towards what I would term a 'panopticon of the victim' and the environment rather than the situational risk management of the offender. This entails a fundamental shift in focus away from applying 'checklists' in recognising patterns of grooming behaviour as others have advocated (van Dam, 2001; Salter, 2003; Sanderson, 2004; Powell, 2007), towards broadening protective efforts around victims, offenders and organisational communities. One interviewee outlined the essence of this broader approach that represents a distinct move away from a focus on individual risk factors:

> Ultimately, I think it is not about individual behaviour, it is about whole organisational behaviour that will extinguish the possibility of grooming, because other than that it takes us into that trying to spot the sex offender and trying to spot grooming, and I just don't believe, by and large, that is possible. So it's not about managing grooming behaviour more effectively, it is about taking a whole organisation approach... It incorporates knowing what's appropriate and what are appropriate boundaries, as opposed to being rule bound, and it becomes much more child friendly.[16]

The balance of victim–offender perspectives

A final strategy to be considered as part of early intervention and identification of risk is the integration of victim and offender perspectives on child sexual abuse. Sex offender risk assessment and management frameworks are premised on the notion of 'joined-up'

---

16 Interview, senior voluntary sector professional, England and Wales, 1 September 2011.

thinking (Cowan, Pantazis and Gilroy, 2001, p.439) and 'partnership' (Crawford, 1997; Gilling, 2007) as part of a multi-agency approach (Kemshall and Maguire, 2001). However, in tandem with broader policy debates on criminal justice more generally, victims and offenders of child sexual abuse are typically framed within oppositional hierarchical discourses (McAlinden, 2014). Equally, for the most part, practitioner discourses, on sex offender risk management on the one hand and child protection on the other, remain disconnected.

In this vein, I would argue for a more integrated approach which encompasses the child protection and offender management ends of the spectrum of policy and professional interventions with child sexual abuse. This would facilitate knowledge exchange about best practice in relation to the protection of individual children as well as the broader management of potential sex offenders. One social worker framed the problem as follows:

> You can't talk about child protection without talking about the offender. The victim and the offender have to be together and that has never been done. We still don't have that in process… the difficulty is there is no one driving that forward. To me it is just very, very clear when I see it…people have a very good understanding of child protection but they don't know how the offender and the risk management fit into that… I think it should be looked at…child protection and offender management as two different sides of the one coin.[17]

Such an approach would also enhance inter-agency cooperation in relation to the care and protection of children and could be further facilitated, for example, through specifically tailored knowledge exchange seminars aimed at both child protection and offender management professionals.

Indeed, for those on the front-line of work with perpetrators or victims of child sexual abuse, this balance of perspectives is even more pertinent. As one interviewee explained:

---

17 Interview, senior social worker, Scotland, 24 August 2011.

> One of the most difficult things in forensic work is trying to stay in the middle all the time...not over-identifying with victims; not over-identifying with offenders. It is not being drawn into... completely seeing the side that the offender wants you to see, but also seeing the other side.[18]

At the level of professional practice this also means giving due consideration to the rights and needs of potential victims and suspected perpetrators within the context of investigations into institutional child sexual abuse. The circumstances surrounding the Savile inquiries, particularly those concerning former allegations made to the police which were not properly followed up (Gray and Watt, 2013), demonstrate that there is a need to take seriously the complaints of victims when they do come forward. At the same time, this must be counterbalanced with concern for the due process rights of suspected offenders during investigations into institutional child sexual abuse in order to avoid the reputational damage following spurious allegations. More broadly, however, there is a need to recognise that institutional child sexual abuse, and the grooming strategies which underpin it, is an ongoing and ubiquitous societal problem.[19] Tackling this issue, therefore, in a meaningful way, means recognising child protection as the responsibility of not only elite-level actors but of all.

References

Baker, A.W. and Duncan, S.P. (1985) 'Child sexual abuse: a study of prevalence in Great Britain.' *Child Abuse and Neglect 9*, 4, 457–467.

Barter, C. (1999) 'Practitioners' experiences and perceptions of investigating allegations of institutional abuse.' *Child Abuse Review 8*, 6, 392–404.

Benneworth, K. (2009) 'Police interviews with suspected pedophiles: a discourse analysis.' *Discourse Society 20*, 5, 555–569.

---

18 Interview, forensic psychiatrist, Scotland, 24 August 2011.

19 See, for example, allegations of widespread institutional child sexual abuse within British football which emerged at the time of writing involving 55 amateur and professional football clubs: *BBC News*, 'Football Child Sex Abuse Claims: What Has Happened So Far?', 6 December 2016.

Ben-Yehuda, N. (2001) *Betrayal and Treason: Violations of Trust and Loyalty*. Boulder, CO: Westview.

Beyer, L., Higgins, D. and Bromfield, L. (2005) *Understanding Organizational Risk Factors for Child Maltreatment: A Review of Literature*. Melbourne, VIC: National Child Protection Clearinghouse, Australian Institute of Family Studies. Accessed on 15 August 2017 at https://aifs.gov.au/cfca/sites/default/files/publication-documents/organisations.pdf

Bithell, S. (1991) *Educator Sexual Abuse: A Guide for Prevention in the Schools*. Boise, ID: Tudor House Publishing Company.

Boffey, D. (2014) 'Revealed: How Jimmy Savile Abused up to 1,000 Victims on BBC Premises.' *The Observer*, 18 January. Accessed on 15 August 2017 at www.theguardian.com/media/2014/jan/18/jimmy-savile-abused-1000-victims-bbc

Burns, J. and Somaiya, R. (2012) 'A Shield of Celebrity Let a BBC Host Escape Legal Scrutiny for Decades.' *The New York Times*, 1 November.

Busch, R. (2002) 'Domestic Violence and Restorative Justice Initiatives: Who Pays if We Get It Wrong?' In H. Strang and J. Braithwaite (eds) *Restorative Justice and Family Violence*. Melbourne, VIC: Cambridge University Press.

Cohen, S. (2001) *States of Denial: Knowing about Atrocities and Suffering*. Cambridge: Polity Press.

Commission of Inquiry (2011) *Sexual Abuse of Minors in the Roman Catholic Church* (the 'Deetman Commission'). Summary of the report in English accessed on 24 August 2017 at www.scribd.com/document/127207981/Deetman-Report-Summary-The-Sexual-Abuse-of-Minors-Within-the-Roman-Catholic-Netherlands-2011

Commission of Investigation (2009) *Report into the Catholic Archdiocese of Dublin*. Chair: Judge Yvonne Murphy. Dublin: Department of Justice and Law Reform.

Commission of Investigation (2011) *Report into the Catholic Archdiocese of Cloyne*. Chair: Judge Yvonne Murphy. Dublin: Department of Justice and Law Reform.

Commission to Inquire into Child Abuse (2009) *Report of the Commission to Inquire into Child Abuse*. Chair: Judge Séan Ryan. Accessed on 21 July 2017 at www.childabusecommission.ie

Corby, B., Doig, A. and Roberts, V. (2001) *Public Inquiries into Abuse of Children in Residential Care*. London: Jessica Kingsley Publishers.

Cowan, D., Pantazis, C. and Gilroy, R. (2001) 'Social housing as crime control: an examination of the role of housing management in policing sex offenders.' *Social and Legal Studies 10*, 4, 435–457.

Craven, S., Brown, S. and Gilchrist, E. (2006) 'Sexual grooming of children: review of the literature and theoretical considerations.' *Journal of Sexual Aggression 12*, 3, 287–299.

Crawford, A. (1997) *The Local Governance of Crime: Appeals to Community and Partnership*. Oxford: Clarendon Press.

Dawson, R. (1983) *The Abuse of Children in Foster Care: Summary Report.* Ontario: Ontario Family and Children's Services of Oxford County.

Douglas, M. (1986) *How Institutions Think.* New York: Syracuse University Press.

Durkin, K. and Bryant, C. (1999) 'Propagandizing pederasty: a thematic analysis of the online exculpatory accounts of unrepentant pedophiles.' *Deviant Behavior: An Interdisciplinary Journal 20*, 2, 103–127.

Elliott, M., Browne, K. and Kilcoyne, J. (1995) 'Child abuse prevention: what offenders tell us.' *Child Abuse and Neglect 19*, 5, 579–594.

Erooga, M. (2009a) *Towards Safer Organisations: Adults Who Pose a Risk to Children in the Workplace and Implications for Recruitment and Selection. Executive Summary.* London: NSPCC. Accessed on 15 August 2017 at www.nspcc.org.uk/globalassets/documents/research-reports/towards-safer-organisations-2009-summary.pdf

Erooga, M. (2009b) *Towards Safer Organisations: Adults Who Pose a Risk to Children in the Workplace and Implications for Recruitment and Selection. Full Report.* London: NSPCC. Accessed on 15 August 2017 at www.nspcc.org.uk/globalassets/documents/research-reports/towards-safer-organisations-2009-report.pdf

Erooga, M., Allnock, D. and Telford, P. (2012) *Towards Safer Organisations II: Using the Perspectives of Convicted Sex Offenders to Inform Organisational Safeguarding of Children.* London: NSPCC. Accessed on 15 August 2017 at www.nspcc.org.uk/globalassets/documents/research-reports/towards-safer-organisations-2012-report.pdf

Exton, L. and Thandi, K. (2013) *Would They Actually Have Believed Me? A Focus Group Exploration of the Underreporting of Crimes by Jimmy Savile.* London: NSPCC. Accessed on 15 August 2017 at www.nspcc.org.uk/globalassets/documents/research-reports/would-they-actually-believed-me-savile-report.pdf

Gallagher, B. (2000) 'The extent and nature of known cases of institutional child sexual abuse.' *British Journal of Social Work 30*, 6, 795–817.

Gilling, D. (2007) *Crime Reduction and Community Safety: Labour and the Politics of Local Crime Control.* Cullompton, Devon: Willan Publishing.

Gray, P. and Watt, P. (2013) *Giving Victims a Voice: A Joint Report into Sexual Allegations against Jimmy Savile.* London: Metropolitan Police. Accessed on 11 August 2017 at www.nspcc.org.uk/globalassets/documents/research-reports/yewtree-report-giving-victims-voice-jimmy-savile.pdf

Grubin, D. (1998) *Sex Offending against Children: Understanding the Risk.* Police Research Series Paper 99. London: Home Office.

Hall, M. (2000) 'After Waterhouse: vicarious liability and the tort of institutional abuse.' *Journal of Social Welfare and Family Law 22*, 2, 159–173.

Hebenton, B. and Seddon, T. (2009) 'From dangerousness to precaution: managing sexual and violent offenders in an insecure and uncertain age.' *British Journal of Criminology 49*, 3, 343–362.

Her Majesty's Inspectorate of Constabulary (HMIC) (2013) *'Mistakes Were Made': HMIC's Review into Allegations and Intelligence Material Concerning Jimmy Savile between 1964 and 2012.* London: HMIC. Accessed on 11 August 2017 at www.justiceinspectorates.gov.uk/hmicfrs/media/review-into-allegations-and-intelligence-material-concerning-jimmy-savile.pdf

Historical Institutional Abuse (HIA) Inquiry (2017) *Historical Institutional Abuse Inquiry Report.* Chairman: Sir Anthony Hart. Accessed on 21 July 2017 at www.hiainquiry.org/historical-institutional-abuse-inquiry-report-chapters

John Jay College (2004) *The Nature and Scope of Sexual Abuse of Minors by Catholic Priests and Deacons in the United States, 1950–2002.* Washington, DC: United States Conference of Catholic Bishops. Accessed on 15 August 2017 at www.usccb.org/issues-and-action/child-and-youth-protection/upload/The-Nature-and-Scope-of-Sexual-Abuse-of-Minors-by-Catholic-Priests-and-Deacons-in-the-United-States-1950-2002.pdf

John Jay College (2011) *The Causes and Context of Sexual Abuse of Minors by Catholic Priests in the United States, 1950–2010: A Report Presented to the United States Conference of Catholic Bishops by the John Jay College Research Team.* Washington, DC: United States Conference of Catholic Bishops. Accessed on 15 August 2017 at www.usccb.org/issues-and-action/child-and-youth-protection/upload/The-Causes-and-Context-of-Sexual-Abuse-of-Minors-by-Catholic-Priests-in-the-United-States-1950-2010.pdf

Johnstone, A. and Dent, C. (2015) *Investigation into the Association of Jimmy Savile with Stoke Mandeville Hospital: A Report for Buckinghamshire Healthcare NHS Trust.* Amersham: Buckinghamshire Healthcare NHS Trust. Accessed on 12 August 2017 at www.speakingoutinvestigation.com/Downloads/Speaking%20out%20investigation/2902210_Investigation%20into%20the%20Association%20of%20Jimmy%20Savile%20with%20Stoke%20Mandeville%20Hospital.pdf

Kemshall, H. (2001) *Risk Assessment and Management of Known Sexual and Violent Offenders: A Review of Current Issues.* Police Research Series Paper No. 140. London: Home Office.

Kemshall, H. and Maguire, M. (2001) 'Public protection, partnership and risk penalty: the multi-agency risk management of sexual and violent offenders.' *Punishment and Society 3*, 2, 237–364.

Kirkup, B. and Marshall, P. (2014) *Jimmy Savile Investigation. Broadmoor Hospital: Report to the West London Mental Health NHS Trust and the Department of Health.* London: West London Mental Health NHS Trust. Accessed on 11 August 2017 at www.gov.uk/government/publications/jimmy-savile-investigation-broadmoor-hospital

Kirkwood, A. (1993) *The Report of the Inquiry into Aspects of the Management of Children's Homes in Leicestershire between 1973 and 1986.* Leicester: Leicestershire County Council.

Law Commission of Canada (2000) *Restoring Dignity: Responding to Child Abuse in Canadian Institutions*. Ottawa: Law Commission of Canada.

Laws, D.R. (2000) 'Sexual offending as a public health problem: a North American perspective.' *Journal of Research and Treatment 8*, 3, 243–248.

Levy, A. and Kahan, B. (1991) *The Pindown Experience and the Protection of Children: The Report of the Staffordshire Child Care Inquiry 1990*. Stafford: Staffordshire County Council.

Lippert, T., Cross, T.P., Jones, L. and Walsh, W. (2010) 'Suspect confession of child sexual abuse to investigators.' *Child Maltreatment 15*, 2, 161–170.

McAlinden, A.M. (2006) '"Setting 'em up": personal, familial and institutional grooming in the sexual abuse of children.' *Social and Legal Studies 15*, 3, 339–362.

McAlinden, A.M. (2010) 'Vetting sexual offenders: state over-extension, the punishment deficit and the failure to manage risk.' *Social and Legal Studies 19*, 1, 25–48.

McAlinden, A.M. (2012) *'Grooming' and the Sexual Abuse of Children: Institutional, Internet and Familial Dimensions*. Clarendon Studies in Criminology. Oxford: Oxford University Press.

McAlinden, A.M. (2013) 'An inconvenient truth: barriers to truth recovery in the aftermath of institutional child abuse in Ireland.' *Legal Studies 33*, 2, 189–214.

McAlinden, A.M. (2014) 'Deconstructing victim and offender identities in discourses on child sexual abuse hierarchies, blame and the good/evil dialectic.' *British Journal of Criminology 54*, 2, 180–198.

McAlinden, A.M. and Naylor, B. (2016) 'Reframing public inquiries as "procedural justice" for victims of institutional child abuse: towards a hybrid model of justice.' *Sydney Law Review 38*, 3, 277–309.

Murphy, F.D., Buckley, H. and Joyce, L. (2005) *The Ferns Report*. Presented by the Ferns Inquiry to the Minister for Health and Children. Dublin: Government Publications.

Nolan, L. (2001) *Report of the Review on Child Protection in the Catholic Church in England and Wales: A Programme for Action*. Accessed on 21 July 2017 at www.cathcom.org/mysharedaccounts/cumberlege/finalnolan1.htm

Parton, N. (2004) 'From Maria Colwell to Victoria Climbié: reflections on public inquiries into child abuse a generation apart.' *Child Abuse Review 13*, 2, 80–94.

Plymouth Safeguarding Children Board (2010) *Serious Case Review, Overview Report, Executive Summary in Respect of Nursery Z*. Accessed on 24 August 2017 at www.cscb-new.co.uk/downloads/Serious%20Case%20Reviews%20-%20exec.%20summaries/SCR_Archive/Plymouth%20SCR%20-%20Nursery%20Z%20(2010).pdf

Powell, A. (2007) *Paedophiles, Child Abuse and the Internet*. Oxford: Radcliffe Publishing.

Proctor, S., Galloway, R., Chaloner, R., Jones, C. and Thompson, D. (2014) *The Report of the Investigation into Matters Relating to Savile at Leeds Teaching Hospitals NHS Trust.* Leeds: Leeds Teaching Hospitals NHS Trust. Accessed on 11 August 2017 at www.leedsth.nhs.uk/assets/Uploads/40482-2901955-Libra-Executive-SUMMARY-accessible2.pdf

Reder, P., Duncan, S. and Gray, M. (1993) *Beyond Blame: Child Abuse Tragedies Revisited.* London: Routledge.

Robben, A.C.G.M. (1995) 'The Politics of Truth and Emotion among Victims and Perpetrators of Violence.' In C. Nordstrom and A.C.G.M. Robben (eds) *Fieldwork Under Fire: Contemporary Studies of Violence and Survival.* Berkeley: University of California Press.

Salter, A. (1995) *Transforming Trauma: A Guide to Understanding and Treating Adult Survivors of Child Sexual Abuse.* Newbury Park, CA: Sage.

Salter, A. (2003) *Predators, Pedophiles, Rapists, and Other Sex Offenders: Who They Are, How They Operate, and How We Can Protect Ourselves and Our Children.* New York: Basic Books.

Sanderson, C. (2004) *The Seduction of Children: Empowering Parents and Teachers to Protect Children from Sexual Abuse.* London and Philadelphia: Jessica Kingsley Publishers.

Savell, J. (2013) *Report into Operation Ornament.* Guildford: Surrey Police.

Savell, J. (2015) *Operation Outreach Report.* Guildford: Surrey Police. Accessed on 11 August 2017 at http://mandatenow.org.uk/wp-content/uploads/2015/04/Operation-Outreach-29-4-2015-11186-link.pdf

Shaw, T. (2007) *Historical Abuse Systemic Review: Residential Schools and Children's Homes in Scotland 1950–1995.* Edinburgh: The Scottish Government.

Siskind, A. (1986) 'Issues in institutional child sexual abuse: the abused, the abuser and the system.' *Residential Treatment for Children and Youth 4*, 2, 9–30.

Smith, J. (2016) *The Independent Review into the BBC's Culture and Practices during the Jimmy Savile and Stuart Hall Years.* London: BBC. Accessed on 11 August 2017 at www.bbc.co.uk/bbctrust/dame_janet_smith

Stanko, E.A. (1990) *Everyday Violence.* London: Virago.

Sullivan, J. and Beech, A. (2002) 'Professional perpetrators.' *Child Abuse Review 11*, 3, 153–167.

Sullivan, J. and Beech, A. (2004) 'A comparative study of demographic data relating to intra- and extra-familial child sexual abusers and professional perpetrators.' *Journal of Sexual Aggression 10*, 1, 39–50.

Sullivan, J. and Quayle, E. (2012) 'Manipulation Styles of Abusers Who Work with Children.' In M. Erooga (ed.) *Creating Safer Organisations.* New York: John Wiley and Sons.

Sullivan, J., Beech, A.R., Craig, L.A. and Gannon, T.A. (2011) 'Comparing intra-familial and extra-familial child sexual abusers with professionals who have sexually abused children with whom they work.' *International Journal of Offender Therapy and Comparative Criminology 55*, 1, 56–74.

Tallon, J.A. and Terry, K.J. (2008) 'Analyzing paraphilic activity, specialization, and generalization in priests who sexually abused minors.' *Criminal Justice and Behaviour 35*, 5, 615–628.

Utting, W. (1997) *People Like Us: The Report of the Review of the Safeguards for Children Living Away from Home*. London: HMSO.

van Dam, C. (2001) *Identifying Child Abusers: Preventing Child Sexual Abuse by Recognizing the Patterns of Offenders*. New York: The Haworth Press.

Vize, C. and Klinck, B. (2015) *Legacy Report – Further Investigation into the Association of Jimmy Savile with Stoke Mandeville Hospital: A Report for Buckinghamshire Healthcare NHS Trust*. Amersham: Buckinghamshire Healthcare NHS Trust. Accessed on 12 August 2017 at www.speakingoutinvestigation.com/Downloads/Speaking%20out%20investigation/2903580_Legacy%20Report%20Accessible%20v2.pdf

Ward, T. and Hudson, S.M. (1998) 'A model of the relapse process in sexual offenders.' *Journal of Interpersonal Violence 13*, 6, 700–725.

Warner, N. (1992) *Choosing with Care*. London: HMSO.

Waterhouse, R. (2000) *Lost in Care: Report of the Tribunal of Inquiry into the Abuse of Children in Care in the Former County Council Areas of Gwynedd and Clwyd since 1974*. London: HMSO.

Williams, G. and McCreadie, J. (1992) *Ty Mawr Community Home Inquiry*. Cwmbran: Gwent County Council.

Wortley, R. and Smallbone, S. (eds) (2006) *Situational Prevention of Child Sexual Abuse*. Crime Prevention Studies, Vol. 19. Monsey, NY: Criminal Justice Press, and Cullompton, Devon: Willan Publishing.

4

THINKING BEYOND A SINGLE TYPE OF ORGANISATIONAL SEX OFFENDER

MARCUS ERODGA

A longstanding stereotype of sex offenders is that of 'a sophisticated and well organised, predatory individual' (Jenkins, 1992) with its implications of intentionality in the process of finding settings where vulnerable children may be accessed. Indeed, one of the effects of a high-profile case like that of Jimmy Savile is that it has the potential to reinforce an archetype of organisational sex offenders more generally. The perception therefore becomes that all 'professional offenders' are characterised as being charismatic, manipulative and highly motivated to abuse. That is undoubtedly true of Savile and some others, for example William Vahey, a teacher at Southbank International School in London who is believed to have abused at least 54 pupils at a school where he was a highly regarded teacher (Wonnacott and Carmi, 2016).

This brief chapter considers the possibility of a different kind of organisational sex offender, what will be termed here 'situational offenders'. The implication of the existence of such offenders is that simply relying on vetting and screening is not sufficient to maximise organisational safeguarding, and different approaches are required. The chapter therefore considers a 'low-level concerns' approach to whole organisation safeguarding.

'Types' of organisational sex offender

The early situational offending literature (Clarke, 1983) describes the interaction of factors that result in decision-making about committing crime, including the environment or situation in which the offending is to take place. In later publications Cornish and Clarke (2003) propose three offender types based on the strength of the offender's criminal disposition and the role situational factors play in their offending, and Beyer, Higgins and Bromfield (2005) suggest that these classifications are useful for understanding a range of maltreatment types, including sexual abuse, which may not classically be considered in literature on crime prevention.

Developing that further, it is possible to think of organisational sex offenders as possibly constituting three types, which differ to some extent from the more general types proposed by Cornish and Clarke – that is, that some are primarily preferential, some are opportunistic and some are situational.

Preferential sex offenders are those who have a conscious desire to sexually abuse children, and who either do not see, or are not easily deterred by, obstacles. Jimmy Savile and William Vahey would appear to be classic examples of preferential offenders.

Opportunistic sex offenders are those who are motivated to abuse and do so because potential victims are available and potentially vulnerable, and the organisational setting either inadvertently facilitates, or fails to prevent, abusive activity. Under Cornish and Clarke's (2003) Rational Choice Theory this category of offender performs an internal 'risk–benefit analysis' to determine whether or not to commit a particular crime. This analysis is influenced by their assessment of the risks associated with committing a crime at a given moment in time. For this category of offender, therefore, if organisational factors are more stringent or less permissive of 'offence conducive behaviour', then it is more likely that they will be deterred.

The final 'type', *situational sex offenders*, are those whose propensity to abuse is previously unknown or unacknowledged, and their offending is specific to the set of institutional factors which potentiates their offending. Situational sex offenders react to particular sets of personal and environmental circumstances, and Cornish and Clarke (2003), who were discussing crime more generally rather than sexual abuse specifically, suggest that in that context the offence may represent an aberration in an otherwise law-abiding life. Transposed to sexual offending it may be that their abuse, whilst very possibly not being an isolated offence, may represent the exception to otherwise offence-free behaviour.

The heterogeneity of organisational sex offenders

It is very human to seek a degree of certainty or predictability about our world and particularly about phenomena that are challenging or troubling. The possibility of abuse of children by those with a responsibility to care for them undoubtedly fits that description. Sullivan and Quayle (2012) note that those who offend in the context of organisations represent a highly heterogeneous group whose motivations for sexually offending are varied. Certainly some (Sullivan and Quayle suggest that it is a majority) are aware of their sexual interest in children before they join the organisation within which they will abuse. It is this 'type' of offender who tends to dominate thinking about approaches to organisational safeguarding.

Whether or not it is a majority, other research suggests that whilst it is a common perception that all organisational offenders are motivated to abuse before joining the organisation, there is a significant proportion for whom that is not the case. In a study of sexual abuse in US day care (nursery) settings, Finkelhor, Williams and Burns (1988) state that it is their impression that 'much sexual abuse in day care does not grow out of a specific, conscious, and pre-existing sexual preference for day-care-age children' (p.65). Rather, they suggest that opportunism may be a defining characteristic of the abuse – that it is motivated by drivers that are more general and diffuse than specific sexual attraction. Rather than sexual attractiveness to the abuser, they suggest that the key factor was the children's availability and vulnerability. Indeed, they go so far as to suggest that 'opportunistic perpetrators probably…would not have abused at all if they had not found themselves in a setting where they were in close and constant interaction with children' (p.66).

That possibly startling finding is echoed in the report of the serious case review of the sexual abuse of numerous children by nursery nurse Vanessa George. The review found that:

> ...it has become clear that there is no evidence that [George] had a sexual interest in children prior to the commencement of her internet relationship with [her male co-accused with whom she shared images of the abuse], and it is therefore unlikely that a sexual interest in children would have been apparent prior to [George] 'meeting' him. (Wonnacott, 2010, para.5.1)

The possibility that not all offenders are predisposed is reinforced by research conducted with organisational sex offenders by this author and colleagues (Erooga, Allnock and Telford, 2012). A significant minority of the sample (n=19) appeared to be what could be described as situational offenders – those who had no apparent predisposition to sexually abuse, but for whom a specific set of personal circumstances, organisational features and often an emotionally intimate relationship with a particular child were the factors which resulted in their offending. It is not possible to quantify the relative proportion of each category of offender in a wider offender population, but in that research ten (53%) reported that they had no awareness of a sexual interest in children prior to the offences; two (11%) reported that they became aware of their sexual interest in children in adulthood; and four (21%) reported that they were under 11 years when they became aware of sexual interest in younger children. A further three (16%) reported that they were aware of a sexual interest in children, but it was unclear when this awareness developed.

Boundaries

If these offenders are not pre-motivated, it is reasonable to assume that there is some process which ultimately results in them abusing, and logically it follows that if that process is interrupted or not 'played out' then the abuse would not occur. A key element of any abuse process will be boundary violation – that boundaries must be broken for abuse to occur. In the case of non-predisposed, or situational, offenders it is possible to conceptualise a 'slippery slope' of boundary violations towards abuse, with a number of stages as precursors to the sexual abuse itself. This model differs from a classic slippery slope argument, in which an initial misstep inevitably leads to progression down the slope (Walton, 2015). Rather, in this version it is suggested that initial infringements are sometimes part of a grooming process, but at other times they are made innocently and with good intention (Subotsky, Bewley and Crowe, 2010). Frequently the violation of boundaries may be excused, or not recognised as potential warning signs, by colleagues (Erooga, 2009).

Once boundaries are breached it then becomes more difficult to restore the relationship to one in which proper boundaries are respected. When expressed diagrammatically (Figure 4.1) it can be seen that the increasingly steep sides of the slope make it more likely that without intervention an individual may progress in a process from a relatively innocent boundary violation, or set of violations, to more serious behaviour or abuse.

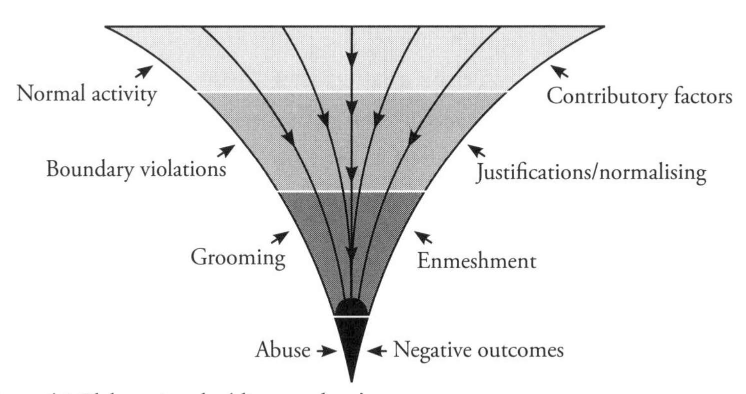

Figure 4.1 Elaborating the 'slippery slope'

This seems likely to be exacerbated by another issue identified by inquiries (e.g. Lampard and Marsden, 2015; Scott-Moncrieff and Morris, 2015), the absence of adequate whistle-blowing arrangements, which can potentially be a protective factor as addressed below. The implication is that organisations should not simply concern themselves with defining boundaries. Rather, the safest environments for children are organisations where boundaries are considered important and adhered to in every aspect of staff performing their role. A frequent issue identified in reviews and inquiries is that colleagues have some level of concern about an individual subsequently known to have abused, but do not have a framework or mechanism to discuss those with someone with the authority to intervene. Chapter 2 considers this issue in relation to Savile, but it is also a feature of other inquiries into cases of abuse in organisations – for example, teacher Nigel Leat (NSSCB, 2012), nursery worker Vanessa George (Plymouth Safeguarding Children Board, 2010) and Chichester Cathedral Head Steward Terence Banks (Carmi, 2014).

Policies to support a positive organisational culture

In 1993 an inquiry into a case of organisational abuse in Northern Ireland (DHSS, 1993) highlighted the importance of a culture of openness and trust in the organisation, and suggested it should be one in which staff are encouraged, through formal and informal channels of communication, to question, express concerns or pass on significant information to management about the protection of children, or the conduct of colleagues, and be assured that those will be received in a sensitive manner. It was not a review that received much attention beyond those directly involved or in the immediate professional arena, but that observation now seems prescient in suggesting an approach which is currently receiving further consideration.

A 'NEUTRAL NOTIFICATION' POLICY

In his 2014 review of the circumstances surrounding the sexual abuse of tens of pupils by teacher William Vahey at Southbank International School, Davies suggests that there was a dominant belief at the school that the type of offending committed by Vahey could not happen there (a perspective which understandably is likely to be found in many child-serving organisations). Whilst some of Vahey's colleagues therefore had concerns about aspects of his behaviour, Davies suggests that the language of 'allegation' (which originates from statutory guidance and is mirrored in organisations' safeguarding policies) operated as a disincentive to notifying those concerns to managers who might be in a position to intervene early and address Vahey's conduct. He suggests that 'this language needs to be changed or extended. Even the language of "whistle-blowing", as distinct from neutral "notification", in my opinion has the same problem' (para.7.32).

Davies therefore recommends a policy he calls 'neutral notification' of activity that is neither led by signs of a specific child being at risk of, or suffering, some form of abuse, or an interpretation that the report amounts to an 'allegation' or 'complaint', which is a 'definitional threshold that students, teachers, staff and parents are understandably reluctant to cross' (para.9.6).

A 'LOW-LEVEL CONCERNS' POLICY

Described as a low-level concerns policy, that process is elaborated on by Eastman and Rigg (2017) as one that enables staff to share any concerns, no matter how small, about their own or a colleague's behaviour. These concerns, they suggest, should not be limited to safeguarding but rather may relate to any behaviour that does not meet the professional standards of the profession or those expected in the organisation.

The purpose of such a policy is to help to create a culture in which the clear values and expected behaviours set out in the organisation's code of conduct are lived, and constantly monitored and reinforced, by all adults working with children, where these adults can be confident about sharing low-level concerns, and so that the organisation can respond to breaches of the rules and code, all of which serve to create a safer and more open culture.

Implementing a 'low-level concerns' policy

Lawyers Eastman and Rigg (2017) suggest that there are a number of areas requiring careful consideration before any policy is implemented. These include the following:

- It is important that the policy should be clear and accessible to all adults working with children, setting out what these adults should do if they have a low-level concern, and how the organisation will investigate and record such concerns.

- The method of implementation and the way in which the policy is communicated to staff are key. Carefully designed training that is engaging and includes scenario-based discussions should encourage buy-in from staff and volunteers and help to achieve the policy's objectives. In contrast, poor communication of the policy, or inappropriate responses to concerns shared (see below), might create suspicion, confusion and toxicity that could be highly damaging to the organisational culture, decreasing rather than increasing reporting.

- Everyone in the organisation should understand the relationship between low-level concerns and allegations, and the distinction between them. For example, the person receiving the low-level concern must always consider whether it meets the threshold for reporting to the designated officer of the local authority as an allegation. If in any doubt they should contact the designated officer of the local authority for advice. Equally, a series of low-level concerns may cumulatively meet the threshold and need to be treated as such.

- Ideally all concerns should be reported to one person so that patterns can be identified. It may inhibit reporting if that person is the head of the organisation, so, for example, for schools it may be appropriate for low-level concerns to be reported to the designated safeguarding lead rather than the head teacher.

- The handling of concerns, if done appropriately and proportionately, will strengthen the confidence of staff and volunteers in the organisation. By contrast, handling concerns disproportionately or inappropriately will decrease rather than increase reporting. The way in which concerns are handled and the identity of the person handling them will necessarily depend on the nature of the concern being raised. If the policy is to make a constructive contribution to the organisational culture it will be important that reported concerns are considered in context and responded to proportionately. Some concerns are likely to be at a level which may not actually warrant disciplinary action but give another adult some cause for discomfort, in which case it may be appropriate simply to note and monitor.

- In other circumstances it will be necessary to investigate and, depending on the nature of the issue, understand the perspective and reasoning of the individual concerned about the boundary breach(es), and clearly explain to the adult who is the subject of the concern why their behaviour is inappropriate, exactly what they should do in future to ensure that boundary breaches are not repeated, and the possible consequences if there are repetitions (e.g. disciplinary action/formal external referral). There should also be clarity about the process for monitoring to ensure that there is no repetition of the behaviour. In some circumstances, it may be appropriate to provide further training to the adult concerned.

- A crucial element of the approach that needs to be considered before implementation is the recording of concerns. There is no official guidance for the recording of concerns that do not meet the threshold for referral as an allegation. Eastman and Rigg suggest that low-level concerns which do not individually or collectively meet the threshold for referral as an allegation, and where no other internal process has been instigated (for example, disciplinary, grievance or whistle-blowing), should not be recorded on personnel files or used on references, but should be retained in a confidential, central safeguarding file. They report that feedback from staff in schools where a low-level concerns policy has been introduced has been that this is central to creating a culture of openness and dialogue between staff and the designated safeguarding lead.

- The final, crucial, element of implementing this approach safely is oversight and review, the regular review of low-level concerns to ensure that concerns are being handled appropriately and proportionately, that no concerns meet the threshold of an allegation and that subtle patterns of behaviour are identified. It will also be important that those with whom low-level concerns are shared and who are responsible for responding to them, as indicated, have a clear understanding of the difference between appropriate and inappropriate behaviour, how to identify possible grooming processes, and of the 'slippery slope' model outlined above to understand the potential relationship between inappropriate behaviour and grooming.

Conclusion

The importance of understanding grooming processes, whether conscious and deliberate as appear to be the case with Savile and Vahey, or those resulting from a more gradual process of progression through violated boundaries, cannot be overstated. In either case inappropriate behaviour needs to be addressed and potential risk assessed. However, an appropriate response is likely to be partially rooted in an understanding of the distinction between motivated devious behaviour and less conscious or deliberate transgressions that, once addressed, may in fact not be repeated.

Sullivan and Quayle's (2012) work may be helpful in identifying ways in which some offenders might attempt to manipulate those around them. It is hoped that the 'slippery slope' process outlined will offer a way of understanding how some other behaviour may be less deliberate but at worst has the potential to result in abuse and, even where it does not progress so far, is likely to erode the clear boundaries and professionalism which are often the hallmark of a successful organisation.

Whilst still largely untested, a 'neutral-notification' or 'low-level concerns' approach to whole organisation safeguarding seems to have the potential to enable early identification of potential problems, to provide a route to address concerns and above all to help create an organisational environment where safeguarding children and young people is a real commitment shared by all.

References

Beyer, L., Higgins, D. and Bromfield, L. (2005) *Understanding Organisational Risk Factors for Child Maltreatment: A Review of Literature*. Melbourne, VIC: National Child Protection Clearinghouse, Australian Institute of Family Studies. Accessed on 15 August 2017 at https://aifs.gov.au/cfca/sites/default/files/publication-documents/organisations.pdf

Carmi, E. (2014) *Case CO1: Case Review*. Chichester: Diocese of Chichester. Accessed on 14 August 2017 at www.chichestercathedral.org.uk/dyn/_assets/_pdfs/CarmiReport.pdf

Clarke, R.V. (1983) 'Situational crime prevention: its theoretical basis and practical scope.' *Crime and Justice: An Annual Review of Research 4*, 225–256.

Cornish, D.B. and Clarke, R.V. (2003) 'Opportunities, Precipitators and Criminal Dispositions: A Reply to Wortley's Critique of Situational Crime Prevention.' In M.J. Smith and D.B. Cornish (eds) *Theory and Practice in Situational Crime Prevention*. Monsey, NY: Criminal Justice Press.

Davies, H. (2014) *Southbank International School Independent Review Arising from the Criminal Conduct of William Vahey: Final Report*. London: Farrer and Co.

Department of Health and Social Services (DHSS) (1993) *An Abuse of Trust: The Report of the Social Services Inspectorate Investigation into the Case of Martin Huston*. Belfast: DHSS.

Eastman, A. and Rigg, K. (2017) *Safeguarding Children: Dealing with Low-Level Concerns about Adults*. London: Farrer and Co.

Erooga, M. (2009) *Towards Safer Organisations: Adults who Pose a Risk to Children in the Workplace and Implications for Recruitment and Selection*. London: NSPCC. Accessed on 15 August 2017 at www.nspcc.org.uk/globalassets/documents/research-reports/towards-safer-organisations-2009-report.pdf

Erooga, M., Allnock, D. and Telford, P. (2012) *Towards Safer Organisations II: Using the Perspectives of Convicted Sex Offenders to Inform Organisational Safeguarding of Children*. London: NSPCC. Accessed on 15 August 2017 at www.nspcc.org.uk/globalassets/documents/research-reports/towards-safer-organisations-2012-report.pdf

Finkelhor, D., Williams, L. and Burns, N. (1988) *Nursery Crimes: A Study of Sexual Abuse in Daycare*. Newbury Park: Sage.

Jenkins, P. (1992) *Intimate Enemies. Moral Panics in Contemporary Great Britain: Social Problems and Social Issues*. Guernsey: The Book Repository.

Lampard, K. and Marsden, E. (2015) *Themes and Lessons Learnt from NHS Investigations into Matters Relating to Jimmy Savile: Independent Report for the Secretary of State for Health.* London: Department of Health. Accessed on 11 August 2017 at www.gov.uk/government/uploads/system/uploads/attachment_data/file/407209/KL_lessons_learned_report_FINAL.pdf

North Somerset Safeguarding Children Board (NSSCB) (2012) *Serious Case Review. The Sexual Abuse of Pupils in a First School: Overview Report.* Weston-Super-Mare: NSSCB. Accessed on 15 August 2017 at www.wigan.gov.uk/Docs/PDF/WSCB/NSSCB.pdf

Plymouth Safeguarding Children Board (2010) *Nursery Z: Serious Case Review.* Plymouth Safeguarding Children Board. Accessed on 15 August 2017 at www.cscb-new.co.uk/downloads/Serious%20Case%20Reviews%20-%20exec.%20summaries/SCR_Archive/Plymouth%20SCR%20-%20Nursery%20Z%20(2010).pdf

Scott-Moncrieff, L. and Morris, B. (2015) *Independent Investigation into Governance Arrangements in the Paediatric Haematology and Oncology Service at Cambridge University Hospitals NHS Foundation Trust following the Myles Bradbury Case.* Cambridge: Cambridge University Hospitals NHS. Accessed on 15 August 2017 at https://southwestlincolnshireccg.nhs.uk/about-us/safeguarding/safeguarding-children/what-s-new

Subotsky, F., Bewley, S. and Crowe, M. (2010) 'Introduction: Mapping the Territory.' In F. Subotsky, S. Bewley and M. Crowe (eds) *Abuse of the Doctor–Patient Relationship.* London: Royal College of Psychiatry.

Sullivan, J. and Quayle, E. (2012) 'Manipulation Styles of Abusers Who Work with Children.' In M. Erooga (ed.) *Creating Safer Organisations: Practical Steps to Prevent the Abuse of Children by Those Working with Them.* Chichester: John Wiley and Sons.

Walton, D. (2015) 'The basic slippery slope argument.' *Informal Logic 35*, 3, 275.

Wonnacott, J. (2010) *Nursery Z Serious Case Review.* Plymouth Safeguarding Children Board. Accessed on 24 October 2017 at www.schools.norfolk.gov.uk/view/ncc180559

Wonnacott, J. and Carmi, E. (2016) *Serious Case Review: Southbank International School.* Hammersmith and Fulham, Kensington and Chelsea and Westminster LSCB. Accessed on 15 August 2017 at www.rbkc.gov.uk/pdf/Southbank%20SCR%20REPORT%2012%201%2016.pdf

5

NEW TECHNOLOGIES AND ORGANISATIONAL OFFENDERS

ETHEL QUAYLE

Introduction

It would be something of an understatement to suggest that the unfolding story of Jimmy Savile's casual and purposeful sexual violence came as a shock to many people. It would also seem to be the case from the large number of reports and commentaries that followed allegations and disclosures (see Appendix) that the shock was often also accompanied by an uncomfortable feeling that there was something 'odd' about his public behaviour as well as his ability to insert himself into public institutions and be given freedoms of movement and access, regardless of the age or vulnerability of many of those he came into contact with. Chadwick (2014) asks of her readers whether this was a case of knowingly turning a blind eye, or simply not seeing what was in front of us. She suggests that both are dangerous and point to the need specifically to address what strategies might be effective in managing the apparent power of celebrity to 'undermine moral judgement' (p.ii). Mann (2015) also makes reference to the benefits of turning a blind eye in relation to serial boundary violation, which removes the responsibility of action and of being a whistle-blower. As with Savile, she suggests that serial boundary violators often appear charming, even charismatic, in how they present to the world, which hides a dark malignancy and which can fool both their world and their victims. The Savile case generated much attention from the media, but much of what came to light was both in the public domain and, to some extent, admitted by Savile before his death (Boyle, 2017). Boyle (2017) suggests that the lack of sustained attention or credibility given to allegations during his life was in part Savile's willingness to threaten to pursue the media through the courts. It is suggested that he also had the capacity to implicate others, particularly men, in his behaviour, and made them his audience to constant bragging about his sexual activities.

Savile managed to achieve and sustain enormous power, both in the organisation that employed him as well as others that gave him access to their employees alongside those in their care. Boyle's (2016) commentary in *The Conversation* about Louis Theroux's second documentary on Savile notes the moment when Savile tells him, 'There's nothing I cannot get.' This was with respect to him having Theroux's ex-directory phone number and sits alongside Smith's (2016) remark: 'He never seems to have had any fear that any of [his victims] would report him' (para.5.338). Such a perception of power must inevitably have been reinforced by both his success and the fear that he managed to instil in others.

In all of the documentation about Savile there seems nothing to document his engagement with digital media and this likely reflects the fact that much of his behaviour predates our current level of Internet use. However, it would seem likely that if Savile had still been alive when the case against him was being prepared his online behaviour, and that of others, would have also come under scrutiny.

Our changing world

In recent years, we have largely stopped referring to online and offline as discrete spaces: in fact, the use of such terms often says more about our own age than our practices. Plowman (2016) makes reference to the 'Internet of Things' in relation to the study of children, and how technology is not only omnipresent in people's lives but is also increasingly invisible. She argues that the embedded nature of the Internet of Things means it can be imperceptible, even though it is manifested in 'things' or material objects. The Internet of Things allows anything that has been tagged with unique identifiers to send and receive data over a network without any apparent form of interaction or mediation. Sensors generate data that can be received and interpreted by a network of interacting 'things' via the cloud, giving rise to incalculable intelligent networks that do not rely on active human input. This connectivity does not need to be via standard digital devices such as phones, tablets or laptops, so it is less obvious than previous forms of networking and blurs the boundaries between physical and digital worlds in new ways (Plowman, 2016). Greenfield (2017) remarks, 'The technologist Mike Kuniavsky, a pioneer of this idea, characterises it as a state of being in which "computation and data communication [are] embedded in, and distributed through, our entire environment". I prefer to see it for what it is: the colonisation of everyday life by information processing.' Greenfield gives concrete examples that relate to the 'quantified self' (such as the gadgets we all routinely use to track our steps, heart rate and time spent inactive or sleeping), our homes (connectivity between our phones and our home heating or refrigerators) and our public spaces (bus times calculated by sensors which are able to anticipate how long the bus will take to reach our stop). Our connected environments and lives are seen to be on the periphery of our awareness. We may not always realise that the toys we buy for our children might have an embedded chip that sends and receives information, and which in the main we perceive as benign. However, the invisibility of devices and how they are intertwined in our lives somewhat challenges how we both perceive and manage the possibility of their misuse. Such technologies are not inherently bad or good but they offer opportunity for social connectivity and the creation of content in ways that have not been seen before and which can be open to sexually aggressive and exploitative acts.

Affordances

The role of the Internet in the online abuse and exploitation of children has, paradoxically, been given little consideration (Quayle, 2016). Finkelhor (2014, p.655) has argued that any problems 'are not unique but, rather, extensions of social interaction or media consumption problems that cut across environments and are best conceptualised holistically rather than as special to the digital technology'. However, it does seem to be the case that technology affords distinctive opportunities to offend (Taylor and Quayle, 2006) and for adolescents to take sexual risks (Staksrud, Ólafsson and Livingstone, 2013), and that engagement with technology affects an individual's behaviour, mood and ways of thinking (Davidson and Gottschalk, 2011; Guitton, 2013). Affordance has been used to describe the quality of an environment (physical and software) that enables, facilitates or makes possible an action (Gibson, 1979; Quayle *et al.*, 2014). For example, social media may be associated with increasing risk of harm (Staksrud *et al.*, 2013) and with children placing themselves at risk (Noll *et al.*, 2009; Sengupta and Chaudhuri, 2011), and Livingstone and Smith (2014) identify affordances of specific online sites and services as one factor important for risks of harm to young people.

Mitchell *et al.*'s (2011) survey of law enforcement indicated that social media have also been used by sexual offenders to initiate sexual relationships, to provide a means of communication between victim and offender, to access information about the victim, to disseminate information or pictures about the victim, and to get in touch with the victim's friends. Social media might be said to 'afford' opportunities for offending. Staksrud *et al.* (2013) talked of these affordances in the context of an interaction between design and usage. An example of this is privacy settings in social media, where affordances shape practice in that privacy settings distinguish between public, private and partially private communications. However, people using social media also shape affordances. We can, for example, set up multiple profiles on social media sites to project different aspects of ourselves to different people (and contexts). Adolescents may use social media to explore sexuality, afforded through the ability to create sexual content, the online applications that support this (e.g. WhatsApp, Snapchat), and peer and adult engagement with the digital content. Livingstone and Smith (2014) suggest that researchers (and practitioners) will need to recognise how this complex interplay among social norms and technological affordances shapes communicative contexts. Blurring of boundaries between many aspects of our lives, especially in relation to social media use in the context of work and recreation, create considerable challenges within organisations. Fuzzy boundaries may lead to deliberate or more nuanced violations of social norms, especially in relation to social affordances, and these will be considered in the rest of the chapter. Weatherbee (2010) has suggested that the permeability of these boundaries means that behaviours learned or practised in one domain can be expected to cross over into the other, posing an escalating challenge to the prevention and management of 'cyber deviant' behaviours in organisations. The very physical environments that might have contained some behaviours may disappear because online abusive practices can take place regardless of geographical or temporal proximity. In addition, abusive practices with origins in the workplace can now easily be maintained outside of that context.

Abusive and exploitative acts: The creation of sexual media

Simply stated, technology-mediated abusive acts in the workplace may involve the use of technology to commit abuse against children within the immediate physical environment as well as acts that exploit opportunities within the workplace to engage in ways which are illegal and involve children both proximally and remotely (Quayle, 2012). The former may include taking photographs of children abused while under the care of an employee. A notable case involving the production and sharing of images was that of Vanessa George, a nursery worker who was jailed in 2009 for an indeterminate period for sexually abusing children in her care (Wonnacott, 2010). George, who had two children of her own, used a mobile phone that she called her 'fun phone' and took pictures of herself abusing children at Little Ted's Nursery in Plymouth. She exchanged more than 7000 images of the abuse, texts and calls with her two co-defendants, one of whom was another woman, over a six-month period (Marsh, 2009). She had contacted Colin Blanchard, one of her co-defendants, on a Facebook page called 'Are You Interested?', and this was followed by a request for her to send pictures of children with whom she worked. She responded initially by sending pictures of herself changing babies' nappies, but these later included images of real, or simulated, penetration of children with objects. The court was told that mobile phones were not allowed in the nursery but that the rules had been relaxed because the in-house phone was unreliable. This case was shocking in part because she was a woman and to date offences related to the creation, distribution and possession of online child sexual abuse images had been seen as exclusively male. This is a largely unexplored phenomenon, although there are a few case studies of female producers of child pornography which suggests that possession of child pornography images by women is unusual, and that their criminal behaviour is not related to paedophilia (Prat *et al.*, 2014). These researchers hypothesise that accessing and producing images enables women perpetrators to satisfy the sexual urges of their partner.

However, while such cases are shocking, they appear to be comparatively rare. By far the larger concern relates to people either accessing online child sexual abuse images while at work, or accessing images in another context while working for an organisation that brings them into close proximity with children. A recent example is a primary school head teacher who was in charge of child protection at his school and who was found to be in possession of over 160,000 images (Hunt, 2017). While he acknowledged being interested in girls aged nine and above, there seemed to be no question of whether he posed a danger to children in his care. This is of interest, as the question that has preoccupied research in the area of possession of online child sexual abuse images is the relationship between possession and the risk of contact offences, and the role that access to children may play in this. Most studies on online abuse and exploitation have focused on individuals to explore the personal characteristics and motivations of offenders who view indecent images of children (Seto, Hanson and Babchishin, 2011) and to prioritise which offenders pose the greatest risk (and presumably offences which we need to prevent). This has led to the development of specific risk appraisal tools, such as KIRAT (Kent Internet Risk Assessment Tool: Long *et al.*, 2016) and CPORT (Child Pornography Offender Risk Tool: Seto and Eke, 2015). Many of these studies ask questions about the ways that these 'online offenders' may be similar to or different from contact offenders against children (Babchishin, Hanson and Van Zuylen, 2015). Differences include greater psychological barriers to offending, higher levels of empathic concern, poorer self-management and socio-affective deficits (Henry *et al.*, 2010), and obsessive-compulsive disorder and loneliness (Marshall *et al.*, 2012).

Sexual images of children also appear to meet needs relating to problems with attachment relationships and intimacy (Armstrong and Mellor, 2016) along with early sexual experiences (Wood, 2011). Reports of less interpersonal warmth (Jung *et al.*, 2013; Magaletta *et al.*, 2014) may make close relationships uncomfortable and anxiety provoking. However, the presence of self-control and supportive marital relationships may act as protective factors (Clevenger, Navarro and Jasinski, 2016). Of interest in relation to risk is that the KIRAT data would point to risk factors specific to child abuse images that include access to children, previous offence history, sexual grooming and possession of IIOC that depicts similar-aged victims (McManus *et al.*, 2014). KIRAT indicates that any close or unsupervised access to children via friends, neighbours or acquaintances significantly increases risk.

Sexting, social media and boundary violations

The creation of media through the use of a hand-held device (such as a smartphone) or a webcam embedded within a laptop or desktop computer is part of the way we relate to others. We exchange pictures or videos of mundane, everyday events (what we are having for dinner) and those that seem significant and worth sharing (our child's first step). There are generational differences in the ways that social media are used, and despite the ubiquity of platforms such as Facebook, applications such as Snapchat and Instagram are more widely used by younger people as a way of sharing. Snapchat is clearly fun to use and does not leave a trail of posts and photographs for others, particularly parents, to find. It is also much easier to hide social media activity on Snapchat, because only the My Story page is visible to all of one's friends at once. Photos, videos and messages disappear by default (although they can be saved). When Snapchat (followed by Instagram) first appeared there was considerable concern that it would be abused by those with a sexual interest in children to create content that may be used as a form of blackmail. There is not a lot of evidence to support this being the case, although the self-production of sexual images by young people appears to account for a lot of the content seized from offender collections. The largest data set is from the US longitudinal National Juvenile Online Victimization Study (NJOV) (Walsh, Wolak and Finkelhor, 2012) collected at three time points (2000, 2006, 2009) over two phases: a postal survey of law enforcement agencies and telephone interviews. Between 2000 and 2006 there was a substantial increase in arrests, with approximately half related to image possession. Arrests for image production increased by 30 per cent between 2000 and 2006 and doubled between 2006 and 2009. This reflected a large increase in *offenders known to their victims* (family and acquaintance offenders) and production associated with 'youth-produced sexual images' (also referred to as sexting), taken by children 17 and under, and which met the US legal definition for child pornography. Most of those arrested were adults who had solicited images from a minor, and many victims were adolescent and known offline to the person arrested. By 2009, 37 per cent of arrests were adults who had taken images of minors, and 39 per cent where minors had been enticed to produce images of themselves (Wolak, Finkelhor and Mitchell, 2012). By 2009 most victims were aged 13–17, and more than half of those arrested had committed a contact sexual offence documented in the images taken. Wolak *et al.* (2012) described most of these offences as 'non-violent', in that children were persuaded or pressured into the activity, rather than forced, although in 2009, 45 per cent of cases involved penetrative sex. Trends in arrests for possession suggested that most arrested offenders had images of children aged 6–12, female and depicting sexual penetration of a child.

Snapchat has, however, also been used as a means of contacting children and inciting them to engage in sexual activity. An example of this is a teacher who in 2016 was jailed after he sent suggestive Snapchat messages to two 14-year-old pupils and tried to meet them for sex. He sent a picture of his face to the girls on the last day of term with the caption 'Make me hard and I'll do you' and a second image of his genitals inside his boxer shorts with text saying, 'You can play with this on Tuesday', when he had suggested meeting the two girls. What is encouraging is that the meeting did not take place because one of the girls sent a message asking whether he felt it was 'weird' having contact with girls of their age when he was much older (West, 2016). Another example in relation to social media was use by a special education teacher who posted on Facebook that he was 'super horny' and an 'A++ in bed'. This posting was not to a particular child, but resulted in a new law in Missouri, subsequently overturned because of possible freedom of speech violations, which restricted educators from using social networking sites that allowed them to communicate privately with students (Decker, 2014). The challenge of inappropriate employee–student relationships is not contingent on technology, but clearly the 'fuzzy boundaries' afforded by the Internet potentially create opportunities for inappropriate conduct that previously would not have been available. DeGroot and Vik (2017) discuss the aspects of Facebook (and presumably other social media) that may be associated with privacy violations and resulting 'boundary turbulence'. They use the online disinhibition effect (Suler, 2004) to account for communication that can violate another person's privacy. Due to the anonymity afforded by Facebook and other social media, the threats associated with face-to-face communication are considerably reduced when they take place online. In addition, perceptions of being invisible reduce one's awareness of the presence and reactions of others, also reducing the perceived risk of disclosing information. In a similar way, the asynchronicity provided by online communication allows people to avoid coping with someone's immediate reaction to a statement (or an image).

However, the factors associated with boundary violations offline are similar to those seen where social media is used. Knoll (2010) described a model of educator sexual grooming in which victim selection is influenced by the compliance of the student and the likelihood of secrecy. Students who are seen as 'controllable' are targeted and are likely to respond to positive attention from their teachers. Grooming has been defined by Craven *et al.* (2006) as a process by which a person prepares a child, significant adults and the environment for the abuse of this child. Whittle *et al.* (2013) suggest that this definition may apply to a real world setting or that which occurs online. Olson *et al.* (2007) proposed a 'luring communication theory' (LCT) that described the communicative processes of entrapment used by child sexual offenders to lure their victims into sexual relationships. They suggested that offenders typically identify children who exhibit low self-esteem or lack of confidence, as they may be easier to emotionally or physically isolate. This is often characterised as alienation from their family or fragile relationships with parental figures, and where unknowingly the young people behave in ways that appeal to perpetrators, responding to promises of affection and attention. Crucially for this model, how a young person responds to an offender's sexual acts makes a significant difference to whether a sexual act will follow. Students who are experiencing difficulties in their relationships with parents may be targeted not only because of being responsive but also because they may be less likely to disclose what is happening. The exchange of images and texts might serve to effectively silence a child, particularly where the adult is in a position of authority within an organisation. The exchange of images can result in 'sextortion', where threats are made of exposure of the child through imaged distribution if a disclosure is made and which, for a smaller number of children, can involve actual threats of physical harm to the child or members of their family (Quayle and Newman, 2016; Kopecký, 2017).

Children who feel marginalised by their sexual orientation may have additional vulnerabilities. While adolescent girls are more likely to be the targets of online solicitation (Jones, Mitchell and Finkelhor, 2012), boys who are gay or are questioning their sexual orientation may also be particularly vulnerable (Wolak *et al.*, 2008). In a nationally representative sample of Swedish youth (16–22 years), Priebe and Svedin (2012) found that, compared to heterosexual youth, males and females with a sexual-minority identity were three times more likely to have experienced some type of problematic sexual meeting offline with person(s) they met online. Rice *et al.* (2015), in a large survey of US high school students aged 12–18, found that bisexual identifying students reported higher rates of being approached online for sex. A further US study of adolescents (aged 12–17) with suspected sexual abuse seen in a child advocacy centre (Rood *et al.*, 2015) revealed that 74 per cent had experienced at least one online problematic experience, with 50 per cent indicating five or more exposures. Of note, over half had been asked to send nude or nearly nude photographs or videos, 21 per cent of the total sample did so, and 42 per cent of the sample had received sexual images. There was a higher level of exposure to problematic experiences in ages ≥ 14 years. This relationship between online-initiated and offline sexual abuse experiences has also been seen in other studies (e.g. Sumter *et al.*, 2012).

Impact of social media use on organisations

Warnik *et al.* (2016) have created a typology of problematic issues in relation to social media use, and while their content is in relation to teaching staff, it has relevance to other organisations. Their typology includes statements made by staff through social media that are taken to reflect badly on their professional judgement. Similarly, problems can arise when social media content appears to show a member of staff doing something illegal or egregiously reckless. Warnik *et al.* give an example of a substitute teacher in Georgia who was dismissed for posting unsolicited pictures of his students on Reddit through a site where users submit content that is subject to popularity ratings. This is particularly problematic as pictures of underage children may also be illegal. Problems also arise where uncomfortable or unwelcome attention is given to students through social media, which in extreme cases may amount to stalking. For example, a high school teacher in the US was charged following bombarding a 15-year-old student with inappropriate text messages professing his love for her and which were sent to 'follow her every move' (Newton, 2016). A further example given by Warnick *et al.* (2016) was a female teacher who was charged with stalking for contact initiated with a student, which was followed by multiple calls and text messages even after a court order had been issued. The teacher also hacked into the student's Facebook account, which she then used to send messages to the student's friends. The final category within this typology includes behaviour that, while not illegal or reckless, goes against community norms, or is thought to represent an undesirable role model to children. This may reflect posts that are extremely personal, or which are perceived as sexually suggestive. An example of this is a teacher posting images on her Facebook page of her drinking and wearing low-cut clothes. These images may be seen as problematic because of the person's employment status.

Social media are increasingly used across many organisational settings that serve children. Social networking sites such as Facebook, it has been argued, encourage egalitarian contributions by users and offer opportunities for collaborative learning (Asterhan and Rosenberg, 2015). These authors suggest that social media allow learners to self-organise and collaborate on shared interests, along with the possibility of linking and sharing online information with ease. For example, students can use Facebook to share logistical information about school or college activities. However, while a case can be made that social media exchange between professionals within organisations and children can improve interpersonal relationships, there are also potential dilemmas. These include blurring and shifting professional boundaries, particularly in relation to what should remain public or can be private. While social media can increase the availability and responsibility of organisations, they can also create problems of maintaining appropriate authority and distance. As we have already seen, these blurred boundaries on occasion can also be associated with sexual violence, especially when public conversations become private ones.

Ecological approaches and prevention

Martin and Alaggia (2013) suggest a need to expand the ecology of the child by including cyberspace into ecological systems theory, as a person-in-environment context (Bronfenbrenner, 1986). This is a developmental model which assumes that individual social, emotional and physical development as well as ongoing functioning can be understood only by considering factors at microsystem (family, peers, school), mesosystem (relationships between systems), exosystem (systems indirectly related to child) and macrosystem (beliefs, values, laws of society and culture) levels. Bronfenbrenner presented this model as concentric circles of context that are set in an overarching system of time (chronosystem). Viewing child development from this perspective allows us simultaneously to consider (a) the child and family context, (b) larger social systems of influence within which the family is embedded and (c) overarching cultural values and belief systems. Johnson and Puplampu (2008) suggested the ecological techno-subsystem as a dimension of the microsystem to examine children's online behaviours and the role of technology in children's cognitive development. Martin and Alaggia (2013) expand on this to consider the dimension of cyberspace across all these person-in-environment contexts.

Kenny and Wurtele (2012) provide an ecological approach to child sexual abuse prevention, which is compatible with person–situation approaches and emphasises that behaviours happen within a context. Bidirectional transactions between human beings and the systems in which they interact move away from examining only individual-level activities to systematic strategies to change macrosystem characteristics, such as legislation and social norms. Parks, Davis and Cohen (2010) suggested that, in this broadest context, levels of prevention include: influencing policy and legislation, changing organisational practices, fostering coalitions and networks, educating providers, promoting community education, and strengthening individual knowledge and skills. Wurtele and Kenny (2016) suggested such an approach in relation to technology-related sexual solicitation of youth, and described cyber-safety websites and educational programmes, resources and information for parents and caregivers. Situational prevention of online abuse and exploitation requires strategies that reduce, for example, opportunities for accessing children, as well as illegal images, by making the activity less rewarding, more difficult and riskier (Leclerc, Feakes and Cale, 2015). This takes a whole population, rather than a risky population, approach.

There is less need to make assumptions about deviant subgroups and this approach acknowledges that interest in sexual media of children might be higher than is seen in the known offender population (largely from conviction data) (Dombert *et al.*, 2015). A situational prevention approach (Clarke, 1997; Cornish and Clarke, 2003) is congruent with public health models. It is designed to prevent a problem before it occurs and is directed at environments that afford opportunities for unwanted behaviour (see Chapter 6). Farrell (2010) suggested the 'situational' approach aims to reduce society's harms and improve quality of life by modifying the design of products, systems and environments, which can range from simple and cheap measures to complex, expensive technologies. In the context of child abuse, society is gradually developing an extensive repertoire of situational responses, from routine practices such as accompanying children, mandatory employee background checks, teaching parents and teachers how to recognise sexual grooming, monitoring Internet chat rooms, glass panels in office doors and supervision of spaces that children use, such as swimming pool changing rooms (Wortley and Smallbone, 2006). This has also extended into the digital environment (Taylor and Quayle, 2006). Wurtele (2012) give, as an example, the Boy Scouts of America's social media guidelines, which make clear that all communication between adult leaders and scouts be via public, not private, social media channels.

Brown and Saied-Tessier (2015) examined the evidence for what works in child protection across several primary intervention approaches, including education programmes for children, parents, carers and professionals; relationship-based interventions (targeting bystanders); situational crime prevention community programmes; and societal-level interventions (media campaigns). While there is some support that educating children helps them identify dangerous situations and prevents abuse, Topping and Barron (2009) found little evidence in their systematic review of education programmes of any change in children's behaviour (including levels of disclosure). Jones, Mitchell and Walsh's (2014) content analysis of four Internet safety education programmes indicated that most were not incorporating proven education strategies and lacked any strong evidence base.

These authors also questioned whether messages would be better delivered through broader prevention programmes for young people targeting interpersonal violence rather than offering stand-alone lessons. There is limited evidence of what works for parents, carers and professionals in relation to child sexual abuse, and to date there have been very few evaluations of effectiveness in relation to online safety.

This focus on education is a recurrent theme in promoting Internet safety (e.g. Moreno *et al.*, 2013; Wurtele and Kenny, 2016). However, while education of children is unlikely to have a direct impact on offender behaviour, directing education campaigns at the general public may (e.g. through online information) encourage potential and actual offenders to seek help (e.g. the campaign by Stop It Now (BBC, 2017) and the Dunkelfeld Project in Germany (Beier *et al.*, 2009)), and the ability of others within both the offender's and the victim's immediate social environment to interrupt this activity. What is important in recent campaigns is the willingness of some large organisations specifically to use the campaign material in relation to their own workforces.

Wurtele and Kenny (2016) examined prevention efforts in relation to online child sexual abuse, with a specific focus on the solicitation of adolescents. They outlined education programmes, cyber-safety sites for young people and the importance of parent–child education to reduce vulnerability to online risks. Whittle *et al.* (2013) concluded in their review that young people whose parents monitored their Internet use experienced fewer negative online events, suggesting that parents' involvement and checking of their children's Internet use appears to be a protective factor. However, the role of parental supervision for adolescents as opposed to younger children remains contested. Sasson and Mesch (2014), in a sample of 495 children aged 10–18, found that after controlling for age, gender, time spent online and online activities, only restrictive parental supervision had a significant effect on cyber-aggression. However, this form of supervision was associated with an increase in adolescent risky online behaviour. Perceived peer approval of risk-taking reduced the effect of parental restrictions. Helsper *et al.* (2013) indicated, from the EU Kids Online data, concern that both too much parental protection through restrictions and lack of support for children's online use might in fact lead to higher levels of harm when risk is encountered.

Wurtele and Kenny (2016) examined prevention efforts, largely in the US, in managing technology-mediated crimes against children. They argue that organisations must develop and implement responsible use of technology policies that outline acceptable and unacceptable uses of digital devices and electronic communications, including guidelines for communication between staff and youth within the same organisation on social networking sites and via mobile phones (Wurtele, 2012). But they also note that within organisations such as schools these may be resisted or seen as difficult to implement because of the adoption and use of technological learning platforms, tools and the use of social media by schools. They note that there has been a bid to limit digital contact between staff and the children in their care, or at least to outline clear policies, which are made explicit to both staff and children in what constitutes acceptable use. They provide as an example of good practice USA Swimming (n.d.) that provides a model policy for electronic communication. This policy makes explicit that any electronic communication with swimmers must be 'transparent, accessible, and professional'. Specific reference is made to drugs or alcohol use, sexual language or activity, personal or relationship problems, or the inclusion of inappropriate or sexually explicit pictures. Young (2010) has outlined a framework for Internet management from proactive to reactive approaches. This framework suggests that policies should be the first level of prevention and would exclude some of the problems associated with screening beyond those of existing vetting procedures. The policy focus can consider new digital technologies to keep pace with change and adds a component of employee training as a more aggressive way to communicate policies, especially to people who are newly employed. Of relevance to child protection, specifically stating what is accepted and allowed within the organisation, and what disciplinary measures will be taken for violations, appear to be central.

There have been several toolkits developed with guidelines for policy and procedures in relation to keeping children safe. The Keeping Children Safe (2016) guidelines and toolkit were designed for people working in child protection and are translated into five languages. The toolkit comprises five tools that cover basic standards for all organisations, guidance and activities to offer help for organisations to achieve those standards, alongside flexible training exercises and materials. Across these tools organisations are also asked to make sure the guidance exists on appropriate use of information technology to ensure that children are not put at risk. Emphasis is given that the police should be involved if a staff member is suspected or found with abusive (pornographic) images of children on a computer or suspected of an Internet crime. Important aspects of the Toolkit in relation to technology-facilitated problems can be summarised in the following (Quayle, 2012):

- Any checklist for recruitment and selection should take account of what other sort of contact the person may have with children (such as email, letter, telephone and other Internet protocols).
- A policy should include procedures for taking, using and storing photographs or images of children.
- There should be agreed procedures for reporting any suspicions or allegations of abuse.
- Training should include information to staff about the use of abusive images of children on the Internet and how digital cameras and mobile phones have become an easy way to access children.

Conclusion

In 2012, when Erooga's book *Creating Safer Organisations* was published, it was already noted that technological advances were posing challenges within organisations in relation to child protection. Since then we have seen further changes that embed technology into most aspects of our lives. It is impossible to say whether this has been associated with more crimes against children being perpetrated within organisations as there is not adequate data that addresses this.

However, the key messages in *How Safe Are Our Children?* (NSPCC, 2017) concerning online harm indicated a 9 per cent increase over the previous year in the number of children having counselling sessions from ChildLine about online safety and abuse; 30 per cent of the reviews by young people of the most popular social media sites reported violence and hatred; and in 2015–2016 the number of recorded offences related to online abuse images increased by 64 per cent in England, 50 per cent in Wales, 71 per cent in Northern Ireland and 7 per cent in Scotland.

It is difficult to evaluate what impact the development and implementation of responsible use of technology policies within organisations have had. The same must be said for other child protection strategies that have been implemented. An additional challenge relates to the pervasiveness and invisibility of the digital connectivity that weaves its way through our lives offering considerable opportunities and some threats. Organisations are increasingly encouraged to make their child protection policies clear to staff, young people and parents so that everyone is aware of what is appropriate behaviour along with consequences for violations.

This book asks the questions post-Savile, 'What do we know?' and 'What do we need to do?' The various Savile inquiries have demonstrated how pervasively one individual managed to subvert the policies, where they existed, of the organisations that he used and the people he abused. Technology, and in particular social media, affords opportunities for us to behave as responsible digital citizens towards the children in our care and it is incumbent on organisations to respond to this, alongside managing the constant, changing impact of ongoing technological change.

References

Armstrong, J. and Mellor, D. (2016) 'Internet child pornography offenders: an examination of attachment and intimacy deficits.' *Legal and Criminological Psychology 21*, 1, 41–55.

Asterhan, C. and Rosenberg, H. (2015) 'The promise, reality and dilemmas of secondary school teacher–student interactions in Facebook: the teacher perspective.' *Computers and Education 85*, 134–148.

Babchishin, K., Hanson, M. and Van Zuylen, R. (2015) 'Online child pornography offenders are different: a meta-analysis of the characteristics of online and offline sex offenders against children.' *Archives of Sexual Behavior 44*, 1, 45–66.

BBC (2017) 'Paedophile Self-Help Site Stop It Now Used 1,530 Times.' *BBC News*, 10 February. Accessed on 31 July 2017 at www.bbc.co.uk/news/uk-scotland-38922239

Beier, K., Neutze, J., Mundt, I.A., Ahlers, C.J., *et al.* (2009) 'Encouraging self-identified pedophiles and hebephiles to seek professional help: first results of the Prevention Project Dunkelfeld (PPD).' *Child Abuse and Neglect 33*, 8, 545–549.

Boyle, K. (2016) 'Louis Theroux's New Jimmy Savile Documentary is a Horrible Misstep.' *The Conversation*, 3 October. Accessed on 24 July 2017 at http://theconversation.com/louis-therouxs-new-jimmy-saviledocumentary-is-a-horrible-misstep-66421

Boyle, K. (2017) 'Hiding in plain sight: gender, sexism and press coverage of the Jimmy Savile case.' *Journalism Studies*, 1–17. http://dx.doi.org/10.1080/1461670X.2017.1282832

Bronfenbrenner, U. (1986) 'Ecology of the family as a context for human development: research perspectives.' *Developmental Psychology 22*, 6, 723–742.

Brown, J. and Saied-Tessier, A. (2015) *Preventing Child Sexual Abuse*. London: NSPCC. Accessed on 15 August 2017 at https://www.nspcc.org.uk/services-and-resources/research-and-resources/2015/preventing-child-sexual-national-strategy

Chadwick, R. (2014) 'Jimmy Savile: the questions for bioethics.' *Bioethics 28*, 7, ii.

Clarke, R.V. (1997) *Situational Crime Prevention: Successful Case Studies.* Monsey, NY: Criminal Justice Press/Willow Tree Press.

Clevenger, S., Navarro, J. and Jasinski, J. (2016) 'A matter of low self-control? Exploring differences between child pornography possessors and child pornography producers/distributers using self-control theory.' *Sexual Abuse: A Journal of Research and Treatment 28*, 6, 555–571.

Cornish, D.B. and Clarke, R.V. (2003) 'Opportunities, precipitators, and criminal decisions: a reply to Wortley's critique of situational crime prevention.' *Crime Prevention Studies 16*, 41–96.

Craven, S., Brown, S. and Gilchrist, E. (2006) 'Sexual grooming of children: review of literature and theoretical considerations.' *Journal of Sexual Aggression 12*, 287–299.

Davidson, J. and Gottschalk, P. (2011) 'Characteristics of the Internet for criminal child sexual abuse by online groomers.' *Criminal Justice Studies: A Critical Journal of Crime, Law and Society 24*, 1, 23–36.

Decker, J.R. (2014) 'Facebook phobia! The misguided proliferation of restrictive social networking policies for school employees.' *Northwestern Journal of Law and Social Policy 9*, 2, 163–205.

DeGroot, J. and Vik, T. (2017) '"We were not prepared to tell people yet": confidentiality breaches and boundary turbulence on Facebook.' *Computers in Human Behavior 70*, 351–359.

Dombert, B., Schmidt, A., Banse, R., Briken, P., *et al.* (2015) 'How common is men's self-reported sexual interest in prepubescent children? *The Journal of Sex Research,* 1–10.

Erooga, M. (ed.) (2012) *Creating Safer Organisations: Practical Steps to Prevent the Abuse of Children by Those Working with Them* (Wiley Child Protection and Policy Series). Chichester: John Wiley.

Farrell, G. (2010) 'Situational crime prevention and its discontents: rational choice and harm reduction versus "cultural criminology".' *Social Policy and Administration 44*, 1, 40–66.

Finkelhor, D. (2014) 'Commentary: cause for alarm? Youth and Internet risk research – a commentary on Livingstone and Smith.' *Journal of Child Psychology and Psychiatry 55*, 6, 655–658.

Gibson, J.J. (1979) *The Ecological Approach to Visual Perception.* Boston: Houghton Mifflin.

Greenfield, A. (2017) *Rise of the Machines: Who Is the 'Internet of Things' Good for?* Accessed on 24 July 2017 at www.theguardian.com/technology/2017/jun/06/internet-of-things-smart-home-smart-city

Guitton, C. (2013) 'A review of the available content on Tor hidden services: the case against further development.' *Computers in Human Behavior 29*, 6, 2805–2815.

Helsper, E.J., Kalmus, V., Hasebrink, U., Sagvari, B. and de Haan, J. (2013) *Country Classification: Opportunities, Risks, Harm and Parental Mediation.* EU Kids Online, The London School of Economics and Political Science.

Henry, O., Mandeville-Norden, R., Hayes, E. and Egan, V. (2010) 'Do Internet-based sexual offenders reduce to normal, inadequate and deviant groups?' *Journal of Sexual Aggression: An International, Interdisciplinary Forum for Research, Theory and Practice 16*, 1, 33–46.

Hunt, K. (2017) *Head Teacher Richard Williams Jailed for Downloading More Than 160,000 Child Abuse Images.* Accessed on 24 July 2017 at www.kentonline.co.uk/canterbury/news/primary-school-head-downloaded-160000-127933

Johnson, G.M. and Puplampu, K.P. (2008) 'Internet use during childhood and the ecological techno-subsystem.' *Canadian Journal of Learning and Technology 34*, 1.

Jones, L.M., Mitchell, K.J. and Finkelhor, D. (2012) 'Trends in youth Internet victimization: findings from three youth Internet safety surveys 2000–2010.' *Journal of Adolescent Health 50*, 179–186.

Jones, L.M., Mitchell, K.J. and Walsh, W.A. (2014) *A Content Analysis of Youth Internet Safety Programs: Are Effective Prevention Strategies Being Used?* Durham, NH: Crimes Against Children Research Center (CCRC), University of New Hampshire.

Jung, S., Ennis, L., Stein, S., Choy, A. and Hook, T. (2013) 'Child pornography possessors: comparisons and contrasts with contact- and non-contact sex offenders.' *Journal of Sexual Aggression 19*, 3, 295–310.

Keeping Children Safe (2016) *Keeping Children Safe: A Toolkit for Child Protection.* Accessed on 11 August 2017 at http://toolkit.ineesite.org/toolkit/INEEcms/uploads/1103/Keeping_Children_Safe_EN.pdf

Kenny, M. and Wurtele, S. (2012) 'Preventing childhood sexual abuse: an ecological approach.' *Journal of Child Sexual Abuse 21*, 4, 361–367.

Knoll, J. (2010) 'Teacher sexual misconduct: grooming patterns and female offenders.' *Journal of Child Sexual Abuse 19*, 4, 371–386.

Kopecký, K. (2017) 'Online blackmail of Czech children focused on so-called "sextortion" (analysis of culprit and victim behaviors).' *Telematics and Informatics 34*, 1, 11–19.

Leclerc, B., Feakes, J. and Cale, J. (2015) 'Child sexual abuse in youth-oriented organisations: tapping into situational crime prevention from the offender's perspective.' *Crime Science 4*, 1, 1–12.

Livingstone, S. and Smith, P. (2014) 'Annual research review. Harms experienced by child users of online and mobile technologies: the nature, prevalence and management of sexual and aggressive risks in the digital age.' *Journal of Child Psychology and Psychiatry, and Allied Disciplines 55*, 6, 635–654.

Long, M., Alison, L., Tejeiro, R., Hendricks, E. and Giles, S. (2016) 'KIRAT: law enforcement's prioritization tool for investigating indecent image offenders.' *Psychology, Public Policy, and Law 22*, 1, 12–21.

Magaletta, P., Faust, E., Bickart, W. and McLearen, A. (2014) 'Exploring clinical and personality characteristics of adult male Internet-only child pornography offenders.' *International Journal of Offender Therapy and Comparative Criminology 58*, 2, 137–153.

Mann, D. (2015) '"Turning a blind eye" on sexual abuse, boundary violations and therapeutic practice.' *Psychodynamic Practice 21*, 2, 126–146.

Marsh, S. (2009) *Vanessa George and the Evil That Women Do.* Accessed on 24 July 2017 at www.thetimes.co.uk/article/vanessa-george-and-the-evil-that-women-do-l5frxb5w0h5

Marshall, L.E., O'Brien, M.D., Marshall, W.L., Booth, B. and Davis, A. (2012) 'Obsessive-compulsive disorder, social phobia, and loneliness in incarcerated Internet child pornography offenders.' *Sexual Addiction and Compulsivity: The Journal of Treatment and Prevention 19*, 1–2, 41–52.

Martin, J. and Alaggia, R. (2013) 'Sexual abuse images in cyberspace: expanding the ecology of the child.' *Journal of Child Sexual Abuse 22*, 4, 398–415.

McManus, M., Long, M., Alison, L. and Almond, L. (2014) 'Factors associated with contact child sexual abuse in a sample of indecent image offenders.' *Journal of Sexual Aggression 21*, 3, 368–384.

Mitchell, K.J., Jones, L.M., Finkelhor, D. and Wolak, J. (2011) 'Internet-facilitated commercial sexual exploitation of children: findings from a nationally representative sample of law-enforcement agencies in the US.' *Sexual Abuse: A Journal of Research and Treatment 23*, 1, 43–71.

Moreno, M.A., Egan, K.G., Bare, K., Young, H.N. and Cox, E.D. (2013) 'Internet safety education for youth: stakeholder perspectives.' *BMC Public Health 13*, 543.

Newton, J. (2016) *High School Teacher Is Arrested after Being Accused of Stalking 15-Year-Old Female Student by 'Bombarding Her with Text Messages Expressing His Love for Her'.* Accessed on 24 July 2017 at www.dailymail.co.uk/news/article-3437177/Teacher-Michael-Sporrer-arrested-stalking-15-year-old-female-student.html

Noll, J.G., Shenk, C.E., Barnes, J.E. and Putnam, F.W. (2009) 'Childhood abuse, avatar choices, and other risk factors associated with Internet-initiated victimization of adolescent girls.' *Pediatrics 123*, e1078–e1083.

NSPCC (2017) *How Safe Are Our Children?* Accessed on 24 July 2017 at www.nspcc.org.uk/globalassets/documents/research-reports/how-safe-children-2017-report.pdf

Olson, L.N., Daggs, J.L., Ellevold, B.L. and Rogers, T.K.K. (2007) 'Entrapping the innocent: toward a theory of child sexual predators' luring communication.' *Communication Theory 17*, 231–251.

Parks, L.F., Davis, R.A. and Cohen, L. (2010) 'Changing Community Environments to Prevent Sexual Violence: The Spectrum of Intervention.' In K.L. Kaufman (ed.) *The Prevention of Sexual Violence: A Practitioner's Sourcebook.* Holyoke, MA: NEARI Press.

Plowman, L. (2016) 'Rethinking context: digital technologies and children's everyday lives.' *Children's Geographies 14*, 2, 190–202.

Prat, S., Bertsch, I., Chudzik, L. and Réveillère, C. (2014) 'Women convicted of a sexual offence, including child pornography production: two case reports.' *Journal of Forensic and Legal Medicine 23*, 22–24.

Priebe, G. and Svedin, C-G. (2012) 'Online or off-line victimisation and psychological well-being: a comparison of sexual-minority and heterosexual youth.' *European Child and Adolescent Psychiatry 21*, 569–582.

Quayle, E. (2012) 'Organisational Issues and New Technologies.' In M. Erooga (ed.) *Creating Safer Organisations: Practical Steps to Prevent the Abuse of Children by Those Working with Them* (Wiley Child Protection and Policy Series). Chichester: John Wiley.

Quayle, E. (2016) *Researching Online Child Sexual Exploitation and Abuse: Are There Links between Online and Offline Vulnerabilities?* London: Global Kids Online. Accessed on 24 July 2017 at www.globalkidsonline.net/sexual-exploitation

Quayle, E. and Newman, E. (2016) 'An exploratory study of public reports to investigate patterns and themes of requests for sexual images of minors online.' *Crime Science 5*, 1, 1–12.

Quayle, E., Allegro, S., Hutton, L., Sheath, M. and Lööf, L. (2014) 'Rapid skill acquisition and online sexual grooming of children.' *Computers in Human Behavior 39*, 368–375.

Rice, E., Winetrobe, H., Holloway, I., Montoya, J., Plant, A. and Kordic, T. (2015) 'Cell phone Internet access, online sexual solicitation, partner seeking, and sexual risk behavior among adolescents.' *Archives of Sexual Behavior 44*, 3, 755–763.

Rood, C.J., Thackeray, J., Letson, M., Leder, R. and Berlan, E. (2015) 'Prevalence of sexting, online solicitations, and offline meetings among adolescents of a large child advocacy center with suspected sexual abuse.' *Journal of Pediatric and Adolescent Gynecology 28*, 2, e41.

Sasson, H. and Mesch, G. (2014) 'Parental mediation, peer norms and risky online behavior among adolescents.' *Computers in Human Behavior 33*, 32–38.

Sengupta, A. and Chaudhuri, A. (2011) 'Are social networking sites a source of online harassment for teens? Evidence from survey data.' *Children and Youth Services Review 33*, 2, 284–290.

Seto, M. and Eke, A.W. (2015) 'Predicting recidivism among adult male child pornography offenders: development of the Child Pornography Offender Risk Tool (CPORT). *Law and Human Behavior 39*, 4, 416–429.

Seto, M., Hanson, R. and Babchishin, K. (2011) 'Contact sexual offending by men with online sexual offenses.' *Sexual Abuse: A Journal of Research and Treatment 23*, 1, 124–145.

Smith, Dame Janet (2016) *The Dame Janet Smith Review Report: Volume 2 – The Jimmy Savile Investigation Report.* London: BBC. Accessed on 24 July 2017 at www.bbc.co.uk/bbctrust/dame_janet_smith

Staksrud, E., Ólafsson, K. and Livingstone, S. (2013) 'Does the use of social networking sites increase children's risk of harm?' *Computers in Human Behavior 29*, 1, 40–50.

Suler, J. (2004) 'The online disinhibition effect.' *CyberPsychology and Behavior 7*, 3, 321–326.

Sumter, S.R., Baumgartner, S.E., Valkenburg, P.M. and Peter, J. (2012) 'Developmental trajectories of peer victimization: off-line and online experiences during adolescence.' *Journal of Adolescent Health 50*, 6, 607–613.

Taylor, M. and Quayle, E. (2006) 'Precriminal Situations and Opportunity.' In R. Wortley and S. Smallbone (eds) *Situational Prevention of Child Sexual Abuse.* Crime Prevention Studies, Vol. 19. Monsey, NY: Criminal Justice Press/Willan Publishing.

Topping, K. and Barron, I. (2009) 'School-based child sexual abuse prevention programs: a review of effectiveness.' *Review of Educational Research 79*, 1, 431–463.

USA Swimming (n.d.) *Model Policy: Electronic Communication.* Accessed on 11 August 2017 at www.usaswimming.org/docs/default-source/safesportdocuments/club-toolkit/1.-policies-and-guidelines/model-policy_electronic-communication.pdf?sfvrsn=12

Walsh, W., Wolak, J. and Finkelhor, D. (2012) *Methodology Report – 3rd National Juvenile Online Victimization Study (NJOV3): Prosecution Study.* Durham, NH: Crimes against Children Research Center.

Warnick, B.R., Bitters, T.A., Falk, T.M. and Kim, S.H. (2016) 'Social media use and teacher ethics.' *Educational Policy 30*, 5, 771–795.

Weatherbee, T. (2010) 'Counterproductive use of technology at work: information and communications technologies and cyberdeviancy.' *Human Resource Management Review 20*, 1, 35–44.

West, A. (2016) 'Teacher sent filthy Snapchat messages to two 14-year-old schoolgirls and tried to meet them for sex.' *The Sun.* Accessed on 4 November 2017 at https://www.thesun.co.uk/archives/news/1072976/teacher-sent-filthy-snapchat-messages-to-two-14-year-old-schoolgirls-and-tried-to-meet-them-for-sex-2

Whittle, H., Hamilton-Giachritsis, C., Beech, A. and Collings, G. (2013) 'A review of young people's vulnerabilities to online grooming.' *Aggression and Violent Behavior 18*, 135–146.

Wolak, J., Finkelhor, D. and Mitchell, K. (2012) *Trends in Arrests for Child Pornography Possession: The Third National Juvenile Online Victimization Study (NJOV-3).* Durham, NH: Crimes against Children Research Center.

Wolak, J., Finkelhor, D., Mitchell, K.J. and Ybarra, M.L. (2008) 'Online predators and their victims: myths, realities and implications for prevention and treatment.' *American Psychologist 63*, 111–128.

Wonnacott, J. (2010) *Nursery Z Serious Case Review.* Plymouth Safeguarding Children Board. Accessed on 15 August 2017 at www.cscb-new.co.uk/downloads/Serious%20Case%20Reviews%20-%20exec.%20summaries/SCR_Archive/Plymouth%20SCR%20-%20Nursery%20Z%20(2010).pdf

Wood, H. (2011) 'The Internet and its role in the escalation of sexually compulsive behaviour.' *Psychoanalytic Psychotherapy 25*, 2, 127–142.

Wortley, R.K. and Smallbone, S. (2006) 'Applying Situational Principles to Sexual Offenses against Children.' In R.K. Wortley and S. Smallbone (eds) *Situational Prevention of Child Sexual Abuse.* Morsey, NY: Criminal Justice Press.

Wurtele, S. (2012) 'Preventing the sexual exploitation of minors in youth-serving organizations.' *Children and Youth Services Review 34*, 2442–2453.

Wurtele, S. and Kenny, M. (2016) 'Technology-related sexual solicitation of adolescents: a review of prevention efforts.' *Child Abuse Review* 25, 5, 332–344.

Young, K. (2010) 'Killer surf issues: crafting an organizational model to combat employee Internet abuse.' *Information Management Journal 44*, 1, 34.

Section 3

PREVENTIVE RESPONSES

6

APPLYING A SITUATIONAL PREVENTION LENS TO THE SAVILE CASE

Enhancing Understanding and Providing a Template for Strengthening Organisational Prevention of Child Sexual Abuse

KEITH L. KAUFMAN, MIRANDA SITNEY, ALYSSA GLACE, KELLY STEWART, JUDITH ZATKIN AND ERIN MCCONNELL

> '...most social acts have to be understood in their setting, and lose meaning if isolated. No error in thinking about social facts is more serious than the failure to see their place and function.'
>
> (Solomon E. Asch, 1952, p.61)

Sir Jimmy Savile may be considered one of the world's most prolific and 'successful' opportunistic sex offenders of all time. Yet, to portray him as simply opportunistic would be to underestimate the very active and strategic manner in which he created opportunities to offend and exploited existing setting-, system-, and person-based vulnerabilities within organisations. Strategic self-promotion and a keen sense of systems and settings were at the heart of his offending. Savile's celebrity and philanthropy allowed him to garner powerful friends and allies in government and in organisations which gave him unfettered access, remarkable latitude to act beyond standard policy and practices, and made him virtually 'untouchable' when his behaviour was questioned. At the same time, he used both his perceived and actual power to create new opportunities for offending and to reduce the potential for detection and reporting. While Savile's individual characteristics (e.g. personality) may account for his motivation to offend, it was his mastery over situational and environmental factors that allowed him so 'successfully' to carry out his abusive intent for more than five decades.

This chapter examines Savile's masterful manipulation of environmental and situational factors to enable his sexually abusive and assaultive behaviour. This exploration will be used as a means of illustrating the importance of a situational approach for the prevention of sexual violence. The chapter will begin by defining situational prevention and providing details regarding its evidence-based nature. Examples of how Savile exploited situation-based risk factors to create opportunities for sexual abuse/assault will be highlighted and practical suggestions for utilising a situational prevention approach for assessment and intervention to create safer organisational settings will be provided.

Defining situational risk factors and understanding theories underlying situational prevention approaches

Situational factors that increase the chances of a crime occurring are typically defined as those associated with environmental risks, risky situations, routine and daily activities, or policies (see Kaufman and Erooga, 2016, for a more in-depth discussion). Environmental risks may be illustrated by isolated building stairwells or playground landscaping that obscures 'line of sight' and makes proper supervision more difficult. Risky situations may include an inadequate staff-to-young person ratio of supervisors, patients' older siblings who are allowed to freely interact with other hospitalised children, or older teen volunteers who are asked to supervise adolescents very close to them in age. Examples of routine and daily activities could include parents dropping children off for camp prior to opening so that they can get to work on time and children walking home from organised activities alone in the dark. Finally, situational factors related to policies are reflected by an absence of policies that limit after-hours fraternisation between organisational staff and children's families, inconsistent summer job orientation to make new staff aware of organisational rules, or policies that need to be updated to incorporate social media.

Situational risks are at the core of criminal justice theories intended to prevent crimes that stem from such environmental and circumstance-based vulnerabilities. Key underlying theories include Routine Activity Theory (RAT: Cohen and Felson, 1979), Defensible Space Theory (DST: Newman, 1972), and Rational Choice Theory (RCT: Cornish and Clarke, 2002).

RAT suggests that crime is not random and three elements are required for it to occur: (1) a motivated perpetrator; (2) a suitable victim; and (3) a lack of adequate supervision (Cohen and Felson, 1979). RAT has been successfully used to understand and address a broad array of crimes, including burglary (Tseloni *et al.*, 2004), kidnapping (Marongiu and Clarke, 1993), robbery (Groff, 2007), and car theft (Rice and Smith, 2002). It has also been applied to sexual violence in many forms (sexual harassment of college students: Clodfelter *et al.*, 2008; sexual assault: Franklin *et al.*, 2012; online harassment: Bossler, Holt and May, 2011; Marcum, Higgens and Ricketts, 2010; and perpetration of child sexual abuse (CSA): Leclerc, Wortley and Smallbone, 2010).

DST states that spaces can be more or less defensible, with the potential of making them more resistant to crime (Newman, 1972). This concept of defensibility is rooted in three key dimensions: (1) territoriality; (2) natural surveillance; and (3) image/milieu. Territoriality refers to the ability to create areas that communicate a belongingness to someone through the erection of barriers, both physical and symbolic. These elements denote a place as public, private, or semi-private. The more 'private', the greater the influence an individual exerts over the area and the activities acceptable for that space (Brower, Dockett and Taylor, 1983). This type of behaviour deters others from intruding and from committing crimes in that area. Natural surveillance refers to the environmental layout of a property or space, and the extent to which this affords opportunities for individuals to regularly and easily observe the space. Greater ability for many people to observe the space is typically associated with reductions in crime (Newman, 1972). Finally, image refers to the general impression the space or building conveys, while milieu speaks to the larger context in which the space or building is situated. For example, Newman (1972) points out that the placement of 'the projects' (i.e. low-income housing) in a 'rundown' neighbourhood (common to many cities) contributes strongly to the impression that crimes can not only easily be committed without being caught, but that few people care about what happens in those 'bad' parts of the city.

DST has been associated with reductions in crime (Brown, 1999; Armitage, 2000; Clarke and Eck, 2005). However, it has also been criticised as too vaguely defined to adequately test (Taylor, Gottfredson and Brower, 1980; Merry, 1981), ignoring other factors that may contribute to creating safer communities (e.g. social, attitudinal, and behavioural commitments to safety: Taylor, Gottfredson and Brower, 1984; McMillan and Chavis, 1986), and failing to attend to important levels of embeddedness (i.e. a building is embedded within a block, which is embedded within a neighbourhood: Ratcliffe, 2003). A more recent review and reconceptualisation by Reynald and Elffers (2009) suggests that DST may be more useful when considered in combination with RAT, which helps incorporate residents' attitudes and behaviours as well as DST's interplay with important factors associated with levels of embeddedness.

Finally, Cornish and Clarke's (2002) RCT states that perpetrators are continually performing an internal 'risk–benefit analysis' to determine whether or not to commit a particular crime. This analysis is influenced by their assessment of the risks associated with committing a crime, at a given moment in time, balanced with the offender's perceptions of their current criminal skills and abilities relative to the demands of the criminal task. RCT has been successfully applied to many criminal behaviours, including: homicide (De Souza and Miller, 2012); assault (Schreck and Fisher, 2004; Reynald and Elffers, 2009); cybercrime (Yar, 2005); and domestic violence (Rotton and Cohn, 2001). It has also been applied to better understand sexual violence, as well (Proulx, Ouimet and Lachaîne, 1995; Beauregard, Proulx *et al.*, 2007; Beauregard, Rossmo and Proulx, 2007).

Clarke's Situational Prevention Model (SPM) drew upon each of these three theories (i.e. RAT, DST, RCT) to create a probabilistic framework for examining situational and contextual risks that predict the likelihood that a crime will occur in a given setting (Clarke, 1995; Clarke and Homel, 1997). The SPM assumes the three components of RAT are present (i.e. a motivated offender, suitable victims, and lack of supervision). It also views the offender as an active decision-maker, balancing risk versus potential gain (i.e. from RCT), and incorporates the contribution of symbolic and/or physical attributes of a setting in determining the likelihood of successfully committing the crime and avoiding detection.

Developing a situational prevention model for the prevention of sexual violence

Originally developed to apply to general criminal behaviour, Clarke's SPM was adapted and expanded upon by Kaufman to apply to child sexual abuse (Kaufman *et al.*, 2006, 2012; see Figure 6.1). This adaptation, referred to as the Situational Prevention Approach (SPA), is rooted in research on child sex offenders' modus operandi (MO) or patterns of perpetration (Kaufman and Patterson, 2010). The SPA is most applicable to extra-familial CSA, particularly in the context of child-serving organisations (Kaufman *et al.*, 2006).

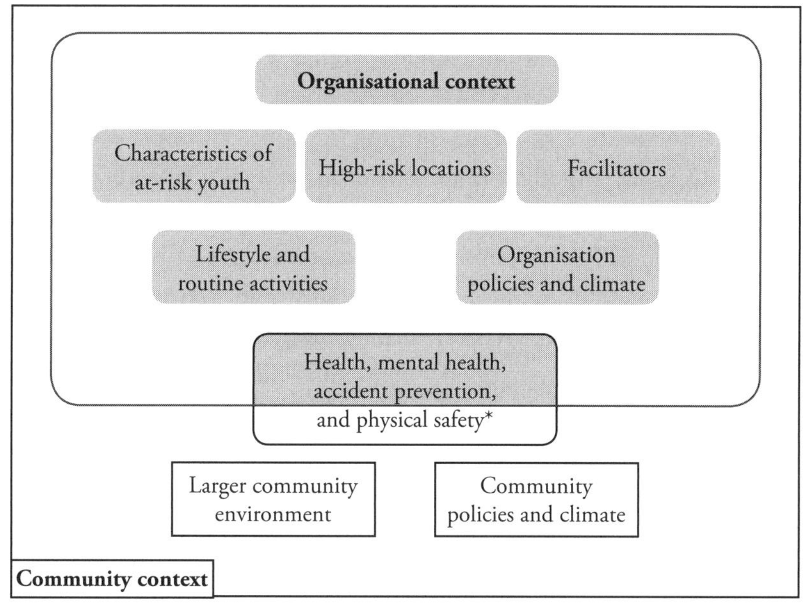

Figure 6.1 Situational Prevention Approach (SPA): Risk factor areas for organisational and community contexts
Source: Kaufman, 2016
Note: *Resides in both organisational and community context

The SPA is designed as a sustainable, four-step process intended to identify situational risk factors and address them with solutions that draw from a combination of existing organisational strengths and protective factors, as well as newly developed prevention strategies to fill the gaps. The SPA's goal is the comprehensive identification of situational risks in a particular organisational setting and the implementation of effective and affordable, tailored prevention and risk-reduction solutions to resolve each identified risk. Where possible, utilisation of multiple key informant groups (e.g. organisational staff and volunteers, board members, older teens involved in programming, children and teens' parents) helps achieve these goals. SPA steps include: (1) utilising a brainstorming process to identify existing safety risks; (2) developing effective and affordable solutions to address identified risks; (3) prioritising risk-solution pairs based on the degree of concern with the risk and available resources for implementing the solution; and (4) creating simple implementation plans and taking action (Kaufman *et al.*, 2012).

Drawing from Clarke's SPM (1995) as well as experience with a number of organisations serving young people (e.g. children's hospitals, Boys & Girls Clubs of America), the SPA uses seven prompts to guide risk brainstorming sessions. Prompts focus on risks within the organisational setting as well as those that reside fully or partially in the organisation's community context. These risk prompts were designed to reflect key situational prevention elements (i.e. environmental, risky situations, daily and routine activities, policies). Environmental risks are prompted by asking about high-risk locations (e.g. isolated classrooms) and the larger community environment (e.g. dangerous neighbourhoods). Risky situations are tapped by inquiring about facilitators (e.g. poor staff-to-child ratio that may cause risks to occur) and characteristics of high-risk young people (e.g. cognitively disabled). Risks related to daily and routine activities are prompted by asking about lifestyle and routine activities (e.g. walking home alone despite being quite young) and policies are inquired about both by asking about organisational climate and policies (e.g. minimal emphasis on safety) and community climate and policies (e.g. a neighbourhood with a high incidence of crime). Finally, the SPA also includes a prompt for risks related to other types of childhood harm (i.e. health, mental health, accident prevention and physical safety). In some cases, these risks may co-occur with CSA and they are included to enhance children's overall health, wellbeing, and safety. Box 6.1 provides definitions for each of the risk brainstorming prompts.

Box 6.1 Situational Prevention Approach brainstorm prompts

1. *High-risk locations* refer to specific rooms, hallways, or spaces within the organisation, on its grounds, or at a field trip site that may increase the chances of an abusive incident occurring. A location may be at risk due to its isolated nature, physical aspects, or even crowds that limit supervision (e.g. your organisation's crowded gym, a

community swimming pool). High-risk locations include any part of the organisation or grounds as well as any setting that youth travel to with staff as part of programming or field trips.

2. *Characteristics of at-risk youth* represent characteristics of the organisation's youth and their families that may increase their risk. Examples include being withdrawn, frequently engaging in attention-seeking behaviour, and having developmental delays. Characteristics of a youth's parents that may increase risks include parents who are neglectful, those who have substance abuse difficulties, and parents who themselves have developmental delays.

3. *Facilitators* may be thought of as the factors that allow or make it easier for someone to carry out child sexual abuse or sexually inappropriate behaviours in organisational settings. These facilitators often reduce the quality of supervision provided to staff and volunteers, negatively impact the amount and quality of youth supervision, allow safety rules to be avoided, create one-to-one situations between staff and youth, make staff and volunteer roles less clear, and allow for the manipulation of youth. It is important to note that facilitators can develop accidentally (e.g. in the case of camp staff who start work before receiving the orientation that clarifies club rules) or in a more purposeful way (e.g. a volunteer who actively works to create situations where he or she is alone with young people). Examples of facilitators include: staff who are poorly screened in their job interview or who don't get an adequate background check; a low staff-to-child ratio; field trips where there are too few staff and volunteers to provide adequate supervision; long-term employees who are not required to follow all of the organisation's rules; missing safety policies; a lack of specific job descriptions that allow staff and/or volunteers to engage in behaviours that shouldn't be part of their job; and poor

communication that contributes to not knowing where staff and young people are during the day.

4. *Organisation and community policies and culture* reflect the organisational climate and policies as well as local city and community policies, procedures, and climate. For the organisation, examples could include an inadequate hiring process, delays in completing background checks for volunteers, little attention to creating a safety culture, or a lack of clear policies on one-to-one time with young people. For the community, an example would be a city park where hedges are overgrown due to cost-saving policies that makes supervision of young people very difficult or a culture that encourages gang involvement.

5. *Lifestyle and routine activities* reflect day-to-day activities of young people as well as organisation staff and volunteers. This area includes *both* risks related to a young person's lifestyle and routine activities *and* the routine activities of organisation staff and volunteers. For a young person, their family lifestyle may require them to wait outside for a ride after closing time due to their parents' work schedule or they may walk through a dangerous neighbourhood each day on the way to the organisation. For staff or volunteers, routine activities that present a risk may include walking with a young person from a club to a local store for candy or pop, giving them a ride home, or waiting with them after hours for their ride to arrive. It is important to be sure that risks in this area are explored both for the young person and for staff and volunteers.

6. *The larger community environment* represents the risks that a young person faces in neighbourhoods and communities that surround the organisation, including any properties and areas next to the organisation, but not owned and managed by them. The *larger physical environment* includes

all of the neighbourhoods that a young person travels through and 'hangs out' in on their way to and from the organisation. These risks can include dangerous places (e.g. poorly lit streets), dangerous people (e.g. gang members), and dangerous situations (e.g. being 'hit on' by older teens). Other examples could include a young person taking shortcuts through alleys or woods, a poorly lit bus or train stop, abandoned buildings that young people frequently stop to play in, walking home alone, and having neighbourhood men saying inappropriate things to them when they're walking to and from the organisation.

7. *Health, mental health, accident prevention, and physical safety concerns* represent all non-child sexual abuse related risks. These include a broad range of concerns that may be associated with maintaining a young person's health (e.g. exposure to mould in a wet facility wall), mental health (e.g. anxiety due to poor social skills), accident prevention (e.g. preventing slips and falls, injury during sports), and ensuring physical safety (e.g. preventing injury due to fights or bullying).

Source: Kaufman, 2016 (used with permission)

The SPA offers a number of distinct advantages. First, and foremost, it represents a systematic approach intended to enhance the organisation's focus on prevention. It encourages organisations to identify safety risks early on and resolve them before they result in harm to the children that they serve. The SPA also contributes to the development of a strong safety climate, communicating to staff and volunteers that safety is part of their daily work and everyone's job. It takes a grass roots approach, encouraging the involvement of multiple stakeholders and allowing for the integration of key perspectives (e.g. parents, young people, staff, board members, community members), as well as taking advantage of the depth and breadth of experience provided by seasoned administrators, staff, and board members. The use of broad-based risk brainstorming as a 'front end' to the approach fosters an examination of the organisation's key safety elements (e.g. policy, physical setting factors, supervision, safety communication, staffing). At the same time, the SPA is self-tailoring. In other words, it focuses on the risks germane to a particular organisational setting and utilises solutions crafted by organisational staff that specifically meet organisational needs, draw upon organisational strengths, and are consistent with available resources. Finally, the SPA is a sustainable process that is simple to use and does not have any monetary cost associated with the process itself. This allows a broad range of organisations to utilise it to enhance safety.

The SPA has been tailored for use with community organisations and has demonstrated promising results. It has been used in consultations with two large metropolitan children's hospitals, in response to the identification of abusive staff members (Kaufman *et al.*, 2012). It has also been used as the focus of a three-year pilot project with Boys & Girls Clubs of America (funded by the Pennsylvania Coalition Against Rape) to tailor the SPA for use with organisations serving young people. Findings from a small comparison of clubs across four US states indicated that clubs using the SPA were able to identify 7–10 times more safety risks as compared to clubs in the same cities conducting business as usual (i.e. eight clubs; Kaufman, 2015). Clubs using the approach also indicated a high level of satisfaction with the SPA (i.e. 3.2 on a 4-point scale) and were able to develop and put into play solutions for identified risks in a timely fashion (Kaufman, 2015). Finally, the SPA is a central component in a large three-year, US Department of Justice SMART (Sex Offender Sentencing, Monitoring, Apprehending, Registering, and Tracking) Office-funded grant designed to develop a situation-based prevention approach to address campus sexual assault. Preliminary work over six months across three US colleges and universities indicated that the SPA has particular strengths in assisting students, faculty, staff, and administrators to identify critical risks on their campus that may lead to student harm, including sexual assault. While early in the project, campus work groups also found the approach useful in guiding the development of prevention and risk-reduction solutions to address identified risks (Erooga and Kaufman, 2016). As with applications of the SPA in organisations serving young people, the emphasis on campus solutions has been to identify effective strategies that are also sustainable (i.e. minimal cost, relatively simple to implement, consistent with existing policies).

Jimmy Savile recruited a large proportion of his sexual abuse and assault victims in organisational contexts. In fact, he went on to commit many of his offences in these same settings. A careful review of Savile's offence history underlines the extent to which he took advantage of situational and environmental vulnerabilities in organisational settings. This fact highlights the importance of a 'situational prevention lens' for not only better understanding Savile's prolific offending, but also for examining how community professionals can utilise a situational-based approach to enhance organisational safety. The next section closely examines Savile's offending from a situational prevention perspective and is followed by a detailed discussion about how this approach can be used by organisations to enhance participant safety.

Jimmy Savile through a situational prevention lens

As already mentioned, the SPA offers a mechanism for systematically identifying and addressing risks in a particular organisational setting. Had it, or a similar process, been available and used in settings such as Broadmoor Hospital, Leeds General Hospital, or the BBC, it would not only have uncovered risks, it might have encouraged the reporting of Savile's many abusive behaviours. The SPA could have helped encourage the many staff and patients who felt too isolated, disempowered, unlikely to be believed, or at risk of sanctions for speaking out.

This section organises key risks related to the Savile case within a situational prevention framework. It utilises the SPA risk brainstorming prompts to further structure this discussion. The intention of this section is both to present the many specific situational behaviours that Savile exhibited in a systematic fashion and, at the same time, to illustrate the use of the SPA process. This section focuses on the presentation of situational risks reflected in Savile's behaviour. It will be followed by a discussion of how these concerns form the foundation for effective prevention strategies tailored to an organisation's particular needs and resources.

Environmental risks

Environmental risks reflect those related to the physical aspects of a particular setting. Environments of interest may include community or organisational settings (e.g. buildings, parks, city streets, green spaces). These risks are critical in assessing the potential for CSA, as they often contribute significantly to victim access, privacy that affords opportunities to abuse, as well as features that minimise detection and facilitate the perpetrator's escape (Wortley and Smallbone, 2006; Terry and Ackerman, 2008). The SPA captures environmental risks by soliciting information about high-risk locations associated with the organisation and the larger community surrounding the organisation. The use of these dimensions is illustrated in the following examination of select examples reflective of Savile's perpetration of sexual abuse and assault.

HIGH-RISK LOCATIONS

Savile exploited a variety of high-risk locations across the many settings in which he offended. In some cases, he took advantage of existing physical features of organisations to facilitate his perpetration of sexual abuse and assaults. For example, the report of findings from Broadmoor Hospital indicates, 'The existence of alternative entrances to some wards and to the female area…allowed [Savile] to reach some patient areas unsupervised and without the knowledge of those in charge' (Kirkup and Marshall, 2014, para.1.4). In another case, an eight-year-old girl describing her abuse by Savile at Stoke Mandeville Hospital recalled 'the hospital as a "maze"… Savile would take her down numerous corridors, and she would feel disorientated and unsure of where in the hospital she was' (Vize and Klinck, 2015, para.50). The expansive size and complexity of the three hospital settings in which Savile perpetrated many of his crimes offered a chance to move quickly between hospital areas, through low-traffic corridors, take advantage of opportunities to isolate victims in sparsely used locations, avoid supervision by staff, and remain virtually invisible. Savile's extensive knowledge of the hospitals' layouts allowed him to maximise the usefulness of these physical features to enable his abuse of patients and staff.

In addition to taking advantage of existing high-risk locations, Savile was able to obtain access to private spaces within organisations that further supported his offending. At each of the hospitals, he managed to be assigned sleeping quarters. In two of them he became a 'volunteer porter', which involved moving patients as needed. In the third hospital, he arranged an administrative position that led to the acquisition of a private office with attached sleeping quarters. At the BBC, he often invited members of his show's audience back to his private dressing room with the intention of abusing them.

Finally, the sophisticated nature of Savile's attention to detail related to high-risk locations and how they could be manipulated is illustrated by his use of ward whiteboards that were used to track patient movements. As a Leeds Hospital staff member described:

> They had a big whiteboard with all the wards on it for patients and when they were going to X-ray, and he'd have a look at the board and nominate himself to go and do that job...the patient's name was on the board, and the ward, so if you were familiar with the hospital, even if it was just a surname, you'd know if it was a male or female ward. (Proctor *et al.*, 2014, p.84)

Little did the hospital know that in posting the movements of patients they were creating a virtual guide to accessing compromised children for Savile. Of course, only a predator with unfettered access to the hospital could have made use of the information in this fashion.

THE LARGER COMMUNITY ENVIRONMENT

In general, Savile was less likely to use aspects of the community environment to further his offending behaviour. That said, there were exceptions. For example, he parked a caravan outside both the BBC building and the Duncroft School (where he was a frequent guest). His caravan represented a private space where he lured some of his victims for the purpose of abusing or assaulting them. The caravan offered the advantage of being in close proximity to a large number of children, while not being under the control or supervision of organisational staff. Savile also used his car in a similar fashion at a number of locations (Gray and Watt, 2013). Finally, there were a number of times when he accessed victims in the community (e.g. young fans of his show) or used restaurants as a means of gaining victims' trust prior to an offence or as a reward following abusive acts (Smith, 2016).

Risky situations

The SPA assesses *risky situations* by asking about *characteristics of high-risk young people*, abuse/assault *facilitators*, and *health, mental health, accident prevention, and physical safety* concerns that may facilitate CSA.

CHARACTERISTICS OF HIGH-RISK YOUNG PEOPLE

A hallmark of much of Savile's offending was his targeting of high-risk children and teens. For example, the Broadmoor Hospital population of 800 patients (i.e. teens as well as adults) was described in one report as 'deemed to be at significant risk of exploitation by reason of their mental health and their incarceration' (Kirkup and Marshall, 2014, para.6.5). Moreover, female Broadmoor patients 'were obliged to strip completely to change into nightwear and to take baths, watched by staff' (Kirkup and Marshall, 2014, para.1.13). Savile used the routine precaution of supervising this high-risk population during baths to normalise his presence and enable him to watch the women bathe without engendering the staff's suspicions.

Savile capitalised on child medical patients' high-risk status at Stoke Mandeville Hospital in a different but equally egregious manner. He sought out patients who were unable to speak, were tied to their beds, or were otherwise immobilised. Savile abused two young women who were incapacitated at the time. First, he abused a 16-year-old car accident victim; while 'in bed with her face heavily bandaged, he stood over her and leaned over her, rubbing her arm and her breast, he did not speak and she was unable to' (Vize and Klinck, 2015, para.41). Second, he climbed through a bedroom window and kissed an 18-year-old sedated woman whose hands had been severely burned and thus was incapable of stopping him (Johnstone and Dent, 2015, para.6.29).

FACILITATORS

Savile employed a broad array of approaches to facilitate his perpetration of sexual crimes. He used his stardom, fundraising efforts, and introductions from highly placed political figures to gain access to a number of organisations and to influence their staff. This included an introduction to Duncroft School from Princess Alexandra (Queen Elizabeth II's cousin), securing funding to help build Stoke Mandeville's National Spinal Injuries Centre from Prime Minister Margaret Thatcher (Johnstone and Dent, 2015), and 'charming' a senior civil servant who then appointed him to chair a task force responsible for a period for the running of Broadmoor Hospital (Kirkup and Marshall, 2014). These introductions not only got him access, but also helped convince staff that his powerful connections made him a man whose actions could not be questioned. In the case of Broadmoor Hospital, he was literally handed the keys to the hospital and granted unlimited access to patient wards. Savile also used his unique position as 'celebrity volunteer porter' at Stoke Mandeville and Leeds General Hospitals as a means of facilitating access to patients, for the purpose of assaulting them in the guise of transporting them throughout the facility. Staff were aware that Savile often untied the dressing gowns of men, women, and child patients, groped them, and made lewd comments. He played upon these facilitators, as well as his reputation as an 'eccentric star', to avoid being held accountable for his inappropriate and illegal sexual behaviour in the hospital settings. His actual and perceived power also gave potency to the threats he used with victims and staff to ensure that he wasn't reported. At the BBC, his 'star power' ensured that his sexually abusive/assaultive behaviours of staff and child audience members were not only condoned but actively covered up.

Of particular note is the way in which Savile used his accumulated power to facilitate his sexual abuse and sexual assault of victims. His acumen in acquiring, consolidating, and utilising actual and perceived power across the perpetration process was without equal. When one considers the combined impact of Savile's status as a TV and radio personality, his political connections (e.g. Prime Minister Thatcher, British royalty), and his fundraising successes, it's not surprising that he was able to offend against an unprecedented number of victims. Moreover, his ability to wield his power in such a strategic and effective fashion (e.g. pandering to key hospital administrators while threatening victims and staff) may explain much about how he managed to offend prolifically over five decades without being arrested.

HEALTH, MENTAL HEALTH, ACCIDENT PREVENTION, AND PHYSICAL SAFETY

As already noted, the physical and mental health vulnerabilities of hospital patients played a significant role in who was targeted for abuse or assault by Savile. Broadmoor patients' incarcerated status and mental health concerns, as well as medical patients' incapacitation due to physical injuries and/or sedation, made it easier for Savile to perpetrate his crimes and less likely that anyone would believe patients' reports of abuse/assault if they were brave enough to challenge 'Sir Jimmy Savile'.

Lifestyle and routine activities

The organisations that Savile targeted were ones that had complex systems requiring rigid routines to run smoothly. Savile exploited the procedure-based and predictable nature of these organisational routines (e.g. staff's supervision of female patients' baths at Broadmoor). Moreover, he was attuned to variations in routine by specific patients that increased their vulnerability. For example, Savile targeted a particular Broadmoor patient whose routine was to shower quickly and return to the patient lounge before staff were finished supervising other patients' showers. Savile was able to assault this patient three or four times in the lounge without fear of being seen (Kirkup and Marshall, 2014).

Savile also made extensive use of night-time routines at Leeds Teaching Hospital as cover for his offending. He was seen visiting the infirmary during night shift when staffing was at a minimum (Proctor *et al.*, 2014). Similarly, he was known to use his keys in the middle of the night to visit patient rooms at Broadmoor, when there was little chance of being seen by the few staff on duty (Kirkup and Marshall, 2014).

His strategy had to be different at the BBC (British Broadcasting Corporation), where he met many of his victims as audience members to his shows. The BBC inquiry (Smith, 2016) describes a number of these encounters. The inquiry found that Savile would strike up a conversation before or after the show and invite an audience member backstage or offer them a tour after the programme finished. Savile's knowledge of the show's routine taping schedule allowed him to maximise access to victims and minimise the chances of detection.

Policy risks

ORGANISATIONAL CLIMATE AND POLICIES

Institutional policies may fail to ensure organisational safety for a number of reasons. Limitations may be due to: (1) key safety areas not being addressed by current policies; (2) a need to update older policies; (3) inconsistent application of policies; and (4) a failure to adequately orient staff to existing policies. Savile capitalised on policies that reflected each of these flaws. For example, Stoke Mandeville introduced an unrestricted visiting policy in 1973 that gave unit heads discretion to allow anyone visiting privileges, including open access to their children's ward (Johnstone and Dent, 2015). Savile exploited this inadequate policy by easily accessing wards and abusing a staggering number of child patients.

In contrast, Broadmoor Hospital had strong policies and a number of staff who consistently applied safety procedures. Savile had much less success abusing children on these wards. The children that he did abuse tended to be on units where policies were inconsistently applied or where he was able to use his status to neutralise security measures (Kirkup and Marshall, 2014). In general, however, strict institutional policies and well-trained staff members accounted for a smaller number of victims at Broadmoor compared with other hospital settings.

Savile's use of his voluntary porter position at both Stoke Mandeville and Leeds Teaching Hospitals to basically do as he wished with patients highlights the risks of policies badly in need of updating and strengthening. In this case, a weak policy actually did more to put patients at risk than no policy at all. Savile was able to use the policy to normalise his behaviour with patients, increase access to victims, and hide behind the façade of an 'altruistic volunteer' (Kirkup and Marshall, 2014; Proctor *et al.*, 2014).

At the BBC, the implicit policy of suppressing all complaints about 'on air talent' amounted to a tacit tolerance of child sexual abuse. In her report on Savile's abuse at the BBC, Dame Janet Smith wrote, 'An important feature of the culture...was the reluctance of staff to complain or raise concerns. Management...did not recognise the sense of insecurity which inhibited staff from speaking out' (Smith, 2016, para.2.90). Of course, Savile took full advantage of this 'cultural norm', knowing that management was not likely to hear about his behaviour, and if they did, they would simply ignore it.

As the ultimate insider Savile knew the limitations of each organisation's policies and how to exploit them for his abusive purposes. His offending is a study in how to use and/or circumvent the rules to successfully 'game the system'.

COMMUNITY CLIMATE AND POLICIES

The willingness to excuse much of Savile's sexually inappropriate (and abusive) behaviour reflects the broad latitude commonly afforded powerful individuals, and especially movie and TV stars. The many 'red flag' behaviours associated with Savile's public persona, that for 'mere mortals' would have triggered law enforcement investigations, only added to his charm as an 'eccentric', with a great history of volunteering and fundraising.

Possible prevention impacts on Savile: If only we could go back in time…

The Situational Prevention Approach (SPA) not only offers a strategy for identifying risks reflecting organisational vulnerabilities, it provides a systematic means of utilising existing (e.g. strong supervision of existing staff) or newly crafted (e.g. the addition of regular training to better orient new staff to safety issues) strengths and protective factors to develop solutions that address identified risks. Table 6.1 illustrates the SPA's integration of theory and practice to provide a more sensitive mechanism for both identifying safety risks and developing effective solutions. As noted previously, the SPA's seven risk brainstorming prompts foster the identification of risks relevant to key situational risk areas. This relationship is represented in the top portion of Table 6.1 (i.e. situational risks, SPA risk prompts, and specific examples of organisational risks exploited by Savile).

The lower half of Table 6.1 demonstrates how prevention, risk reduction, and policy development strategies can be utilised to provide a solution for identified risks. In practice, prevention-based solutions are given priority over risk-reduction strategies, given the more permanent nature of prevention efforts. At times, however, prevention is not possible (e.g. an organisation's annual open house), and risk-reduction strategies (e.g. having guests sign in) can offer some degree of protection. Policy development often provides the framework for putting preventive approaches in place, and in some instances a new policy may in and of itself enhance safety (e.g. restricting use of the toilets to the programme's child participants, rather than visiting adults as well). Finally, it's important to recognise that the SPA also incorporates a process for prioritising risk-solution pairs based on the level of concern with the risk and the availability of resources to address the risk, as well as guidance for developing brief implementation plans to guide intervention.

Table 6.1 Prevention and policy strategies to address organisational safety risks in the Savile case

Organisational risk identification				
Situational risk area	Environmental risks	Risky situations	Risks due to routine activities	Policy-related risks
Situational prevention approach risk prompt	High-risk location	Facilitators	Lifestyle and routine activities	Organisational and community policies and culture
Specific identified risk to address	Paediatric hospital units with multiple access points that are very difficult to monitor	'Powerful staff' are able to circumvent rules about accessing the paediatric wards and taking patients on outings	Volunteer porters are allowed to select the patients that they transport and are rarely supervised	Safety policies are inconsistently implemented across wards
Safety enhancement strategy development				
Prevention	Close off all but the main access door and control access through the nurses' station	Provide staff with a memo and training to clarify that policies regarding ward access and taking patients on outings applies to all staff, administrators, and guests	Replace volunteer porters with better screened and more closely supervised porters who are full-time hospital employees	Reorient staff to existing safety policies. Institute monthly ward self-audit to track. Hold staff accountable
Risk reduction	Limit access to two doors and install key card reader on both doors	Require powerful staff to sign the ward's logbook and indicate any exceptions to rules regarding visits and outings	Nurse manager assigns volunteer porters to transport patients. Porters must carry a hospital mobile phone with GPS for monitoring	Institute monthly ward self-audit to track
Policy development	Establish a policy that supports either the prevention or risk-reduction strategy selected for implementation	Rewrite existing policies to clarify that ward policies apply to all staff, administrators, and visitors	Modify the existing policy to reflect the implementation of either the prevention or risk-reduction option (above)	Review and update existing policy. Create a complementary policy for self-monitoring

Applying the Situational Prevention Approach to enhance child safety in your organisation

This chapter has examined the case of Jimmy Savile through a situational prevention lens, in part, as a means of enhancing our understanding of Savile's insidious modus operandi. At the same time, we have strived to provide the reader with an introduction to situational theory, the development of the Situational Prevention Approach (SPA), and how SPA can be applied in an organisational context. As previously noted, the SPA has shown promising results in organisational settings (e.g. Boys & Girls Clubs of America) and is the focus of a large-scale prevention project on US college campuses to address sexual assault and other forms of student harm. While an in-depth discussion of the SPA's application in organisational settings is beyond the scope of this chapter, Figure 6.2 briefly outlines the steps involved in the process. The interested professional is also encouraged to read additional information on the SPA (Kaufman and Patterson, 2010; Kaufman *et al.*, 2012) and to contact the first author who is willing to provide forms and additional details on conducting the SPA.

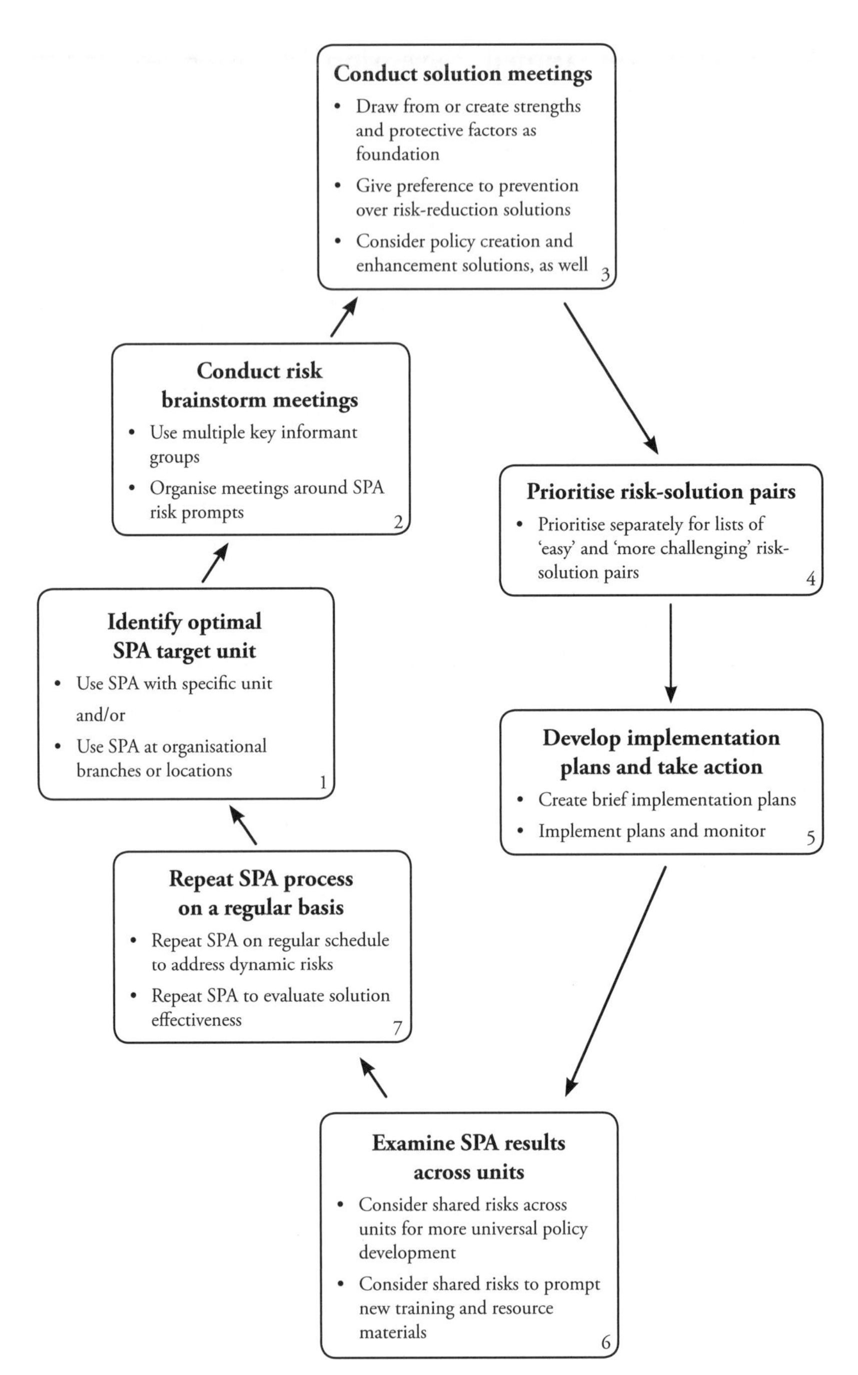

Figure 6.2 Applying the Situational Prevention Approach (SPA) to enhance your organisation's safety
Note: SPA process begins with box #1 and proceeds clockwise

References

Armitage, R. (2000) 'An Evaluation of Secured by Design Housing within West Yorkshire.' *Home Office Briefing Note 7/00*. Policing and Reducing Crime Unit Home Office Research, Development and Statistics Directorate.

Asch, S.E. (1952) *Social Psychology*. New York: Prentice-Hall.

Beauregard, E., Proulx, J., Rossmo, K., Leclerc, B. and Allaire, J. (2007) 'Script analysis of hunting process of serial sex offenders.' *Criminal Justice and Behaviour 34*, 8, 1069–1084.

Beauregard, E., Rossmo, K. and Proulx, J. (2007) 'A descriptive model of the hunting process of serial sex offenders: a rational choice perspective.' *Journal of Family Violence 22*, 6, 449–463.

Bossler, M., Holt, T.J. and May, D.C. (2011) 'Predicting online harassment victimization among a juvenile population.' *Youth and Society 44*, 4, 500–523.

Brower, S., Dockett, K. and Taylor, R.B. (1983) 'Residents' perceptions of territorial features and perceived local threat.' *Environment and Behavior 15*, 4, 419–437.

Brown, J. (1999) 'An Evaluation of the Secured by Design Initiative in Gwent, South Wales.' MSc. Scarman Centre for the Study of Public Order, University of Leicester.

Clarke, R. and Eck, J. (2005) *Crime Analysis for Problem Solvers: In 60 Small Steps*. Washington, DC: Office of Community Oriented Policing.

Clarke, R. and Homel, R. (1997) 'A Revised Classification of Situational Crime Prevention Techniques.' In S.P. Lab (ed.) *Crime Prevention at a Crossroads*. Cincinnati, OH: Anderson Publishing Co. and Academy of Criminal Justice Sciences.

Clarke, R.V. (1995) 'Situational crime prevention.' *Crime and Justice 19*, 91–150.

Clodfelter, T., Turner, M.G., Hartman, J.L. and Kuhns, J.B. (2008) 'Sexual harassment victimization during emerging adulthood: a test of Routine Activities Theory and a general theory of crime.' *Crime and Delinquency 56*, 3, 455–481.

Cohen, L. and Felson, M. (1979) 'Social change and crime rate trends: a routine activity approach.' *American Sociological Review 44*, 4, 588–608.

Cornish, D.B. and Clarke, R.V. (2002) 'Analyzing Organized Crimes.' In A.R. Piquero and S.G. Tibbetts (eds) *Rational Choice and Criminal Behavior: Recent Research and Future Challenges*. New York: Routledge.

De Souza, E. and Miller, J. (2012) 'Homicide in the Brazilian Favela: does opportunity make the killer?' *British Journal of Criminology 52*, 4, 786–807.

Erooga, M. and Kaufman, K. (2016) 'Creating Safer Organizations: Practical Implications of Research Regarding Child Sexual Abuse in Youth Serving Settings.' Half-Day Pre-Conference Workshop. 35th Annual ATSA Research and Treatment Conference, Orlando, FL.

Franklin, C., Franklin, T.W., Nobles, M.R. and Kercher, G. (2012) 'Assessing the effect of Routine Activity Theory and self-control on property, personal, and sexual assault victimization.' *Criminal Justice and Behavior 39*, 10, 1296–1315.

Gray, D. and Watt, P. (2013) *Giving Victims a Voice – Joint Report into Sexual Allegations Made against Jimmy Savile*. London: The Metropolitan Police and National Society for the Prevention of Cruelty to Children. Accessed on 11 August 2017 at www.nspcc.org.uk/globalassets/documents/research-reports/yewtree-report-giving-victims-voice-jimmy-savile.pdf

Groff, E.R. (2007) 'Simulation for theory testing and experimentation: an example using Routine Activity Theory and street robbery.' *Journal of Quantitative Criminology 23*, 2, 75–103.

Johnstone, A. and Dent, C. (2015) *Investigation into the Association of Jimmy Savile with Stoke Mandeville Hospital: A Report for Buckinghamshire Healthcare NHS Trust*. Amersham: Buckinghamshire Healthcare NHS Trust. Accessed on 12 August 2017 at www.speakingoutinvestigation.com/Downloads/Speaking%20out%20investigation/2902210_Investigation%20into%20the%20Association%20of%20Jimmy%20Savile%20with%20Stoke%20Mandeville%20Hospital.pdf

Kaufman, K. (2015) 'Applying the Situational Prevention Approach: Enhancing Safety in Youth Serving Organizations.' Safer Childhoods Network Symposium, October, Atlanta, GA.

Kaufman, K. (2016) 'Using the Situational Prevention Approach to Enhance Club Safety.' Safer Childhoods Network Symposium, August, Los Angeles, CA.

Kaufman, K. and Erooga, M. (2016) *Risk Profiles for Institutional Child Sexual Abuse: A Literature Review*. Royal Commission into Institutional Responses to Child Sexual Abuse, Sydney. Accessed on 25 July 2017 at www.childabuseroyalcommission.gov.au/getattachment/399a6b99-aa14-449e-bf6d-2d5d5beb773f/Risk-profiles-for-institutional-child-sexual-abuse

Kaufman, K, and Patterson, L. (2010) 'Using Sex Offenders' Modus Operandi to Plan More Effective Prevention Programs.' In K.L. Kaufman (ed.) *The Prevention of Sexual Violence: A Practitioner's Sourcebook*. Holyoke, MA: NEARI Press.

Kaufman, K., Mosher, H., Carter, M. and Estes, L. (2006) 'An Empirically Based Situational Prevention Model for Child Sexual Abuse.' In R. Wortley and S. Smallbone (eds) *Situational Prevention of Child Sexual Abuse Crime Prevention Studies*, Vol. 19. Monsey, NY: Criminal Justice Press.

Kaufman, K., Tews, H., Schuett, J. and Kaufman, B. (2012) 'Prevention Is Better Than Cure: The Value of Situational Prevention in Organisations.' In M. Erooga (ed.) *Towards Safer Organisations – Practical Steps to Prevent the Abuse of Children by Those Working with Them*. London: Wiley Press.

Kirkup, B. and Marshall, P. (2014) *Jimmy Savile Investigation. Broadmoor Hospital: Report to the West London Mental Health NHS Trust and the Department of Health*. London: West London Mental Health NHS Trust. Accessed on 11 August 2017 at www.gov.uk/government/publications/jimmy-savile-investigation-broadmoor-hospital

Leclerc, B., Wortley, R. and Smallbone, S. (2010) 'An exploratory study of victim resistance in child sexual abuse: offender modus operandi to sexual behaviors.' *Sexual Abuse: A Journal of Research and Treatment 22*, 1, 25–41.

Marcum, C.D., Higgins, G.E. and Ricketts, M.L. (2010) 'Potential factors of online victimization of youth: an examination of adolescent online behaviors utilizing Routine Activities Theory.' *Deviant Behavior 31*, 5, 1–31.

Marongiu, P. and Clarke, R. (1993) 'Ransom Kidnapping in Sardinia, Subcultural Theory and Rational Choice.' In R. Clarke and M. Felson (eds) *Routine Activity and Rational Choice*. Piscataway, NJ: Transaction Publishers.

McMillan, D. and Chavis, D. (1986) 'Sense of community: a definition and theory.' *Journal of Community Psychology 14*, 6–23.

Merry, S.E. (1981) *Urban Danger*. Philadelphia: Temple University Press.

Newman, O. (1972) *Defensible Space*. New York: Macmillan.

Proctor, S., Galloway, R., Chaloner, R., Jones, C. and Thompson, D. (2014) *The Report of the Investigation into Matters Relating to Savile at Leeds Teaching Hospitals NHS Trust*. Leeds: Leeds Teaching Hospitals NHS Trust. Accessed on 11 August 2017 at www.leedsth.nhs.uk/assets/Uploads/40482-2901955-Libra-Executive-SUMMARY-accessible2.pdf

Proulx, J., Ouimet, M. and Lachaîne, N. (1995) 'Criminologie de l'acte pédophilie' [Criminology in action and paedophilia]. *Revue Internationale de Criminologie et de Police Technique 48*, 294–310.

Ratcliffe, J.H. (2003) 'Suburb boundaries and residential burglars.' *Trends and Issues in Crime and Criminal Justice, Australian Institute of Criminology 246*, 1–6.

Reynald, D. and Elffers, H. (2009) 'The future of Newman's Defensible Space Theory.' *European Journal of Criminology 6*, 1, 25–46.

Rice, K.J. and Smith, W.R. (2002) 'Socioecological models of automotive theft: integrating routine activity and social disorganization approaches.' *Journal of Research in Crime and Delinquency 39*, 304–336.

Rotton, J. and Cohn, E.G. (2001) 'Temperature, routine activities, and domestic violence: a reanalysis.' *Violence and Victims 16*, 2, 203.

Schreck, C.J. and Fisher, B.S. (2004) 'Specifying the influence of family and peers on violent victimization: extending routine activities and lifestyles theories.' *Journal of Interpersonal Violence 19*, 9, 1021–1041.

Smith, J. (2016) *The Independent Review into the BBC's Culture and Practices during the Jimmy Savile and Stuart Hall Years*. London: BBC. Accessed on 11 August 2017 at www.bbc.co.uk/bbctrust/dame_janet_smith

Taylor, R.B., Gottfredson, S.D. and Brower, S. (1980) 'The Defensibility of Defensible Space: A Critical Review and a Synthetic Framework for Future Research.' In T. Hirschi and M. Gottfredson (eds) *Understanding Crime.* Beverly Hills: Sage.

Taylor, R.B., Gottfredson, S.D. and Brower, S. (1984) 'Block crime and fear: defensible space, local social ties, and territorial functioning.' *Journal of Research in Crime and Delinquency 21*, 303–331.

Terry, K.J. and Ackerman, A. (2008) 'Child sexual abuse in the Catholic Church: how situational crime prevention strategies can help create safe environments.' *Criminal Justice and Behavior 35*, 5, 643–657.

Tseloni, A., Wittebrood, K., Farrell, G. and Pease, K. (2004) 'Burglary victimization in England and Wales, the United States and the Netherlands.' *The British Journal of Criminology 44*, 1, 66–91.

Vize, C. and Klinck, B. (2015) *Legacy Report – Further Investigation into the Association of Jimmy Savile with Stoke Mandeville Hospital: A Report for Buckinghamshire Healthcare NHS Trust.* Amersham: Buckinghamshire Healthcare NHS Trust. Accessed on 12 August 2017 at www.speakingoutinvestigation.com/Downloads/Speaking%20out%20investigation/2903580_Legacy%20Report%20Accessible%20v2.pdf

Wortley, R. and Smallbone, S. (2006) 'Applying situational principles to sexual offenses against children.' *Crime Prevention Studies 19*, 7–35.

Yar, M. (2005) 'The novelty of "cybercrime": an assessment in light of Routine Activity Theory.' *European Journal of Criminology 2*, 4, 407–427.

7

ENGAGING THE PUBLIC THROUGH MESSAGING AND BYSTANDER ACTIONS

JOAN TABACHNICK AND KAREN BAKER

The importance of framing

How we think about child sexual abuse in particular, and all types of sexual violence in general, determines how we respond. It affects how we think about who commits sexual abuse, who is victimised, and why and how it occurs (O'Neil and Morgan, 2010). It also determines whether or not we believe that preventing sexual abuse is possible and, if so, what strategies we may consider feasible and potentially effective. The way we generally think about an issue can be referred to as 'the frame' (FrameWorks Institute, 2016).

In the case of Jimmy Savile, in the 1950s when he began to sexually abuse, there was only limited awareness of the problem. The 'frame' for sexual abuse was limited. The general thinking was that sexual abuse was rare, and that if it happened it was to other people and other children and certainly was not done by people we love and care about. Albeit decades later, a similar story took place in the USA with Jerry Sandusky, a nationally known and admired sports coach at Penn State University who sexually abused multiple boys over a period of decades. Neither Jerry Sandusky nor Jimmy Savile fit the idea of a 'monster' that was, and often still is, the typical frame in the media (McCartan, Kemshall and Tabachnick, 2015). When the media portrays a sex offender as a monster it is difficult for people to see that the adults, adolescents, and children they love and admire are at risk of sexually harming a child. In these situations, when someone is looking for a dangerous criminal, they may not see what is happening in their own family or community or, in the case of Jimmy Savile or Jerry Sandusky, by a high-profile celebrity (Tabachnick and Klein, 2011).

The 'swamp' of public opinion

Strategic Frame Analysis (FrameWorks Institute, 2016) is a relatively new research approach used in the United States to help understand how the public views complex social issues and to assist organisations with more effective messaging. Understanding how people will react is essential to creating the right message, the right appeal, and generate the desired actions.

Strategic Frame Analysis suggests that we all have many (sometimes competing) frames readily available to use as shortcuts for organising incoming messages. For example, with the issue of gun control there are varying and competing frames. Some of them are associated with public safety, violence, crime; others with individual rights, self-defence, governmental control, etc. (Pew Research Center, 2016). For someone proposing a particular initiative it would be helpful to know the public's main frames of understanding and to be able to then tailor messages in such a way that activates the desired response, an approach apparently well understood by politicians on both sides of the Atlantic.

In 2010, the National Sexual Violence Resource Center (NSVRC) commissioned a report entitled *American Perceptions of Sexual Violence: A FrameWorks Research Report* (O'Neil and Morgan, 2010). The report's findings identified significant gaps between experts' understanding of sexual violence and the ideas and beliefs commonly held by the public. These cognitive gaps cover all aspects of sexual violence including the causes of sexual abuse, what we know and don't know about the people who commit sexual abuse, the adults and children who are victimised by sexual abuse, the impact and trauma caused by sexual abuse, and the possible solutions.

FrameWorks Institute identified two key concepts (O'Neil and Morgan, 2010) that are widely held public frames related to sexual violence. In a 'mentalism' frame people perceive actions as being solely the responsibility of individuals. Problems are seen as being the result of personal weakness, moral or character flaws, and negative motivations. The concepts of 'a few bad apples' and of people who commit sexual abuse as being 'evil monsters' stem from this mentalism frame. This notion has persisted in the public understanding, despite consistent evidence to the contrary showing that most child sexual abuse is committed by trusted people who are familiar to and known by the child and his or her family (Breiding *et al.*, 2014). It persists in many child safety programmes today where children are told that if someone is touching them in sexual ways, they should tell their parents – which apparently discounts the possibility that the person abusing them is a parent. Many other programmes have expanded their training to say, tell a trusted adult, to ensure they are not sending the wrong message to children.

The second primary frame is the 'family bubble'. This is the notion that family, primarily parents, is the only significant source of influence in a child's growth and development. There is little or no consideration given to the influence or responsibility of peers, media, pop culture, athletics, faith leaders, culture, or other potential areas of influence. The family bubble is reflected in attitudes such as 'It's a private family matter' or 'It's none of my business.' This type of thinking can inhibit proactive interventions by the people surrounding a child, the bystanders who may see the warning signs of sexual behaviour problems but are not in a position to break into that 'family bubble'.

Taken together, these two predominant frames lead people to think about sexual violence as being the result of poor parenting resulting in 'bad actors' or dangerous criminals. When this is the prevalent image of a sex offender it will be difficult for people to see that the adults, adolescents, and children they love are at risk of causing harm or have sexually abused a child. In these situations, when someone is looking for dangerous criminals, they may not see what is happening in their own family or community. The only logical solutions people using these frames can think of are punishment, parent education, and teaching children to avoid strangers. While these have historically been the primary solutions offered in the United States and around the world, there may be other effective solutions outside of this frame. If we want people to intervene when they see or hear something, we need to provide an alternative frame where actions such as bystander engagement are expected and fully supported.

Changing the frames

These notions or frames, of mentalism, family bubble, and stranger danger, are at odds with the evidence about child sexual abuse from experts, researchers, and child advocates. These include the fact that child sexual abuse is, unfortunately, quite prevalent and that in most instances is committed by people who are known and trusted by the victim. A meta-analysis of 75 studies over 22 countries found that 7.9 per cent of men and 19.7 per cent of women had experienced some form of sexual abuse prior to the age of 18 (Pereda *et al.*, 2009). According to the US Centers for Disease Control and Prevention's 2010 *National Intimate Partner and Sexual Violence Survey* data (Black *et al.*, 2011), nearly one in five women have been raped at some point in their lives and nearly one in two women (44.6%) and over one in five men (22.2%) have experienced sexual violence victimisation other than rape in their lifetime. This large-sample survey, conducted in the United States, also revealed that many first experiences with sexual violence occur in childhood. Almost half of the female victims reported their first rape occurring prior to age 18; for over 25 per cent of male victims it occurred before age ten. These incidents of child sexual abuse are the least likely cases to be reported to authorities (Black *et al.*, 2011).

The concepts and misperceptions that the public carries may cause people to look in the wrong places and to ignore important clues or patterns of behaviour, thereby inadvertently exposing children to dangerous situations. As a result, when sexual abuse does come to the public's attention, people feel blindsided by events. This is evident, time and again, in high-profile cases of sexual abuse, such as with Jimmy Savile, Stuart Hall, and Rolf Harris in the UK.

One frame that is especially problematic is the 'stranger-danger frame'. This concept, promoted for many years, puts families at a disadvantage for many reasons. For example, people will look in the wrong places for those who might be a danger to children; it is also problematic for children because they tend to make friends easily, and once someone introduces themselves, and engages in some conversation or activity, they likely will no longer be seen by the child as being a stranger.

Frames that correctly portray the issue of sexual abuse can lead to creative solutions and safer communities. An important pivot we need to make is to change the perception that we can accurately judge people or profile a sex offender. People are complex – research about the people who sexually abuse reinforces this concept. As much as we would want to be able to easily identify a sex offender, our frames must clarify that there is no one profile to describe everyone who sexually abuses a child (US Department of Justice, 2014). The remedy for, or protection against, this is for us to focus on specific *behaviours*.

The family bubble frame noted above offers people a chance to turn away from a situation with thoughts such as 'not my problem', 'not my business', 'those poor people', 'couldn't happen here', etc. This type of thinking does not lend itself to becoming more informed, to developing skills to protect children, report abuse, and hold adults accountable. If someone outside the immediate family sees problematic behaviours or warning signs of sexual abuse, the family bubble makes it difficult to intervene or even begin a conversation unless there is the urgency of an allegation of sexual abuse.

Belief in the mentalism (or individual) frame also prevents us from understanding the important role that organisations, systems, communities, bystanders, and media can play. This frame does not allow us to think of creative primary prevention activities that could impact large numbers of people and to change cultural behavioural norms. In order to be effective we must think more broadly and consider employing public health strategies aimed at entire populations, such as those promoted by the Centers for Disease Control and Prevention (CDC, 2004).

Prevention is possible

In the past, child sexual abuse has primarily been framed as an individual problem, to be addressed one person at a time and ideally by parents (even with the knowledge that a majority of sexual abuse occurs within the family). For decades the media offered skewed coverage of child sexual abuse, focusing on 'newsworthy' stories of extra-familial 'stranger danger' rather than the intra-familial abuse which the research clearly showed was more prevalent (Shavit *et al.*, 2014; Mejia *et al.*, 2015). The primary response to child sexual abuse was to teach children about appropriate touch and what to do if someone violated their boundaries in some way. While important, these initial efforts put all the responsibility on children to respond to people who might cause them harm. More recently, programmes have also been addressing adult responsibilities to understand the warning signs in a child who may be sexually abused and how to respond to disclosures of sexual abuse. Starting in the 1990s, as awareness of sexual abuse increased, new laws were put into effect to manage, monitor, register, and notify the public about sex offenders.

All these efforts were focused on how to more effectively respond to sexual abuse *after* a child is harmed. However, if we are to find ways to prevent adults, adolescents, and children from perpetrating sexual violence the first time (referred to as primary prevention), we need to see solutions that reach those at risk to sexually abuse as well as the people who know them. With this new frame, prevention is not only possible but is, in fact, critical.

There are at least three categories of strategies that, when combined, will significantly reduce the prevalence of child sexual abuse.

1. We can provide treatment for children and young people who have exhibited sexual behaviour problems or who have indicated a sexual attraction to children. When more than one-third of children are sexually abused by other children or

teens, this has a high potential for impact (Finkelhor, Ormrod and Chaffin, 2009). Some examples of innovative programmes include the national Youth with Sexual Behavior Problems Program, funded by the Office of Juvenile Justice and Delinquency Prevention (OJJDP), that targets children and early adolescents with sexual behaviour problems with an evidence-based intervention strategy focusing on the child and their family (National Center on the Sexual Behavior of Youth [NCSBY], 2017); the Help Wanted Program at the Moore Center at Johns Hopkins University that is researching treatment and other resources for young people who have self-identified as having paedophilic interests, but who have not abused a child (Moore Center for the Prevention of Child Sexual Abuse, n.d.); and a number of other programmes such as Stop It Now! (n.d.) in the US and the UK, which offer educational materials, critical programmes, and a helpline that people can call if they are concerned about their own behaviours or the behaviours of someone they care about.

2. We can strengthen organisations, systems, and communities by implementing policies, procedures, protocols, and environments that enhance safety and protection. This approach was described in a report by the Centers for Disease Control and Prevention, *Preventing Child Sexual Abuse within Youth-Serving Organizations* (Saul and Audage, 2007). A number of programmes have demonstrated promising results by applying the 'situational prevention model' to organisations serving young people, colleges, hospitals, and other settings in order to prevent child sexual abuse by addressing environmental factors (Wortley and Smallbone, 2006; Kaufman, 2012).

3. We can educate adults to be informed to identify problematic *behaviours*, rather than thinking they can recognise dangerous people. We can build skills and shift cultural expectations by encouraging people to become active bystanders. They can be prepared to intervene when they observe problematic sexual

> behaviours or behaviours of concern because they violate a code of conduct or a physical or emotional boundary, preferably long before they reach the level of a reportable sexual crime. In the US, there has been growing interest in the use of bystander engagement programmes, especially on college campuses and more recently in high schools and middle schools (serving young people aged 12–18).

The promise of bystander programmes

The word 'bystander' usually conjures the image of a chance spectator or an innocent stranger in the wrong place at the wrong time. The term 'bystander apathy' was coined after a shocking case in 1964, when during a 30-minute episode a young woman, Kitty Genovese, was attacked multiple times, raped, and murdered. The next day, the *New York Times* reported that 38 men and women saw the assault and did nothing to help. The incident captured the country's attention and prompted a massive public inquiry into how caring people could watch an attack yet remain helplessly inactive.

After the Genovese case, social scientists Darley and Latane (1968) published groundbreaking research about 'bystander apathy'. They introduced five steps a bystander will consider before they intervene – a model still in use by researchers and programme developers today. The concept is that, for someone to take action, they must be able to do each of the following:

1. Notice the event.
2. Consider whether the situation demands action.
3. Decide if he/she has responsibility to act.
4. Choose what form of assistance he/she should use.
5. Understand how to implement the choice.

In other words, the bystander must see what is going on, decide that the situation is serious, and then decide to get involved. If they do decide to get involved, the bystander must then be able to choose an action and feel that they can perform it. For many bystanders, these five steps present an overwhelming sequence of decisions and the result is to choose to do nothing at all.

Darley and Latane's (1968) model focuses on the decisions and actions of individuals who are in a position to prevent a crime. Their framework describes a daunting burden, especially in a situation as charged and complex as sexual abuse. This notion of 'apathy' has been reinforced by media that tend to report dramatic situations where someone is tragically harmed rather than the small moments in time when someone did intervene and, as a result, nothing happened.

During the last decade, however, there has been a significant shift to encourage peers, adults, and people in places of responsibility to speak up, to say or do something. A recent re-investigation into the original case of Kitty Genovese reinforces this shift from the concept of apathy to one of engagement. Researchers found that the original newspaper reporting was incorrect and that some people did in fact respond to Kitty's calls for help by calling the police, yelling out the window, and a number of other tactics (Lemann, 2014). Clearly, none of these actions was enough to save Kitty's life, but with this new premise that some did respond, the deeper question is, how do we ensure that bystanders respond effectively to situations of harassment or abuse?

In the last decade, programmes across the United States have begun to explore that question – how to effectively respond to risky situations – especially on college campuses and in high schools and middle schools (Banyard, Plante and Moynihan, 2004; Berkowitz, 2004; Foubert and Newberry, 2006; Hoffman, 2016). They are finding that it is possible to teach people how to move from being an apathetic or powerless bystander to being an engaged and effective bystander, equipped to take action.

These bystander programmes reach a much broader audience than previous programmes because they can be applied to anyone and everyone. Unlike prevention programmes that often identify women and children as victims and men as perpetrators, bystander programmes involve all women and men who surround an abuse situation as players in prevention. In a bystander intervention programme audiences are offered a way to get involved without identifying anyone as either a potential perpetrator or a potential victim, making the issue relevant to everyone. Furthermore, the positive messaging resonates well, making it easier to garner community-wide buy-in with this strategy than with some others (Hoffman, 2016).

Other advantages of a bystander approach include:

- expanding the role of community so that everyone can get involved in prevention
- discouraging victim-blaming by broadening the questions to a family and community responsibility
- offering a chance to give everyone the skills necessary to effectively intervene or reach out for help.

(Tabachnick, 2008b)

What is a bystander intervention?

While most programmes are targeting either the victim or perpetrator of a crime (or the person who is at risk to harm or be harmed), a bystander intervention approach is broadened to address the behaviours of others – the friends, family, co-workers, and other witnesses that surround any act or pattern of abuse – and, by doing so, offers an opportunity to address at-risk behaviours *before* sexual abuse has been perpetrated in the first place (Tabachnick, 2008a). Furthermore, the bystander approach creates opportunities to establish the social norms and expectations within an organisation and a community that does not allow sexual violence (Banyard *et al.*, 2004). It gives a role to each individual to question and address behaviours that fall outside of the social norm or, from a policy perspective, fall outside of the formal code of conduct for that organisation. This approach has been successfully used with a variety of other public health issues such as combating racism and stopping drinking and driving.

When we first consider ways to stop child sexual abuse we typically think about stopping a crime, but rarely is that individual act seen, and if it is observed it is rarely an easy, safe, or effective time and place to intervene. Rather, bystander interventions target the hundreds of small comments, harassments, emotional and physical boundary violations, and other signs that may precede sexual abuse – what may be considered in the broadest sense to be the grooming process (see Chapter 3). If the entire focus of a bystander programme is on the crime then we may miss the multiple opportunities to do something or say something before someone is harmed (Tabachnick, 2008a). Furthermore, creating a bystander intervention programme establishes an organisational culture that expects all staff, volunteers, and participants to speak up, ask questions, and respond to the behaviours they see – these small comments, harassments, and boundary violations test the limits of a culture, thereby protecting our most vulnerable populations.

Within an organisational context, the code of conduct provides the blueprint for what are acceptable behaviours for interactions between adults and children and also between the children and young people. It is typically a straightforward guide of dos and don'ts to inform staff and volunteers about how to conduct themselves within the organisation (Wurtele, 2012). The code of conduct explains behaviours that fit within the organisation's culture as well as the behaviours which break the boundaries of that culture. When developing the code of conduct, it is important to set clear boundaries to address possible violations – emotional (e.g. giving special or personal gifts to an individual young person), communication (e.g. a young person's physical attributes or development), and physical boundary (e.g. photographing or videotaping minors while dressing or showering).

When empowering individuals to become engaged bystanders, and take specific actions, it is equally important to consider the environment surrounding those individuals. If the policy is clear and yet the administration does nothing to enforce the code of conduct or address violations, then it is difficult for any individual to take the actions necessary to prevent harm. One study suggests, 'It is unreasonable to expect that people will change their behaviour easily when so many forces in the social, cultural and physical environment conspire against such change' (Smedley and Syme, 2000, p.4). A simple educational training session around bystander behaviours will not be enough to sustain a significant change within an organisation or community. Training and incentives to take responsibility must be coupled with clear policies and commitment from leadership to adhere to, enforce, and reinforce the code of conduct.

What affects a bystander's sense of responsibility?

Over the years, bystander research has explored the various factors that affect whether an individual perceives that they have a responsibility to act (Banyard *et al.*, 2004). The factors identified in the research include:

- perception of the social norms in the situation
- number and characteristics of other bystanders
- perception of risk that is involved with the intervention
- perceived severity of the incident
- empathy with the victim.

The perception of how others in a broad social group may think or act will significantly affect an individual's decisions to act (Fabiano *et al.*, 2003; Berkowitz, 2004). If there is an expectation that people will act, or there is some social pressure that taking an action is the 'right thing to do', then it will increase their willingness and likelihood to intervene as an active bystander.

In the bystander literature, the number and characteristics of other bystanders may have a significant impact on whether or not someone takes action. When a person encounters an ambiguous situation, they may look to others' behaviour (Darley and Latane, 1968). On seeing inaction in others they may choose to judge the situation to be less dangerous or decide that others are in a better position to act. In fact, one study (Fischer *et al.*, 2006) showed that in situations of low perceived danger only 50 per cent of the observers tried to help the victim if there were no other bystanders in proximity. However, if other bystanders were present and did not do anything, the percentage of observers who tried to help dropped dramatically to 6 per cent.

Some research also indicates that an increased sense of severity tends to motivate bystanders to action. In the same study by Fischer and his colleagues, in situations of perceived high danger 46 per cent of people acted when alone and 40 per cent still acted when other bystanders were present, compared to only 6 per cent when the perceived danger was low (Fischer *et al.*, 2006). As research describes the long-term impact of sexual abuse over a lifetime and as survivors describe the severe, painful, and long-term impact sexual abuse had in their lives, the public's perception of severity and urgency may begin to shift (Ports, Ford and Merrick, 2016).

Many consider empathy with the victim key to bystander engagement: does the bystander identify in some way with the victim or potential victim? Christy and Voigt (1994) conducted one of the few bystander studies regarding child abuse specifically. They surveyed 300 adults and found that half had witnessed child abuse, but only 26 per cent of them intervened or reported it. However, the people who did intervene were more likely to have had personal experience with abuse and, therefore, felt more responsible and were more likely to know what to do. Understanding the situations, having experienced the situation, and/or having thought about the situation prior to facing problematic sexual behaviours means that an individual will be more likely to know what to do and have the skills and the information to respond.

Promising programmes

Bystander programmes are designed to motivate people to intervene safely and effectively (e.g. say something or do something) when they see behaviours that put others at risk and, it is hoped, before any crime has been committed.

In recent years, these programmes have begun to demonstrate a significant impact on reducing victimisation and sexually aggressive behaviours (Foubert, 2005) and on participants' willingness to intervene (Banyard, Moynihan and Plante, 2007).

Consistently across the various models, communities with higher levels of engagement (e.g. trust that the system will work) had more young adults who reported bystander action and interventions (Coker *et al.*, 2015). Overall, the programmes that are most effective are those with the following elements: clear community ownership and repeated exposure to solutions through multiple channels and multiple components delivered in a variety of community settings (World Health Organization [WHO], 2007).

Three programmes that have been closely evaluated are the following:

1. *Bringing in the Bystanders* (Banyard *et al.*, 2007) is a multi-session programme (4.5 hours) focusing on skills to help participants act when they see behaviours that put others at risk of victimisation or perpetration. Research on this programme showed that it was effective in increasing knowledge, decreasing rape-supportive attitudes, and increasing bystander intervention behaviour (e.g. offering assistance or stepping in to help) over time (Banyard *et al.*, 2007; Moynihan *et al.*, 2015). Although there were no direct questions that would measure the decrease in sexually abusive behaviours, it is an ideal place to begin to monitor the impact on those at risk to abuse.

2. The *Green Dot* programme involves both a motivational speech by key leadership as well as a four- to six-hour curriculum delivered by peer opinion leaders. Initial evaluation results indicate that both victimisation and perpetration rates were lower among college students attending the campuses that received the *Green Dot* intervention (Coker *et al.*, 2015). Specifically, the evaluations showed an 11 per cent lower rate of

sexual harassment and stalking victimisation and a 19 per cent lower rate of sexual harassment and stalking perpetration in comparison with other college campuses (Coker *et al.*, 2015). Similar results were found when the *Green Dot* programme was used at high school level (Basile *et al.*, 2016).

3. *Coaching Boys into Men* (Miller *et al.*, 2012, 2013) provides eleven 10–15-minute sessions on dating violence and respectful relationships delivered by athletic coaches to young men. Initial results showed a positive effect on decreasing negative bystander behaviour (e.g. laughing at sexist jokes), reducing dating violence perpetration, and increasing high school young men's intention to intervene in situations that they see might be abusive. The link to sexually abusive behaviours is clearly articulated in these programmes targeting young men.

Examples of other programmes with promising results that have not yet been as rigorously evaluated include: It's on Us Campaign, One in Four, Mentors in Violence Prevention, and the Step UP! Program (University of Arizona, n.d.).

What we can learn from high-profile cases

Tragic as they are, cases of sexual abuse committed by well-known public figures afford opportunities to support victims, to expose and analyse dynamics that are usually hidden, for organisations to explore additional ways to strengthen their policies and procedures, and for all of us to learn together about more effective prevention strategies. We can learn to navigate the swamp and to introduce new strategies (concepts, skills, footpaths) to safely navigate these difficult situations.

The Jimmy Savile and Jerry Sandusky cases both rocked a nation and both have important, and similar, lessons to teach. Jimmy Savile was an established British television and radio personality and DJ, respected for his extensive charitable work and his children's entertainment, efforts which resulted in him being honoured by both the Queen and the Pope. Jerry Sandusky, an award-winning coach at

Penn State University, was also well known for his generosity to young people, and created a residential programme for disadvantaged young people. Like Savile, there were numerous concerns about his behaviours throughout his career, but even when they were reported they were ignored, overlooked, or not substantiated.

Both men had a certain 'celebrity' status (although this was a far greater dynamic in the Savile case). This status, along with manipulative behaviours carefully crafted over decades, afforded both men unsupervised contact with large numbers of children and young people over many years. In addition, because of their celebrity status, the accusations against both men caused national interest in how this could have happened. Because of this national interest and media attention, each case prompted inquiries into the policies and procedures of organisations that allowed such unsupervised contact with these vulnerable populations (Freeh, 2012; Lampard and Marsden, 2015). From what we know about framing and bystander intervention, what can be learned from these and similar cases?

Lesson learned: Policies and procedures and especially a code of conduct should be in place and implemented consistently *every time* with *no* exceptions.

If a code of conduct is in place, an organisation can focus on the behaviours of every individual and confront those behaviours that do not adhere to what is acceptable. Although it is difficult to confront people with power, celebrities, or those with financial ties to an organisation, any attempt to bypass security procedures should be addressed regardless of that person's status. In fact, these individuals should be supervised *more* closely because the response (or lack of response) to their violations will set an example for everyone.

Organisations should encourage all employees to be engaged as active bystanders, to reinforce prosocial behaviours, and to report inappropriate behaviours by other staff, administrators, the board, donors, volunteers, children and young people, vendors, or guests. Taking this a step further, the Davies review of the circumstances of the abuse committed by William Vahey at Southbank International School in London (Davies, 2014) recommended the implementation of mandatory neutral reporting of such matters. Given both human nature and the culture of professional loyalties, he suggests that if reporting is not mandatory it may either not be made or not be adequately investigated or recorded. Furthermore, Davies highlights the importance of neutral language; thus reports are not 'complaints', 'allegations', or 'whistleblowing' but rather just a description of behaviours outside of the code of conduct that need further explanation of circumstances and/or further exploration. The neutral language of describing behaviours will also help to encourage staff, parents, and young people to ask questions and start a conversation rather than have to decide whether this rises to the level of a complaint or allegation. Finally, these descriptions of behaviours outside of the code of conduct, whether by staff or by parents, should be believed, explored, and rewarded rather than punished. Each one should be addressed and, when necessary, seriously investigated.

Lesson learned: Monitor *behaviours* rather than judging *people*.

Both Jerry Sandusky and Jimmy Savile were deemed to be altruistic, valuable to the community, role models, and especially good with children (e.g. Savile at Duncroft School). Over time, these accolades resulted in even more access, less oversight, and fewer restrictions. This type of unquestioning trust placed in certain people who are deemed to be heroes makes it even less likely that victims will report abuse, or that they will be taken seriously when they do (Exton and Thandi, 2013). It also makes it very difficult for bystanders who observe sexually problematic behaviours (e.g. inappropriate comments, touching, intrusions, boundary violations, etc.) to speak up, say something, or ask for the institutions to respond to these personal boundary violations. The NSPCC, which ran the Operation Yewtree Helpline, conducted focus groups with 25 Savile survivors. They reported that:

> a key reason given for not disclosing abuse was an overwhelming belief that if the abuse had been reported, victims would not have been believed. Jimmy Savile was a powerful and influential adult, who was seen as a 'charitable, good guy', raising a lot of money for charity. This led to feelings of helplessness and inferiority in his victims, who felt there was no way that their word would have been believed over his. This was true for those victims who had been adults when they were abused, as well as for those who were children. (Exton and Thandi, 2013, para.4.3)

First, staff and volunteers should be trained on the specific behaviours to look for, the behaviours to reinforce that are positive, and then be provided with the skills necessary to ask questions about areas of concern and to report problematic behaviours. When the focus of supervisions, training, and staff meetings is a clear discussion of behaviours, it is easier to ask questions of anyone, at any level, when those behaviours are outside of the organisational norm.

Lesson learned: Everyone, every bystander, has a critical role to play in prevention.

Jimmy Savile apparently used his fundraising skills and celebrity to curry favour with hospital administrators, which resulted in unsupervised access to certain wards. His relationship with top administrators also reportedly impeded staff's willingness to report inappropriate behaviours. It is interesting to note that, once security systems were improved, he apparently stopped visiting altogether. In the case of Jerry Sandusky, he had created a programme for troubled young people which allowed him to take children out alone without parental permission – against organisational policy. This was a failure of the organisation to consistently implement its own well-intended policies. Sandusky also maintained keys to locker rooms at Penn State University, even after his employment there ended. In the Sandusky case, there were many people throughout the years who noted suspicious behaviours – some of them reported those suspicions and some did not, but ultimately it was a report by a bystander that prevailed and helped to protect children.

Lesson learned: The media has an important role to play in helping the public better understand and accurately frame sexual abuse.

Initially in both of these shocking national cases, the media continued to report on the incidents over long periods of time, digging deeper and deeper into the details, providing context, and talking to experts. In these instances, the media helped the public become better informed about sexual abuse, the importance of believing and supporting victims, and the roles that organisations and bystanders can play in intervention and prevention. Analysis by the Berkeley Media Studies Group (Dorfman *et al.*, 2011) of news coverage about sexual violence in the United States discovered that typically news coverage is sparse, centres on a criminal justice incident (such as an arrest), provides little context, uses vague language, and rarely mentions anything about solutions or prevention. However, after the Sandusky case, a second study (Dorfman *et al.*, 2012) found that reporters other than criminal justice were writing about the incident and offering more information about trends. Because of use of the inquiry transcripts as a source of information, the language to describe child sexual abuse became less ambiguous and more accurate, albeit more graphic (e.g. the anal rape of a child in the shower). The media began to frame the issues away from stranger danger to someone we know and trust and also identified numerous opportunities where individuals (bystanders) did speak up as well as ways to ensure that, in the future, they are also heard.

References

Banyard, V.L., Moynihan, M.M. and Plante, E.G. (2007) 'Sexual violence prevention through bystander education: an experimental evaluation.' *Journal of Community Psychology 35*, 463–481.

Banyard, V.L., Plante, E.G. and Moynihan, M.M. (2004) 'Bystander education: bringing a broader community perspective to sexual violence prevention.' *Journal of Community Psychology 32*, 61–79.

Basile, K.C., DeGue, S., Jones, K., Freire, K., *et al.* (2016) *STOP SV: A Technical Package to Prevent Sexual Violence.* Atlanta, GA: Centers for Disease Control and Prevention. Accessed on 25 July 2017 at www.cdc.gov/violenceprevention/pdf/sv-prevention-technical-package.pdf

Berkowitz, A.D. (2004) *The Social Norms Approach: Theory, Research, and Annotated Bibliography.* Accessed on 25 July 2017 at www.alanberkowitz.com/articles/social_norms.pdf

Black, M.C., Basile, K.C., Breiding, M.J., Smith, S.G., *et al.* (2011) *The National Intimate Partner and Sexual Violence Survey: 2010 Summary Report.* Atlanta, GA: Centers for Disease Control and Prevention. Accessed on 25 July 2017 at www.cdc.gov/violenceprevention/pdf/nisvs_report2010-a.pdf

Breiding, M.J., Smith, S.G., Basile, K.C., Walters, M.L., Chen, J. and Merrick, M.T. (2014) 'Prevalence and characteristics of sexual violence, stalking, and intimate partner violence victimization – National Intimate Partner and Sexual Violence Survey, United States, 2011.' *Morbidity and Mortality Weekly Report 63*(SS08), 1–18. Atlanta, GA: Centers for Disease Control and Prevention. Accessed on 25 July 2017 at www.cdc.gov/mmwr/preview/mmwrhtml/ss6308a1.htm?s_cid=ss6308a1_e

Centers for Disease Control and Prevention (CDC) (2004) *Sexual Violence Prevention: Beginning the Dialogue.* Atlanta, GA: CDC. Accessed on 25 July 2017 at www.cdc.gov/ViolencePrevention/pdf/SVPrevention-a.pdf

Christy, C.A. and Voigt, H. (1994) 'Bystander responses to public episodes of child abuse.' *Journal of Applied Social Psychology 24*, 824–847.

Coker, A.L., Fisher, B.S., Bush, H.M., Swan, S.C., *et al.* (2015) 'Evaluation of the Green Dot bystander intervention to reduce interpersonal violence among college students across three campuses.' *Violence Against Women 21*, 1507–1527.

Darley, J.M. and Latane, B. (1968) 'Bystander intervention in emergencies: diffusion of responsibility.' *Journal of Personality and Social Psychology 8*, 377–383.

Davies, H. (2014) *Southbank International School Independent Review Arising from the Criminal Conduct of William Vahey: Final Report.* London: Farrer and Co.

Dorfman, L., Mejia, P., Cheyne, A. and Gonzalez, P. (2011) *Issue 19. Case by Case: News Coverage of Child Sexual Abuse, 2007–2009.* Berkeley Media Studies Group. Accessed on 25 July 2017 at www.bmsg.org/sites/default/files/bmsg_issue19.pdf

Dorfman, L., Mejia, P., Gonzalez, P. and Cheyne, A. (2012) *Breaking News on Child Sexual Abuse: Early Coverage of Penn State.* Berkeley Media Studies Group. Accessed on 25 July 2017 at www.bmsg.org/sites/default/files/bmsg_report_breaking_news_on_child_sexual_abuse_0.pdf

Exton, L. and Thandi, K. (2013) *Would They Actually Have Believed Me? A Focus Group Exploration of the Underreporting of Crimes by Jimmy Savile.* London: NSPCC. Accessed on 15 August 2017 at www.nspcc.org.uk/globalassets/documents/research-reports/would-they-actually-believed-me-savile-report.pdf

Fabiano, P.M., Perkins, H.W., Berkowitz, A., Linkenbach, J. and Stark, C. (2003) 'Engaging men as social justice allies in ending violence against women: evidence for a social norms approach.' *Journal of American College Health 52*, 105–112.

Finkelhor, D., Ormrod, R. and Chaffin, M. (2009) 'Juveniles Who Commit Sex Offenses against Minors' (NCJ 227763). *Juvenile Justice Bulletin.* Rockville, MD: National Criminal Justice Reference Service. Accessed on 25 July 2017 at www.ncjrs.gov/pdffiles1/ojjdp/227763.pdf

Fischer, P., Greitemeyer, T., Pollozek, F. and Frey, D. (2006) 'The unresponsive bystander: are bystanders more responsive in dangerous emergencies?' *European Journal of Social Psychology 36*, 267–278.

Foubert, J.D. (2005) *The Men's Program: A Peer Education Guide to Rape Prevention* (3rd edn). New York: Routledge.

Foubert, J.D. and Newberry, J.T. (2006) 'Effects of two versions of an empathy-based rape prevention program on fraternity men's rape survivor empathy, attitudes, and behavioral intent to commit rape or sexual assault.' *Journal of College Student Development 47*, 133–148.

FrameWorks Institute (2016) *Strategic Frame Analysis*. Accessed on 25 July 2017 at www.frameworksinstitute.org/sfa-overview.html

Freeh, L. (2012) *Report of the Special Investigative Council Regarding the Actions of the Pennsylvania State University Related to Child Sexual Abuse Committed by Gerald A. Sandusky*. Washington, DC: Freeh, Sporkin and Sullivan. Accessed on 15 August 2017 at http://media.pennlive.com/midstate_impact/other/REPORT_FINAL_071212.pdf

Hoffman, L. (2016) *Sexual Assault Prevention on US College Campuses: A National Scan*. California Coalition Against Sexual Assault. Accessed on 25 July 2017 at www.calcasa.org/download/25211

Kaufman, K.L. (2012) Situational prevention of child sexual abuse: Strategies to reduce risks in community organizations [PowerPoint slides]. Accessed on 25 July 2017 at www.scouting.org/filestore/nyps/presentations/Kaufman-Situation-Prevention-Presentation-For-Scouts.pdf

Lampard, K. and Marsden, E. (2015) *Themes and Lessons Learnt from NHS Investigations into Matters Relating to Jimmy Savile: Independent Report for the Secretary of State for Health*. London: Department of Health. Accessed on 11 August 2017 at www.gov.uk/government/uploads/system/uploads/attachment_data/file/407209/KL_lessons_learned_report_FINAL.pdf

Lemann, N. (2014) 'A Call for Help: What the Kitty Genovese Story Really Means.' *New Yorker*, 10 March. Accessed on 25 July 2017 at www.newyorker.com/magazine/2014/03/10/a-call-for-help

McCartan, K.F., Kemshall, H. and Tabachnick, J. (2015) 'The construction of community understandings of sexual violence: rethinking public, practitioner and policy discourses.' *Journal of Sexual Aggression 21*, 100–116.

Mejia, P., Somji, A., Nixon, L., Dorfman, L. and Quintero, F. (2015) *Issue 22. What's Missing from the News on Sexual Violence? An Analysis of Coverage, 2011–2013.* Berkeley Media Studies Group. Accessed on 25 July 2017 at www.bmsg.org/resources/publications/issue-22-sexual-violence-news-analysis-2011-2013

Miller, E., Tancredi, D.J., McCauley, H.L., Decker, M.R., *et al.* (2012) '"Coaching boys into men": a cluster-randomized controlled trial of a dating violence prevention program.' *Journal of Adolescent Health 51*, 431–438.

Miller, E., Tancredi, D.J., McCauley, H.L., Decker, M.R., *et al.* (2013) 'One-year follow-up of a coach-delivered dating violence prevention program: a cluster randomized controlled trial.' *American Journal of Preventive Medicine 45*, 108–112.

Moore Center for the Prevention of Child Sexual Abuse (n.d.) *Help Wanted Study: A Prevention Program Advancing the Healthy and Safe Development of Adolescents Attracted to Younger Children.* Moore Center for the Prevention of Sexual Abuse, Johns Hopkins University. Accessed on 25 July 2017 at www.jhsph.edu/research/centers-and-institutes/moore-center-for-the-prevention-of-child-sexual-abuse/research/help-wanted-project.html

Moynihan, M.M., Banyard, V.L., Cares, A.C., Potter, S.J., Williams, L.M. and Stapleton, J.G. (2015) 'Encouraging responses in sexual and relationship violence prevention: what program effects remain 1 year later?' *Journal of Interpersonal Violence 30*, 110–132.

National Center on the Sexual Behavior of Youth (2017) Accessed on 25 July 2017 at www.ncsby.org

O'Neil, M. and Morgan, P. (2010) *American Perceptions of Sexual Violence: A FrameWorks Research Report.* Accessed on 25 July 2017 at www.frameworksinstitute.org/assets/files/PDF_sexualviolence/AmericanPerceptionsofSexualViolence.pdf

Pereda, N., Guilera, G., Forns, M. and Gomez-Benito, J. (2009) 'The prevalence of child sexual abuse in community and student samples: a meta-analysis.' *Clinical Psychology Review 29*, 328–338.

Pew Research Center (2016) *Opinions on Gun Policy and the 2016 Campaign.* Accessed on 25 July 2017 at www.people-press.org/2016/08/26/opinions-on-gun-policy-and-the-2016-campaign

Ports, K.A., Ford, D.C. and Merrick, M.T. (2016) 'Adverse childhood experiences and adult sexual victimization.' *Child Abuse and Neglect 51*, 313–322.

Saul, J. and Audage, N.C. (2007) *Preventing Child Sexual Abuse within Youth-Serving Organizations: Getting Started on Policies and Procedures*. Atlanta, GA: Centers for Disease Control and Prevention. Accessed on 25 July 2017 at www.cdc.gov/violenceprevention/pdf/preventingchildsexualabuse-a.pdf

Shavit, Y., Weinstein, A.Q., Reiss-Davis, Z. and Cheit, R.E. (2014) 'Television newsmagazine coverage of child sexual abuse: 1990–2005.' *Journal of Mass Communication and Journalism 4*, 196–204.

Smedley, B.D. and Syme, S.L. (eds) (2000) *Promoting Health: Intervention Strategies from Social and Behavioral Research*. Washington, DC: National Academy of Sciences Press.

Stop It Now! (n.d.) Accessed on 25 July 2017 at www.stopitnow.org

Tabachnick, J. (2008a) *Engaging Bystanders in Sexual Violence Prevention*. Enola, PA: National Sexual Violence Resource Center. Accessed on 25 July 2017 at www.nsvrc.org/sites/default/files/Publications_NSVRC_Booklets_Engaging-Bystanders-in-Sexual-Violence-Prevention.pdf

Tabachnick, J. (2008b) 'The Promise and Potential for Engaging Bystanders in Primary Prevention.' In D. Prescott (ed.) *Applying Knowledge to Practice: Treating and Supervision of Sexual Abusers*. Oklahoma City, OK: Wood 'N' Barnes.

Tabachnick, J. and Klein, A. (2011) *A Reasoned Approach: Reshaping Sex Offender Policy to Prevent Child Sexual Abuse*. Beaverton, OR: Association for the Treatment of Sexual Abusers. Accessed on 25 July 2017 at www.atsa.com/pdfs/Policy/AReasonedApproach.pdf

University of Arizona (n.d.) *STEP UP!* Accessed on 25 July 2017 at www.stepupprogram.org

US Department of Justice, Office of Sex Offender Sentencing, Monitoring, Apprehending, Registering, and Tracking (2014) *Sex Offender Management, Assessment and Planning Initiative* (NCJ 247059). Accessed on 25 July 2017 at https://smart.gov/SOMAPI/pdfs/SOMAPI_Full%20Report.pdf

World Health Organization (2007) *Rape: How Women, the Community and the Health Sector Respond. Research Summary*. Sexual Violence Research Initiative. Accessed on 25 July 2017 at www.svri.org/sites/default/files/attachments/2016-01-19/Rapehowwomenbooklet.pdf

Wortley, R. and Smallbone, S. (2006) 'Applying Situational Principles to Sexual Offences against Children.' In R. Wortley and S. Smallbone (eds) *Situational Prevention of Child Sexual Abuse* (Crime Prevention Studies, Vol. 19). Monsey, NY: Criminal Justice Press.

Wurtele, S.K. (2012) 'Preventing the sexual exploitation of minors in youth-serving organizations.' *Children and Youth Services Review 34*, 2442–2453.

8

WHAT SURVIVORS TELL US ABOUT FACILITATING EARLY DISCLOSURE

JON BROWN

> 'There were so many times when I thought about telling someone but it was just like, how do you bring it up? How do you just walk into a room and go to someone, "oh by the way this happened"?'
>
> (Warrington *et al.*, 2017, p.39)

> 'Like for me as I said I didn't tell anyone for eight years. I think it's because I blocked it out because it was such a young age. So I think I blocked it out, but I still remembered but I don't know how to explain it... Even though I understood but I didn't understand, like it was mixed feelings. I couldn't believe it and I was just like, "oh no one's ever going to believe me".'
>
> (Warrington *et al.*, 2017, p.41)

This chapter will begin with an overview of what the literature tells us about the impact of child sexual abuse on children, young people and adult survivors. It will then go on to examine how victims/survivors can be silenced by abuse and what is likely to enable disclosure. It will then identify what victims/survivors tell us is likely to enable early or earlier disclosure and what is currently in place to facilitate disclosure. The chapter will close with a discussion of what next steps might be necessary to enable earlier disclosure. It should be recognised that because sexual abuse is inextricably linked with the abuse of power, the impacts of abuse can be significantly informed by the nature of the power imbalance. Celebrity can of course further sharpen the power imbalance that already exists between an adult and a child or young person, and it is therefore not surprising to hear victims of Savile and other high-profile and celebrity abusers talk about their fear of never being believed and of being told they were fantasising about and fabricating the abuse if they attempted to disclose.

A note on language: The chapter will refer to 'victims' and 'survivors' in recognition of the different descriptions people prefer to use and of the stage of someone's recovery. Children and young people will be referred to in recognition of the fact that child sexual abuse can and does occur from 0 to 18 years; child sexual abuse will on occasions be referred to as CSA; and finally sexual abuse will be taken to include a wide range of abusive behaviour that includes child sexual exploitation.

Defining child sexual abuse

The NSPCC (2017) identifies two different types of child sexual abuse which can occur on and offline: contact abuse and non-contact abuse.

- *Contact abuse* involves touching activities where an abuser makes physical contact with a child, including penetration. It includes: sexual touching of any part of the body whether the child is wearing clothes or not; rape or penetration by putting an object or body part inside a child's mouth, vagina or anus; forcing or encouraging a child to take part in sexual activity; and making a child take their clothes off, touch someone else's genitals or masturbate.

- *Non-contact abuse* involves non-touching activities, such as grooming, exploitation, persuading children to perform sexual acts over the Internet and flashing. It includes: encouraging a child to watch or hear sexual acts; not taking proper measures to prevent a child being exposed to sexual activities by others;

meeting a child following sexual grooming with the intent of abusing them; online abuse; including making, viewing or distributing child abuse images; allowing someone else to make, view or distribute child abuse images; showing pornography to a child; and sexually exploiting a child for money, power or status (child exploitation).

Prevalence of child sexual abuse

An estimated 150 million girls and 73 million boys under 18 worldwide have experienced forced sexual intercourse or other forms of sexual violence involving physical contact. A review of epidemiological surveys from 21 countries found that 7–36 per cent of females and 3–29 per cent of males reported sexual victimisation in their childhood (Pinheiro, 2006). In 2011, the NSPCC maltreatment survey found 24.1 per cent of 18–24-year-olds reported experiencing sexual abuse (either contact or non-contact) during their childhood.

While it is not known for certain how many children and young people are currently affected by sexual abuse there is evidence from many sources[1] which suggests that sexual abuse, of children is still common and that opportunities for abusers to access children through new technologies continue to increase.

In July 2014, the Children's Commissioner for England launched an inquiry into child sexual abuse in the family environment. This was a critical analysis of the scale and nature of this form of child sexual abuse. Based on data examined by the Commissioner, it is likely that only one in eight victims of sexual abuse come to the attention of the police and children's services (Children's Commissioner for England, 2015). Up to two-thirds of all sexual abuse happens in and around the family. A statistical estimation model called Multiple Systems Estimation found that, over the two-year period from April 2012 to March 2014, there were between 400,000 and 450,000 victims of

1 For example, in 2005–2006, 11,995 children calling ChildLine (8% of all callers) spoke about sexual abuse in their call (NSPCC, 2007); 36 per cent of all rapes recorded by the police are committed against children under 16 years of age (Nicholas, Kershaw and Walker, 2006).

child sexual abuse in England. This represents all forms of child sexual abuse, not only sexual abuse which occurs within the family. It must also be stressed that this confidence interval depends on a number of assumptions, which, while sensible, cannot be completely confirmed from the data, and so it may be that its accuracy is optimistic. Over the same time period, approximately 50,000 victims of child sexual abuse were known to statutory agencies.

Child sexual abuse can and should be seen as a public health problem which requires a coordinated, concerted and sustained response (Brown and Saied-Tessier, 2015). There is growing support for the use of a public health approach to address the sexual abuse of children (Mercy, 1999; Pinheiro, 2006; World Health Organization, 2006). Rather than suggesting a medical or disease-based model, public health in this context is used to describe a coordinated range of multifaceted interventions designed to impact on a significant proportion of the population.

A public health approach involves a long-term strategy, emphasising the importance of prevention in ending child sexual abuse; it seeks to involve the whole community in finding solutions; and it is multidisciplinary and encompasses a wide range of interventions, from prevention strategies to treatment approaches.

If similar proportions of children and young people were being affected by, for example, an environmental risk such as pollution, government-led action would be taken to understand, quantify and reduce the risk and to treat its consequences. There is currently little such coordinated action by government to address the problem of child sexual abuse despite what is known about its damaging long-term consequences and its cost to society.

The prevalence of child sexual abuse is notoriously difficult to estimate because of the significant level of under-reporting and delayed disclosure. Notwithstanding definitional problems, every methodology has significant limitations. As can be seen with the Office of the Children's Commissioner report, official records don't capture the majority of child sexual abuse incidents, as most are not disclosed for many years, *let alone* reported (Allnock *et al.*, 2009), and those using retrospective reports of survivors are subject to participants choosing not to disclose, forgetting abuse or reconstructing past experiences to make sense of current events (Williams, 1994). Overall, the limitations to each of the methodologies lead to the conclusion that most prevalence figures are likely to be significant underestimates.

The incidence and prevalence[2] of child sexual abuse is difficult to quantify in absolute terms. Using broad definitions, some authors have estimated that between 30 and 45 per cent of adult women will have experienced sexual abuse during their childhoods (Anderson *et al.*, 1993).

There is some evidence that the incidence of child sexual abuse may be declining, following a peak in the early 1990s. Jones and Finkelhor (2001) found a 39 per cent reduction in substantiated child sexual abuse cases between 1992 and 1999. The 2011 NSPCC prevalence study provides valuable data in relation to the prevalence of violence and abuse against children in the UK and some indications of a reduction in child sexual abuse (Radford *et al.*, 2011). Despite these apparently encouraging indications from North America and from the 2011 NSPCC prevalence study, child sexual abuse remains a serious and pervasive public health problem, affecting millions of children worldwide.

Impact of child sexual abuse

What children need to grow, develop and be healthy is well documented. Sexual abuse of a child will have a direct impact on this development. The impact may be psychological, social or behavioural. These impacts can be compounded when sexual abuse is combined with physical abuse and/or neglect. Emotional abuse can be seen as being implicitly present in all sexual abuse (Wiffin and MacIntosh, 2005). The impact of the associated emotional abuse

---

2 Incidence refers to occurrence or frequency over a specific period; prevalence is the degree to which something exists in a population and is usually specified as a percentage.

is significantly mediated by the relationship between the abuser and victim.

When a child is sexually abused their body is used by others to meet another person's need. The abuse means they are touched or treated in a way that is not consistent with their development or their own needs. Their world becomes unsafe, their reactions distorted and their relationships with adults and others around them skewed. The child's internal working models, unlike adults', are still being formed, and these become permeated with abuse-related information about their self, the abuser and the world.

Child sexual abuse has a more negative impact on child victims if it involves a greater degree of contact, a higher number of perpetrators, the use of force or threats of death, occurs more frequently and over a longer duration (Caffaro-Rouget, Reuben and Lang, 1989) and, as mentioned above, if the already existing power imbalance is heightened by celebrity status and with that the increased fear of not being believed and of fabricating the abuse. The most consistent finding in research is the link between adverse outcomes and the degree of contact involved in the abuse. Abuse perpetrated by a mother or father figure can also lead to more psychological problems (Cosentino *et al.*, 1995; Trickett *et al.*, 2001).

The physical impact of sexual abuse can be sexually transmitted disease, pregnancy or infection and sterility in later life. Increased understanding of neuroscience has revealed the extent to which children's brain development and brain activity are affected by the associated trauma. It has been shown that core stress response systems are affected and startle reflexes are inhibited, impacting on the child's more general development, affecting their capacity for learning and focusing attention. They may then come to live in 'a state of preparedness for negative emotions', which affects their general information processing (Krystal *et al.*, 1989; Kagan, 1991).

An important part of a child's development is being able to form secure attachments. If their abuse is by a significant caregiver, the impact of the trauma on their developing mind may result in distorted cognitive schema and impaired coping abilities (Wieland, 1998).

In seeking to sexually abuse a child the perpetrator may seek to interfere in the child's normal attachment relationships in order to abuse them, or indeed may spend time building their own attachment relationship. This is referred to as the grooming process. This can then lead to the formation of a 'trauma bond', an unhealthy, unsafe attachment to the perpetrator.

A younger age at the onset of abuse is more likely to lead to sexualised behaviour, anxiety and hyperarousal in children (McClellan *et al.*, 1996), whereas an older age of onset is associated with higher rates of post-traumatic stress disorder (PTSD) and lower general psychological functioning (Ruggiero, McLeer and Dixon, 2000).

During the abuse children may learn to block out the experience in the moment through dissociation and consequently may also tend to dissociate in other parts of their life. They may feel sexually aroused during abuse (Hall, Mathews and Pearce, 1998); they may also seek arousal as a means of soothing their distress and to experience positive feelings. Research indicates that around 50 per cent of children who develop harmful sexual behaviour have themselves been sexually abused (Jones and Ramchandani, 1999).

All these impacts of sexual abuse on children must inform and influence treatment design. The development and evaluation of a treatment manual, commissioned by the NSPCC for work with children who have been sexually abused, will reflect this research and practice knowledge base.

Intervention

Therapeutic work needs to be explicitly informed by:

- *Safety*: The primary immediate aim of intervening in child sexual abuse must be to stop the abuse and make the child safe. Securing their safety will only be the beginning of addressing their needs.
- *Protection*: Children's ongoing protection and the ability of their carers or substitute carers to keep them safe need to be assessed.

This happens as part of the child protection processes in the UK, and assessment must be a continuous process, not an event (HM Government, 2015).

It is known that in order to abuse the child the perpetrator may have damaged their relationship with their parent/carer or may have isolated the child within the family system. Having been the victim of abuse increases vulnerability and the likelihood of re-victimisation (Jones and Ramchandani, 1999). The identified risk factors all reinforce the need for an assessment which addresses the child's need for protection.

Belief and support

Children who have been sexually abused will be sensitive to the responses of adults when they disclose (Malloy, Lyon and Quas, 2007). Retraction of an allegation is likely to be a result of the child's lack of support from the non-offending caregiver, and a desire to protect the perpetrator where they are a family member. Inappropriate adult responses will serve to reinforce any sense of guilt, shame and powerlessness they already feel.

A relatively reliable finding is that currently 50 per cent or less of mothers provide consistent belief, support and protection of their child following disclosure (Everson *et al.*, 1989; Leifer, Shapiro and Kassem, 1993). Reaction to a disclosure appears to be critical to the child's future wellbeing (Roesler, 1994; Everill and Waller, 1995; Bernard-Bonnin *et al.*, 2008), but more longitudinal studies of the impact of disclosure and the effect of a variety of social reactions would be valuable.

Child sexual abuse is an event or series of events which happen to a child, rather than a mental health problem per se, and unattended to or unresolved the harm to the child may be compounded. One model which identifies the characteristics of the abuse experience identifies four areas: betrayal, stigmatisation, traumagenic sexualisation and powerlessness (Finkelhor and Browne, 1985). The wide range of problems for the child, symptoms that may be exhibited and coping strategies which lead to behavioural problems all pose a challenge in assessing the impact of the abuse and the real distress of the child.

Over the last three decades there have been significant developments in understanding what works in the assessment and treatment of children and young people who have been sexually abused, of children and young people with harmful sexual behaviour, and of adult sex offenders.

In the 1960s and 1970s, with the development of feminism and the beginnings of a recognition of children's rights, the scale of sexual abuse, initially that within the family, began to be recognised. The potential amenability of the treatment of adult perpetrators to cognitive behavioural therapy (CBT) and the key role of cognitive distortions began to be recognised (Mann, 2004).

Work by researchers and practitioners such as Finkelhor (1984), Wolf (1984), Bentovim (1988), Laws (1989), Berliner (1991), Marshall, Anderson and Fernandez (1999), Hanson and Morton-Bourgon (2004), Ward and Marshall (2004), Briere and Scott (2006), Vizard *et al.* (2007) and Smallbone, Marshall and Wortley (2008) has been influential in developing knowledge about the aetiology of sexual abuse, the static and dynamic areas to assess when considering treatment need and risk, and what works with treatment.

In 1999 the Department of Health issued *Child Sexual Abuse: Informing Practice from Research* (Jones and Ramchandani, 1999). This noted the research evidence that, for the sexually abused child, psychological treatments are more effective than the passage of time, but that treatment cannot work in isolation. Children must remain safe from further maltreatment in order to benefit from therapeutic interventions, and treatments must involve the non-abusive parent or carer. It also noted that a variety of treatment approaches must be available to cover 'the disparate needs' these children will have.

The National Institute for Health and Care Excellence (NICE) recommends trauma-focused CBT for sexually abused children (NICE, 2005). There is evidence of positive effects on some of those symptoms commonly experienced by sexually abused children. CBT treatment programmes typically include revisiting traumatic memories in order to both reduce the negative emotions surrounding them and challenging distorted beliefs (e.g. self-blame for the abuse); developing self-soothing skills; and overcoming avoidance of trauma reminders. CBT may also involve sessions with non-abusing carers and may include teaching behavioural management skills, addressing maladaptive beliefs, and reducing the negative impact of the abuse on the family (Cohen *et al.*, 2000).

Within the NSPCC a trauma-focused approach to victims of child sexual abuse has been supported since 2007 when a standardised measure, the 'Trauma Symptom Checklist for Children' (TSCC) (Briere, 1996), was introduced. An integrative trauma-focused approach based on a therapeutic relationship combined with a mixture of psychodynamic and cognitive behavioural models has been similarly supported. Analysis of the TSCC data shows a significant improvement in reported difficulties between the beginning and end of service received (Cotmore and D'Souza, 2010). In the most recent NICE guideline on child abuse and neglect (2017), the NSPCC's *Letting the Future in* therapeutic guide (Carpenter *et al.*, 2016) combining play therapy, elements of CBT and psychotherapy is recommended following its RCT evaluation.

There is evidence from other studies that other types of therapy may be helpful. Eye Movement Desensitisation Reprocessing (EMDR) involves processing traumatic memories whilst moving one's eyes to bilaterally stimulate the brain (Jaberghaderi *et al.*, 2004). Individual or group psychotherapy (Trowell *et al.*, 2002; McCrone *et al.*, 2005) and non-directive, supportive sessions appear to facilitate positive change (Deblinger, Stauffer and Steer, 2001). With younger children, there is sparse and conflicting evidence about best approaches.

Parental support has been correlated with a positive outcome for sexually abused children (Macdonald, 2000), and as noted parental distress and disbelief can have a negative impact. A number of studies have reported positive changes in parents participating in CBT alongside their children, such as a reduction in blame of the child, and improvements in their parenting (Deblinger *et al.*, 2001; Cohen *et al.*, 2004).

Questions that still need to be addressed include: For how long are positive changes maintained following therapy? Is therapy beneficial for sexually abused boys as well as girls, for those with multiple difficulties, for victims of multiple forms of abuse, for those from a range of cultures, and for those with learning disabilities? Which therapies and therapeutic processes are most useful for reducing problems beyond PTSD, depression and anxiety? Can therapy be used to prevent problems before they emerge? Which children are most likely to benefit from which form of therapy?

There remains a serious shortfall in provision in the UK for any of the range of therapies or treatments. NSPCC research (see Allnock *et al.*, 2009) found significant gaps in services and a system unable to meet and fulfil a child's right to help when they have been harmed. Resources were particularly inaccessible in some geographical regions and also inaccessible for those children with physical and learning disabilities.

What is likely to inhibit and enable disclosure?

Research findings highlight significant delays between the onset of all forms of abuse and children disclosing (Allnock and Miller, 2013; Children's Commissioner, 2015; Smith, Dogaru and Ellis, 2015). One of the few other pieces of qualitative research interviewing children about experiences of CSA found that less than a third of victims told a peer or a parent immediately after an incident occurred; a third delayed disclosure up to five years; and a third waited longer than five years (Schönbucher *et al.*, 2012).

The silencing impact of abuse before disclosure or identification is eloquently described by one eight-year-old interviewee in the *Making Noise* research, who picked a series of images, words and phrases to explain how it felt before she'd told anyone about the abuse by her brother. Images she chose included a set of keys, a library book, a 'dead end' sign and various faces and words signifying negative emotions.

> [Before telling someone] you want to lock your mouth up...you feel like you have a dead end, you've hit a dead end and you don't

> know what to do and you're trapped and your feelings are trapped inside you and you don't know what to do...you're worried and you're scared...and you might feel angry, confused and also you might feel like you've locked yourself in like a prison that is keeping your worries from coming out. (IV13 Female, 8 years) (Warrington *et al.*, 2017, p.41)

Allnock and Miller (2013) identify a number of factors that can inhibit disclosure and others that can facilitate disclosure. From what children and young people and adult survivors of abuse tell us, the following factors are likely to inhibit disclosure:

- *Unsupportive and poor family relationships and family stress*: Particularly where sexual abuse has occurred within the family environment, lack of support and/or belief – particularly by the primary caregivers – can be a significant factor in stopping or delaying disclosure. This can range from overt hostility to ambivalence. Children can be hyper-vigilant and alert to these signs as a consequence of the abuse they have experienced.

- *Not feeling heard*: Children and young people will often make initial attempts to disclose and will test receptiveness through sometimes oblique comments which, if they are not picked up on, may leave them feeling not heard. Accepting that they may already feel to blame for and ashamed of the abuse, it can sometimes take what others may see as minor oversights to be enough for disclosure to be delayed, sometimes significantly.

- *Over-protective messages to children and young people*: Children and young people hearing messages such as 'If anything like that happened to you I'd literally kill him' can leave them feeling overly responsible for the consequences and aftermath of their disclosure in a way similar to Maya Angelou's silencing and elective muteness in *I Know Why the Caged Bird Sings* (Angelou, 1969).

- *Confidentiality*: Sexual abuse removes a sense of control and therefore a feeling of some control over the process, and what is said and conveyed and when is important.

The following factors are likely to facilitate disclosure:

- *An expectation of belief*: If the child or young person believes that they will be heard, this can be significant in enabling disclosure. Belief is important and should be seen as separate from thorough assessment and investigation.

- *Safety*: If a child or young person feels physically and psychologically safe, they are significantly more likely to disclose. In fact, they are unlikely to disclose until they do feel safe. Many children and young people disclose sexual abuse in a way that others can hear once they have been accommodated by the local authority and are in a foster or residential setting.

- *Belief in a response*: Believing that a disclosure will be responded to, particularly in a way and at a pace that the child or young person has some influence over, can be significant in facilitating disclosure.

- *A non-judgemental response*: Not surprisingly, believing that a familial and professional response to a disclosure will be non-judgemental and non-blaming is important, taking into account the fact that victims and survivors of abuse will often feel in some way to blame or guilty for the abuse as a result of the grooming process and messages they might have internalised from the person or people who abused them.

Allnock and Miller (2013, p.8) identify six key themes which can be significant in facilitating disclosure:

1. interest by others – noticing signs and early attempts at disclosure

2. relationships and sex education at school

3. emotional needs being met and support from friends
4. changes in the nature of the abuse; these junction points can be important opportunities for disclosure
5. recognition that others need to be protected, for example younger siblings or friends – 'it happened to me and I must make sure it doesn't happen to them…'
6. remembering previously forgotten or suppressed memories of abuse.

The NSPCC's *Would They Actually Have Believed Me?* (Exton and Thandi, 2013) is a report of five focus groups in the aftermath of the Savile disclosures that highlights the need for victims and survivors to feel confident that they will be believed, that their disclosures will be thoroughly investigated and that advice and support will be available as soon as a disclosure has been made. The report vividly describes the silencing power of abuse and how this is compounded by the celebrity status of the abuser. The acute feelings of powerlessness that can result should be countered with robust and sufficient support, and advice and help that explicitly recognises the impacts of this particular type of sexual abuse.

The voices of children and young people

Making Noise (Warrington *et al.*, 2017) aimed to improve understanding of children and young people's experiences of the following and to ascertain children and young people's views on how such processes could be improved:

- recognition, identification and disclosure of CSA in the family environment
- help-seeking and support
- contact with services as a result of reporting/identification of CSA

- care systems
- criminal justice procedures.

Significantly, the research found that professionals and other adults continue to miss signs of children's sexual abuse; this unfairly places responsibility on children and young people themselves to actively seek help in the event of CSA in the family environment. Also, while the overwhelming majority of interviewees recognised the desirability of a safe adult finding out about their experiences of CSA in the family environment, the majority did not feel purposeful or direct disclosure was likely or possible for most children in their position.

Children reported being most likely to disclose their experiences of abuse to their non-abusing mother or (in the case of female children) a friend, and there is evidence that particular groups of children and young people – for example, disabled children and young people, those from some minority ethnic communities, boys and young men, and care-experienced children and young people – are likely to face additional barriers to identification or disclosure.

The research concludes that efforts to support the identification of child sexual abuse in the family environment should address: children's knowledge and understanding of abuse; their confidence in being believed; stigma and shame; and their accessibility to and confidence in the provision of support.

Identification and disclosure of CSA in the familial environment often represents the beginning of challenging and difficult processes for children and young people, and recognising the particular vulnerabilities associated with identification or disclosure is vital for professionals wishing to provide effective support in the aftermath of CSA in the family environment. Services are not yet fully equipped to support children through these challenging and difficult processes.

Support to non-abusing family members is critical for helping children and young people after experiences of CSA in the family environment. The research identifies its benefits as being fourfold:

1. addressing parents' and carers' own support needs
2. helping parents and carers to better understand and respond to their children's needs
3. promoting family stability and safe positive relationships
4. reducing the additional burden on children and young people for the responsibility they feel for their families' wellbeing.

The key factors identified in *Making Noise* (Warrington *et al.*, 2017) that inhibit disclosure include: fear of not being believed, family reputation and 'honour', protecting already marginalised communities from further stigma, and difficulties discussing relationships and sex.

Factors identified as facilitating disclosure include (for parents and families) a close and trusting relationship, a propensity to listen, and belief in the family member's ability to advocate for the child or young person and to support children and young people to stay safe. For friends, key factors are trust and confidence in the friendship, anticipation of a less judgemental response, emotional support and advice, and an opportunity to test out responses to a disclosure.

After family and friends, those children and young people identified as most likely to disclose to were the police, ChildLine and teachers.

What is currently in place to facilitate disclosure?

Since the 'discovery' of child sexual abuse in the 1970s and 1980s there has been a gradual move towards putting in place processes and systems with the aim of enabling disclosure, in recognition of the growing knowledge that disclosure of sexual abuse can be a difficult process with many opportunities for retraction.

Achieving Best Evidence in criminal proceedings

Achieving Best Evidence (ABE) was first introduced in 2002 (Ministry of Justice *et al.*, 2011) when the majority of the provisions in the Youth Justice and Criminal Evidence Act 1999 were brought into force. It is significant in that it represents the first coordinated effort to address the needs of vulnerable and intimidated witnesses and recognises the particular challenges of getting best evidence from sexual abuse victims and survivors.

ABE addresses preparing and planning for interviews with witnesses, decisions about whether or not to conduct an interview and whether the interview should be video recorded or a written statement should be taken following the interview. It covers interviewing witnesses both for making a video-recorded statement and for taking a written statement, their preparation for court and the subsequent court appearance. It applies to both prosecution and defence witnesses and is intended for everyone involved in relevant investigations, including the police, adults and children's social care workers, and members of the legal profession. Children are defined as vulnerable by reason of their age. The Act makes all children under 18 years of age, appearing as defence or prosecution witnesses in criminal proceedings, eligible for *special measures* to assist them to give their evidence in court.

The examination by Bunting *et al.* (2015) of ABE practice in Northern Ireland identifies a number of themes that are likely to facilitate good practice: planning, preparation and flexibility; taking into account the specifics of the child or young person; rapport building; training in interview skills; feedback; and review. ABE practice continues to be quite varied across the UK with interviews often being police led, sometimes and not infrequently without an ABE-trained social worker present due to a shortage of social workers with the necessary experience and training. There does therefore need to be a focus on the recruitment, training and retention of suitably trained and qualified social workers who can undertake joint ABE interviews with the police.

Section 28 of the Youth Justice and Criminal Evidence Act 1999 allows for cross-examination of vulnerable witnesses to be filmed prior to trial and then used as evidence in chief in recognition of the fact that cross-examination in court, particularly in sexual abuse cases, often does not achieve best evidence. After almost two decades, section 28 is now being piloted in a number of courts with a view to it being implemented across the UK. This has been too long in coming, particularly when the impact of the trial and cross-examination in court by multiple defence barristers on the victims appearing as witnesses (e.g. the Oxford child sexual exploitation trial held at the Old Bailey in May 2013) is considered.

The Child House

The idea of the Child House originated in the development of Child Advocacy Centres in the US and in the *Barnahus* (Child House) originally developed in Iceland and now used in a number of Scandinavian and Northern European countries. The idea of both Child Advocacy Centres and the Barnahus is that services for children who have experienced abuse should be organised around the child in a welcoming and friendly setting and should provide a continuum of services including joint investigative interviews, court statements, prosecution interviews, medical examinations, video-linked evidence to trials, victim therapy, family counselling, consultation and advice to local prosecutors, the police, education and research. In short, the Centres or Houses should provide an integrated 'one stop shop' service and should be centres of excellence and expertise in the investigation and treatment of sexual abuse.

Evaluation data so far has been positive and has shown improved outcomes for the children and young people who have been referred to and received services from these resources (Gudjonsson *et al.*, 2010; Children's Commissioner for England, 2016). The waiting time from disclosure to case conclusion has been significantly reduced in many cases, and increases in successful prosecutions have also been identified. Further evaluation is necessary, and the working assumption is that resources such as these will not only improve outcomes for children and young people who have been abused but will also encourage more to disclose earlier, knowing that there are resources in place that can provide help and support.

Currently in the UK there is a Child Advocacy Centre operating in Durham, and in London two proof of concept Child Houses are planned, to demonstrate effectiveness, with a plan to roll out further Houses following initial evaluation.

Ten steps to enable earlier disclosure

The two examples above are significant developments that are contributing to early disclosure. The chapter concludes with ten developments which, if implemented, would contribute significantly to enabling earlier disclosure.

1. ABE best practice should be embedded across the UK. Currently interview practice varies and is quite inconsistent. A concerted programme to ensure what has been learned about best ABE practice could make a significant contribution to improving the confidence of children and young people to disclose if they hear of other cases where there have been positive experiences following disclosure.

2. Recognition by key professionals can be important in enabling disclosure. More consistent and routine training is necessary for social workers, police officers, teachers and all those working with children and young people to be confident in identifying signs that could indicate that abuse might have taken place.

3. The Child House model should be rolled out if the initial evaluation shows it to be effective in a UK context.

4. Funding needs to be made available for sufficient therapeutic help for all children and young people who have been abused at a time when they need it. Current provision continues to be patchy and fragmented, and this lack of help is the focus of the NSPCC's 'It's Time' campaign.

5. More suitably qualified and experienced practitioners are needed to provide the necessary help to children and young people who have experienced abuse.

6. More routine training is necessary for judges and lawyers on the signs, symptoms and impacts of sexual abuse. What children and young people see and hear from lawyers and judges and the resulting actions and decisions can be very significant in deciding whether to disclose.

7. For those working with children and young people in higher risk environments, for example residential schools and homes, value-based interviews should be a standard component of all recruitment. Well selected, trained and supported staff, especially in residential settings, can be key in enabling and supporting disclosure.

8. We need to see greater engagement of local authorities and the private sector in enabling children and adults to speak out.

9. There is scope to build on some of the prevention campaigns that have been run, for example in York and Hounslow (www.saferchildrenyork.org.uk; www.hounslow.gov.uk/home), which have included clear messaging about speaking out.

10. Helplines, and increasingly online help, advice and signposting, are often one of the first places children and young people go to when they are thinking about disclosing. There should be sufficient resource to enable all calls and contacts to be answered and for those who have sought help to receive a response that will be experienced as supportive.

References

Allnock, D. and Miller, P. (2013) *No One Noticed, No One Heard: A Study of Disclosures of Childhood Abuse.* London: NSPCC. Accessed on 14 August 2017 at www.nspcc.org.uk/globalassets/documents/research-reports/no-one-noticed-no-one-heard-report.pdf

Allnock, D. with Bunting, L., Price, A., Morgan-Klein, *et al.* (2009) *Sexual Abuse and Therapeutic Services for Children and Young People: The Gap between Provision and Need.* London: NSPCC. Accessed on 14 August 2017 at www.nspcc.org.uk/globalassets/documents/research-reports/sexual-abuse-therapeutic-services-children-young-people-summary.pdf

Anderson, J., Martin, J., Mullen, P., Romans, S. and Herbison, P. (1993) 'Prevalence of childhood sexual abuse experiences in a community sample of women.' *Journal of the American Academy of Child and Adolescent Psychiatry 32*, 911–919.

Angelou, M. (1969) *I Know Why the Caged Bird Sings*. New York: Random House Trade Paperbacks.

Bentovim, A. (1988) *Child Sexual Abuse within the Family. Assessment and Treatment: The Work of the Great Ormond Street Sexual Abuse Team*. London: Wright.

Berliner, L. (1991) 'Effects of sexual abuse on children.' *Violence Update 1*, 10, 1, 8, 10–11.

Bernard-Bonnin, A.C., Hebert, M., Daignault, I.V. and Allard-Dansereau, C. (2008) 'Disclosure of sexual abuse, and personal and familial factors as predictors of post-traumatic stress disorder symptoms in school-aged girls.' *Paediatrics and Child Health 13*, 6, 479–486.

Briere, J. (1996) *Trauma Symptom Checklist for Children*. Odessa, FL: Psychological Assessment Resources.

Briere, J. and Scott, C. (2006) *Principles of Trauma Therapy: A Guide to Symptoms, Evaluation, and Treatment*. London: Sage.

Brown, J. and Saied-Tessier, A. (2015) *Preventing Child Sexual Abuse: Towards a National Strategy for England*. London: NSPCC. Accessed on 14 August 2017 at https://www.nspcc.org.uk/globalassets/documents/research-reports/preventing-child-sexual-abuse-towards-a-national-strategy.pdf

Bunting, L., Carr, N., Hayes, D. and Marshall, J. (2015) *Good Practice in Achieving Best Evidence Interview with Child Witnesses in Northern Ireland: Criminal Justice Perspectives*. Belfast: Department of Justice. Accessed on 14 August 2017 at http://cdn.basw.co.uk/upload/basw_30340-6.pdf

Caffaro-Rouget, A., Reuben, R.A. and Lang, V. (1989) 'The impact of child sexual abuse on victims' adjustment.' *Annals of Sex Research 2*, 1, 29–47.

Carpenter, J., Jessiman, T., Patsios, D., Hackett, S. and Phillips, J. (2016) *Letting the Future in. A Therapeutic Intervention for Children Affected by Sexual Abuse and Their Carers: An Evaluation of Impact and Implementation*. London: NSPCC. Accessed on 14 August 2017 at www.nspcc.org.uk/globalassets/documents/research-reports/letting-the-future-in-evaluation.pdf

Children's Commissioner for England (2015) *Protecting Children from Harm: A Critical Assessment of Child Sexual Abuse in the Family Network in England and Priorities for Action*. London: Office of the Children's Commissioner for England. Accessed on 14 August 2014 at www.childrenscommissioner.gov.uk/wp-content/uploads/2017/06/Protecting-children-from-harm-full-report.pdf

Children's Commissioner for England (2016) *Barnahus: Improving the Response to Child Sexual Abuse in England*. London: Office of the Children's Commissioner for England. Accessed on 14 August 2017 at www.childrenscommissioner.gov.uk/wp-content/uploads/2017/06/Barnahus-Improving-the-response-to-child-sexual-abuse-in-England.pdf

Cohen, J.A., Deblinger, E., Mannarino, A.P. and Steer, R.A. (2004) 'A multisite randomised controlled trial for children with sexual abuse related PTSD symptoms.' *Journal of the American Academy of Child and Adolescent Psychiatry 43*, 4, 393–402.

Cohen, J.A., Mannarino, A.P., Berliner, L. and Deblinger, E. (2000) 'Trauma-focused cognitive behavioural therapy for children and adolescents: an empirical update.' *Journal of Interpersonal Violence 15*, 11, 1202–1223.

Cosentino, C.E., Meyer-Bahlburg, H.F.L., Alpert, J.L., Weinberg, S.L. and Gaines, R. (1995) 'Sexual behavior problems and psychopathology symptoms in sexually abused girls.' *Journal of the American Academy of Child and Adolescent Psychiatry 34*, 8, 1033–1042.

Cotmore, R. and D'Souza, P. (2010) Report on the implementation of TSCC in the NSPCC and preliminary analysis of data. Unpublished report, NSPCC.

Deblinger, E., Stauffer, L.B. and Steer, R.A. (2001) 'Comparative efficacies of supportive and cognitive behavioural group therapies for young children who have been sexually abused and their nonoffending mothers.' *Child Maltreatment 6*, 4, 332–343.

Everill, J. and Waller, G. (1995) 'Disclosure of sexual abuse and psychological adjustment in female undergraduates.' *Child Abuse and Neglect 19*, 1, 93–100.

Everson, M.D., Hunter, W.M., Runyan, D.K., Edelsohn, G.A. and Coulter, M.L. (1989) 'Maternal support following disclosure of incest.' *American Journal of Orthopsychiatry 59*, 2, 197–207.

Exton, L. and Thandi, K. (2013) *Would They Actually Have Believed Me? A Focus Group Exploration of the Underreporting of Crimes by Jimmy Savile.* London: NSPCC. Accessed on 15 August 2017 at www.nspcc.org.uk/globalassets/documents/research-reports/would-they-actually-believed-me-savile-report.pdf

Finkelhor, D. (1984) *Child Sexual Abuse: New Theory and Research*. New York: Free Press.

Finkelhor, D. and Browne, A. (1985) 'The traumatic impact of child sexual abuse: a conceptualization.' *American Journal of Orthopsychiatry 55*, 4, 530–541.

Gudjonsson, G., Sveinsdottir, T., Sigurdsson, J.F. and Jonsdottir, J. (2010) 'The ability of suspected victims of childhood sexual abuse (CSA) to give evidence: findings from the Children's House in Iceland.' *The Journal of Forensic Psychiatry and Psychology 21*, 4, 569–586.

Hall, D.K., Mathews, F. and Pearce, J. (1998) 'Factors associated with sexual behavior problems in young sexually abused children.' *Child Abuse and Neglect 22*, 10, 1045–1063.

Hanson, K. and Morton-Bourgon, K. (2004) *Predictors of Sexual Recidivism: An Updated Meta-Analysis*. Ottawa, Canada: Department of the Solicitor General, Corrections Research.

HM Government (2015) *Working Together to Safeguard Children.* London: Department for Education. Accessed on 15 August 2017 at www.gov.uk/government/uploads/system/uploads/attachment_data/file/592101/Working_Together_to_Safeguard_Children_20170213.pdf

Jaberghaderi, N., Greenwald, R., Rubin, A., Zand, S.O. and Dolatabadi, S. (2004) 'A comparison of CBT and EMDR for sexually abused Iranian girls.' *Clinical Psychology and Psychotherapy 11*, 5, 358–368.

Jones, D. and Ramchandani, P. (1999) *Child Sexual Abuse: Informing Practice from Research.* Abingdon, Oxon: Radcliffe Medical Press.

Jones, L. and Finkelhor, D. (2001) 'The decline in child sexual abuse cases.' *Juvenile Justice Bulletin*, January.

Kagan, J. (1991) 'A conceptual analysis of the affects.' *Journal of the American Psychoanalytic Association 39*, 109–130.

Krystal, J.H., Kosten, T.R., Perry, B.D., Southwick, S., Mason, J.W. and Giller, E.L. (1989) 'Neurobiological aspects of PTSD: review of clinical and preclinical studies.' *Behaviour Therapy 20*, 177–198.

Laws, D.R. (ed.) (1989) *Relapse Prevention with Sex Offenders.* New York: Guilford Press.

Leifer, M., Shapiro, J.P. and Kassem, L. (1993) 'The impact of maternal history and behavior upon foster placement and adjustment in sexually abused girls.' *Child Abuse and Neglect 17*, 6, 755–766.

Macdonald, G. (2000) *Effective Interventions for Child Abuse and Neglect: An Evidence-Based Approach to Planning and Evaluating Interventions.* Chichester: Wiley.

Malloy, L.C., Lyon, T.D. and Quas, J.A. (2007) 'Filial dependency and recantation of child sexual abuse allegations.' *Journal of the American Academy of Child and Adolescent Psychiatry 46*, 2, 162–170.

Mann, R. (2004) 'Innovations in sex offender treatment.' *Journal of Sexual Aggression 10*, 2, 141–152.

Marshall, W.L., Anderson, D. and Fernandez, F. (1999) *Cognitive Behavioural Treatment of Sexual Offenders.* Chichester: Wiley.

McClellan, J., McCurry, C., Ronnei, M., Adams, J., Eisner, A. and Storck, M. (1996) 'Age of onset of sexual abuse: relationship to sexually inappropriate behaviors.' *Journal of the American Academy of Child and Adolescent Psychiatry 35*, 10, 1375–1383.

McCrone, P., Weeramanthri, T., Knapp, M., Rushton, A., *et al.* (2005) 'Cost-effectiveness of individual versus group psychotherapy for sexually abused girls.' *Child and Adolescent Mental Health 10*, 1, 26–31.

Mercy, J. (1999) 'Having new eyes: viewing child sexual abuse as a public health problem.' *Sex Abuse 11*, 317.

Ministry of Justice, Crown Prosecution Service, Department for Education, Department of Health and Welsh Assembly Government (2011) *Achieving Best Evidence in Criminal Proceedings: Guidance on Interviewing Victims and Witnesses, and Guidance on Using Special Measures* (3rd edn). London: Ministry of Justice. Accessed on 14 August 2017 at www.cps.gov.uk/publications/docs/best_evidence_in_criminal_proceedings.pdf

National Institute for Health and Care Excellence (NICE) (2005) *The Management of PTSD in Adults and Children in Primary and Secondary Care: National Clinical Practice Guideline Number 26*. London: NICE. Accessed on 14 August 2017 at https://www.ncbi.nlm.nih.gov/pubmed/21834189

National Institute for Health and Care Excellence (NICE) (2017) *Child abuse and neglect*. NICE guideline [NG76]. Accessed on 7 November 2017 at https://www.nice.org.uk/guidance/ng76

Nicholas, S., Kershaw, C. and Walker, A. (eds) (2006) *Crime in England and Wales 2006/2007*. Home Office Statistical Bulletin, 4th Edition. London: Home Office.

NSPCC (2007) *NSPCC Annual Report, 2007*. London: NSPCC. Accessed on 7 November 2017 at https://www.nspcc.org.uk/globalassets/documents/annual-reports/nspcc-annual-report-2007.pdf

NSPCC (2017) *Sexual Abuse: What is Sexual Abuse*. Accessed on 25 July 2017 at www.nspcc.org.uk/preventing-abuse/child-abuse-and-neglect/child-sexual-abuse/?utm_source=meganavandutm_medium=andutm_campaign

Pinheiro, P.S. (2006) *World Report on Violence against Children*. Geneva, Switzerland: United Nations Secretary-General's Study on Violence against Children. Accessed on 14 August 2017 at www.unviolencestudy.org

Radford, L., Corral, S., Bradley, C., Fisher, H., *et al.* (2011) *The Maltreatment and Victimisation of Children in the UK: NSPCC Report on a National Survey of Young People's, Young Adults' and Caregivers' Experiences*. London: NSPCC. Accessed on 14 August 2017 at www.nspcc.org.uk/globalassets/documents/research-reports/child-abuse-neglect-uk-today-research-report.pdf

Roesler, T.A. (1994) 'Reactions to disclosure of childhood sexual abuse: the effect on adult symptoms.' *Journal of Interpersonal Violence 9*, 3, 327–338.

Ruggiero, K.J., McLeer, S.V. and Dixon, J.F. (2000) 'Sexual abuse characteristics associated with survivor psychopathology.' *Child Abuse and Neglect 24*, 7, 951–964.

Schönbucher, V., Maier, T., Mohler-Kuo, M., Schnyder, U. and Landolt, M.A. (2012) 'Disclosure of child sexual abuse by adolescents: a qualitative in-depth study.' *Journal of Interpersonal Violence 27*, 17, 3486–3513.

Smallbone, S., Marshall, W.L. and Wortley, R. (2008) *Preventing Child Sexual Abuse: Evidence, Policy and Practice*. Cullompton, Devon: Willan Publishing.

Smith, N., Dogaru, C. and Ellis, F. (2015) *Hear Me. Believe Me. Respect Me: A Survey of Adult Survivors of Child Sexual Abuse and Their Experiences of Support Services*. Ipswich: University Campus Suffolk. Accessed on 14 August 2017 at http://cdn.basw.co.uk/upload/basw_122305-1.pdf

Trickett, P.K., Noll, J.G., Reiffman, A. and Putnam, F.W. (2001) 'Variants of intrafamilial sexual abuse experience: implications for short- and long-term development.' *Development and Psychopathology 13*, 4, 1001–1019.

Trowell, J., Kolvin, I., Weeramanthri, T., Sadowski, H., *et al.* (2002) 'Psychotherapy for sexually abused girls: psychopathological outcome findings and patterns of change.' *British Journal of Psychiatry 180*, 234–247.

Vizard, E., Hickey, N., French, L. and McCrory, E. (2007) 'Children and adolescents who present with sexually abusive behaviour: a UK descriptive study.' *Journal of Forensic Psychiatry and Psychology 18*, 1, 59–73.

Ward, T. and Marshall, W.L. (2004) 'Good lives, aetiology and the rehabilitation of sex offenders: a bridging theory.' *Journal of Sexual Aggression 10*, 2, 153–169.

Warrington, C. with Beckett, H., Ackerley, E., Walker, M. and Allnock, D. (2017) *Making Noise: Children's Voices for Positive Change after Sexual Abuse.* Luton: University of Bedfordshire. Accessed on 14 August 2017 at www.beds.ac.uk/ic/recently-completed-projects/making-noise

Wieland, S. (1998) *Techniques and Issues in Abuse-Focused Therapy with Children and Adolescents: Addressing the Internal Trauma.* Ottawa: Sage.

Wiffin, V. and MacIntosh, H. (2005) 'Mediators of the link between childhood sexual abuse and emotional distress: a critical review.' *Trauma, Violence and Abuse 6*, 1, 24–39.

Williams, L.M. (1994) 'Recall of childhood trauma: a prospective study of women's memories of child sexual abuse.' *Journal of Consulting and Clinical Psychology 62*, 1167–1176.

Wolf, S. (1984) 'A Multifactor Model of Deviant Sexuality.' Paper presented at the Third International Conference on Victimology, Lisbon.

World Health Organization (WHO) (2006) *Preventing Child Maltreatment: A Guide to Taking Action and Generating Evidence.* Geneva: WHO. Accessed on 14 August 2017 at http://apps.who.int/iris/bitstream/10665/43499/1/9241594365_eng.pdf

Section 4

PREVENTIVE RESPONSES IN SPECIFIC SETTINGS

9

OPERATION YEWTREE

A Watershed Moment

PETER SPINDLER

This chapter examines the policing response to the revelations about Sir Jimmy Savile's predatory sexual behaviour, considers what lessons have been learnt, and how the policing landscape has changed as a result. It will focus initially on what we know and then consider what we need to do, and indeed what the police service has already done under the leadership of the National Police Chiefs' Council to ensure that victims are never left to suffer alone for so long again. Written from the perspective of the strategic policing lead for Operation Yewtree, it provides a 'behind the scenes' view of the multi-agency approach, the decision-making, and highlights the key issues that helped ensure the success of this unprecedented initiative. It concludes with an analysis of the so-called 'Yewtree effect' and looks at some of the extraordinary outcomes from this enquiry, not least the 124 per cent increase in the reporting of rape since 2012.

This story begins with a former child abuse investigator from Surrey Police, Mark Williams-Thomas, doggedly pursuing a line of enquiry that few wanted to hear or acknowledge. He was convinced that a British icon, a celebrity created through the medium of the BBC, was an unconvicted serial sexual abuser. His hypothesis was based on the evidence of a group of women who, as adolescents, had attended the Duncroft School for Girls in Surrey. Developing the story in his new role as investigative journalist, he took his findings first to the BBC and, following their rejection, on to ITV. It later emerged that the BBC were on the horns of a dilemma, whether to celebrate the life of Sir Jimmy Savile following his death in November 2011 or castigate him as an abuser based on the testimony of a small number of alleged victims. They chose the former, a decision which prompted such debate within the BBC that an independent review (Pollard, 2012) was commissioned to try to understand why the *Newsnight* programme walked away from Williams-Thomas's original pitch.

One of the fascinating issues emerging from these events is how the media respond to, and magnify, allegations about celebrities in our society. Although transmission of the documentary by the ITV Exposure team *The Other Side of Jimmy Savile* wasn't scheduled until Wednesday 3 October 2012, media coverage started the weekend before with tabloid newspapers running the story well in advance of broadcast. From a policing perspective, with 43 forces responsible for a multi-agency approach to the investigation of sexual abuse locally in England and Wales, a coherent national response was always going to be a challenge. With no overarching national police service responsible for the coordination of police investigative activity, it fell to the Child Exploitation and Online Protection (CEOP) centre, based within what was then known as the Serious and Organised Crime Agency (SOCA), to provide a central point of contact for the service. Non-recent abuse of this nature was not, however, one of their areas of expertise and they contacted the Metropolitan Police Service (MPS) Child Abuse Investigation Command to request specialist advice and support from their dedicated intelligence unit. CEOP also took what was to become a key decision, to engage the support of the National Society for the Prevention of Cruelty to Children (NSPCC) who were assisting ITV with the provision of a 24/7 helpline.

Several early meetings took place, hosted by CEOP Chief Executive Peter Davis, involving Assistant Chief Constable Jerry Kirkby from Surrey Police, the force that had interviewed Savile under caution in 2009 under Operation Ornament (Surrey Police, 2016), and the MPS, together with the intelligence analysts, to prepare the national policing response. After the broadcast, it became clear from information provided by the public that the allegations were not limited to Duncroft School and numerous other victims of Savile's offending felt empowered to speak out after seeing the testimony of the women involved on their screens. For the first time, Savile's victims had begun to feel that their claims were being given credence and that for once they might be believed.

This concept of belief was to take on even greater significance in November 2014 with the inception of the now infamous Operation Midland, led by the MPS Homicide and Major Crime Command, which ran between November 2014 and March 2016. Their task was to investigate claims of abuse-related homicides involving a group of powerful men from politics, the military and law enforcement agencies across southern England and in London during the 1970s and 1980s. Initially, however, many of those involved turned to the press or the NSPCC to report their abuse rather than the police, perhaps feeling that in the past they had been failed by the criminal justice system.

By the end of the first week of publicity regarding Savile's offending it was clear that a significant miscarriage of justice had taken place and not in this instance against the suspect, Savile, but to the many victims who had ultimately been denied justice by his death. Reports came in from across the country to the NSPCC's helpline outlining the abuse that primarily, but not exclusively, women had suffered as girls, and a robust policing response was required. The MPS had 20 per cent of the capacity of policing in England and Wales and its Child Abuse Investigation Command had a major investigation capability equipped with the Home Office Linked Major Enquiry System (HOLMES) which could manage a large-scale or complex enquiry such as this. It would have been churlish of the MPS to have left the case with Surrey Police, who were coming under ever-increasing scrutiny for the quality of their response in 2009 as the public started to understand the potential of the scale of Savile's abuse. There was, however, one major issue to overcome: Savile was dead and there could be no criminal justice outcome from any police enquiry. Questions and challenges were likely to arise from any perceived disproportionality in the policing response, so a measured and proportionate approach was required.

On the evening of 4 October 2012 the Met decided to take the lead and Operation Yewtree was born. That decision has ramifications for the British public to this day, and the consequences of that approach have ensured a sustained focus on revelations about child sexual exploitation in our institutions and wider society, including sport, children's homes and other youth organisations as well as in other establishments.

What do we know?

To turn to the first question (What do we know?), it is quite clear that Savile escaped justice because of a failure by so many in our society to challenge, report or confront his criminal activity. If they did summon the courage to speak out they faced the prevailing culture of denial and disbelief that is so often associated with this type of crime, whether from friends, family or officialdom. Indeed, Her Majesty's Inspectorate of Constabulary's review of police knowledge of, and response to, historical allegations made against Savile, the bluntly titled *Mistakes Were Made*, states that 'we have conducted enquiries of all 43 police forces in England and Wales. The results are stark. As far as their records disclose, only five allegations of sexual assault were made against Savile to a police force between 1955 and 2009' (HMIC, 2013, para.2.3).

As described in more detail in Chapter 1, the report goes on to identify seven incidents, two based solely on intelligence records and five based on complaints made by victims where concerns about Savile had been brought to police attention.

It is important to remember that the police service did not begin to digitise its crime and intelligence records until the mid-1990s. It was the tragic murders of Holly Wells and Jessica Chapman in Soham, in August 2002, and the subsequent critical report by Sir Michael Bichard (Bichard, 2004), that led to the creation of the Police National Database that enabled forces for the first time to share information electronically across force boundaries. No such system existed when Savile was at his most prolific and no single police force had a clear picture of his offending behaviour. It was, however, remarkable that so few were surprised when the story finally broke and that there was minimal pushback from the public and the media about the true nature of his character.

The HMIC's critical report on recorded concerns about Savile contrasts dramatically with the findings of the MPS and the NSPCC in their joint report *Giving Victims a Voice* published in February 2012, which identified over 450 victims with 214 substantive crimes recorded including 34 rapes (Gray and Watt, 2013). Those offences covered five decades and demonstrate that something was significantly wrong in both our society and with the systems and processes in our institutions that allowed someone to offend for so long, and so prodigiously, with only minimal reporting of these crimes. These official figures are a snapshot taken in 2013 and will have risen as other organisations and institutions consolidated their data. Indeed, Dame Janet Smith in her review of Savile's time at the BBC (Smith, 2016) identified 72 victims, a significant increase on police data released in 2013.

Several factors inhibited victims from reporting sexual assaults during Savile's lifetime. These were evident from NSPCC focus groups with Savile survivors who contacted the helpline (Exton and Thandi, 2013) and include:

- embarrassment and shame
- self-blame and misguided feelings of some form of responsibility for the assaults
- fear of reprisals from a high-profile and powerful figure
- the lack of safeguarding policies and procedures
- the absence of alternative pathways for reporting
- a prevailing culture in society of denial and disbelief
- a perceived tolerance of such behaviour by celebrities
- a lack of confidence in the criminal justice system to take these issues seriously.

Savile's offending peaked in the mid-1970s when he was at his most powerful both in terms of profile and access to the vulnerable. However, it is important to understand the context of that period when attitudes towards children and young people were nowhere near as developed as they are today. The language of the day then would have included words and phrases such as 'child prostitute', 'child pornography' and 'rent boys' (who could be found at the so-called 'meat-rack' in London's Piccadilly). Young people engaged in sexual activity with older men then were often seen to have made a 'lifestyle choice', whereas today we would recognise them as vulnerable victims of child sexual exploitation.

Our current approach to safeguarding children was not developed until the early 2000s. The shift from traditional child protection to a more all-encompassing approach was influenced by the first Joint Chief Inspectors' safeguarding children report (Social Services Inspectorate *et al.*, 2002) and the Victoria Climbié Inquiry (Laming, 2003). The Every Child Matters programme outlined in the Children Act 2004 formalised these changes in approach into a legislative framework and our institutions such as the BBC began to develop their safeguarding policies and procedures.

Clearly, Savile's victims lacked a voice until 2012 but felt empowered by those who did speak out to come forward and share their experience of his criminal behaviour. With the high public profile provided by the media to Operation Yewtree, the numbers of people coming forward to report non-recent abuse grew incrementally. At the initial press conference on 9 October 2012, 35 people had already reported offences to the police or the NSPCC. Ten days later the numbers had risen to 200 and more than doubled a week later to 450, rising to 589 by mid-December. The reports didn't all relate to Savile as public confidence grew to report offences about other prominent individuals in society. The Yewtree team established three categories of offender: Savile; Savile and others; and others. This simple labelling, suggested by the Head of News at the Met as part of a complex communications strategy, was quickly picked up by journalists in their commentary on the subject and gave greater credence to law enforcement activity.

In early 2013, at a meeting with a senior representative from Rape Crisis hosted by the Duchess of Cornwall at Clarence House, detectives were heartened to be told their work on Yewtree was not in vain. Their view was that although Savile had avoided facing any form of criminal justice, many victims felt a degree of satisfaction from what they saw as 'social justice'. More broadly, this was explained as a sense of relief by the victim or survivor of abuse that some or all of the following objectives were likely to have been achieved:

- They had for the first time been believed.
- The issue was now out in the open and no longer a 'dirty secret'.
- The allegation had been recorded as a crime.
- The public had accepted that what happened was wrong.
- The perpetrator was no longer able to keep abusing.
- Intelligence had been gathered and could be shared across agencies.
- Therapeutic care had been made available.

The 2015/16 HMIC-led Rape Monitoring Group report noted that:

> Following the disclosure of Jimmy Savile's offending history, hundreds of survivors contacted police and agencies across the country to report sexual offences that Savile and other high-profile individuals had committed against them. Many of those survivors may have contacted police with a low expectation of a judicial outcome but, for the first time, many were provided with an opportunity to discuss the offending and they were listened to and believed. Some were then able to access vital support services... In addition, a number of survivors have reported non-recent abuse that they were subjected to in their childhoods. In some of these cases they have disclosed not with a view to a

> prosecution but because they have discovered the perpetrator may now have access to children. In cases of this nature, a criminal prosecution may not be the outcome that would necessarily have been sought by the survivor. However, they rightly expect police and other agencies to ensure that the children are safeguarded and that robust measures are taken to deny the perpetrator an opportunity to reoffend. (HMIC, 2016, p.10)

It is important that this concept of achieving social justice for victims is fully understood by those in law enforcement who will no doubt be concerned that the conviction ratio for reports of rape is generally regarded to be about 6 per cent (HMIC, 2015). It is likely that victims will not always be seeking a criminal justice outcome and the absence of a conviction for an offender such as Savile can still lead to a degree of victim satisfaction.

One important piece of learning from the work of Yewtree was the recognition that the celebrity sex offenders preyed on the vulnerable, exploiting either a person or a situation for their sexual gratification. Phoenix Survivors, a charity providing support to the adult survivors of abuse, coined the phrase 'the uncredibles' to describe those who Savile had preyed upon. He would seek out those in institutions such as Broadmoor, Leeds General Infirmary, Stoke Mandeville Hospital and Duncroft School who lacked the ability and opportunity to speak out or challenge his behaviour. This was described at a joint MPS/NSPCC press conference in November 2012 as 'the collision between power and vulnerability'.

This took on more significance when the then Director of Public Prosecutions (DPP), Keir Starmer, who had been in dialogue with senior Met officers to see what lessons could be learnt, recognised that the Crown Prosecution Service (CPS) were using criteria similar to those used in relation to the alleged offender when selecting victims as part of their 'full code test' to establish whether a case should go to trial. His concern was that CPS staff examined the credibility of the witness and, where it was lacking, the case was unlikely to proceed without significant corroborative evidence. Savile either sought out those who were vulnerable or 'uncredible' and created circumstances where the chances of corroboration were minimised.

The DPP consequently commissioned Alison Levitt QC to review the decision not to prosecute Savile in 2009 and her report raises a number of concerns about the investigative approach and identified a failure to build an effective case by Surrey and Sussex police and prosecutors. The report is indicative of the past police approach to investigating allegations of non-recent abuse involving high-profile individuals. In particular, Levitt highlights the misunderstanding of the need for corroboration (Levitt, 2013) and believes the decision by investigators not to tell victims that others had reported offences inhibited their decision-making on whether or not to give evidence against Savile. Furthermore, officers appear not to have allayed victims' concerns by failing to explain the special measures that could be put in place to protect their identity (Levitt, 2013). Her conclusion was that 'having spoken to the victims I have been driven to conclude that had the police and prosecutors taken a different approach a prosecution might have been possible' (Levitt, 2013, para.6.vi).

On 11 January 2013, the DPP announced several initiatives to improve their response to sexual violence and changed the credibility test to one that examined the whole case, not focusing solely on the victim. These can now be found in the Crown Prosecution Service (2013) *Guidelines on Prosecuting Cases of Child Sexual Abuse*.

The debate on how Savile could have offended for so long with impunity will run and run. Phrases such as 'hiding in plain sight' and 'he groomed the nation' have provided the public with easy-to-understand concepts to try to describe his behaviour at a time when the media were seeking to blame someone other than Savile for his abuse, for example the BBC or hospital management teams. Savile used his charity work and the cloak of celebrity not just to shield himself from scrutiny but to earn himself an OBE in 1971 and knighthoods from both the Queen and the Pope in 1990, after he had committed the majority of the recorded sexual assaults. It is fair to say he captivated royalty, politicians, the media and social and healthcare professionals, as well as wider society. Louis Theroux, in his documentary *Looking Back on Jimmy Savile* broadcast by the BBC on 2 October 2016, was challenged by one of Savile's victims as to whether he felt he had been groomed by Savile. Theroux, misunderstanding the nature of grooming, responded that he was not groomed as he wasn't abused but did feel 'beguiled' by him.

In conclusion, we have learnt that Savile was one of the UK's most prolific sexual predators who offended for over five decades with impunity. Savile was, however, not unique and other high-profile predators in positions of power managed to escape justice for many years. Nevertheless, it should be recognised that he successfully manipulated those around him to exploit the vulnerable and managed to escape justice throughout his lifetime by a combination of factors that include:

- a failure by those in positions of responsibility and authority to challenge or confront his behaviour
- contexts and environments in which he was operating that valued celebrity over safeguarding the vulnerable (indeed, awareness of child sexual exploitation was far more limited than it is today)
- British society failing to take those reporting abuse seriously or provide them with effective mechanisms to speak out and be heard
- law enforcement and social/healthcare agencies either failing or being unable to capture, record and share information about his behaviour.

To turn to the second and most critical challenge (What needs to be done?), the following section will look at these four issues in more detail to see how the police and their partners have collectively responded and what more potentially could be done.

What needs to be done?

> A failure by those in positions of responsibility and authority to challenge or confront his behaviour.

There has been much debate in the media and amongst professionals about the need for legislation to mandate the reporting by those in positions of responsibility who suspect child sexual abuse. At present, there is statutory guidance in place to report abuse (HM Government, 2015) but it is not a legal requirement, although in 2016 the government introduced a specific legal requirement on teachers, health professionals and social workers to report known cases of female genital mutilation (Home Office, 2016). In July 2016, the government issued a consultation document, *Reporting and Acting on Child Abuse and Neglect*, which examined the options of mandatory reporting and an alternative proposal, a duty to act regarding child sexual abuse (HM Government, 2016).

Several risks and issues are identified in the paper, including diversion of resources away from support for victims of abuse, the likely quality of reporting, the potential to inhibit disclosure and fear of being forced into legal proceedings. Far more issues are highlighted in the mandatory reporting section than those for the duty to act, which may suggest which way the government is leaning. As with any discussion of new legislation, the media focus is often on enforcement and sanction when non-compliance is identified.

As an interim measure, in 2016 the NSPCC launched a Whistleblowing Advice Line to provide support for professionals who are worried about children in the workplace. The aim is to encourage those who feel that an organisation is putting children at risk to talk through their concerns even if they lack the certainty required to make a formal referral. The Public Interest Disclosure Act 1998 sets out a framework for supporting whistle-blowers and the NSPCC has been a prescribed whistle-blowing body for child welfare and protection since 2014, so can seek to protect individuals against unfair treatment at work.

From a policing perspective, the service needs to ensure that it clearly promotes its established pathways for reporting concerns and ensures partnerships with both the statutory and third sectors are effective in their sharing of information. Crime reporting is now far less likely to take place at a police station front counter as telephone and online reporting processes become more cost efficient. Other routes such as Crimestoppers and third sector 24/7 helplines allow the public to pass intelligence to police via a third party, but the service must ensure that such information is acted upon, and more importantly that the victims, survivors and witnesses of abuse know that action has been taken.

Police already take a prominent role in multi-agency safeguarding hubs (MASH) where information is shared, assessed and actioned, primarily by statutory agencies at the local level. However, more needs to be done at a strategic level to work across county and local authority borders. ICT systems lack integration, and information sharing processes can often be bureaucratic and laborious. It is essential that the agencies involved adopt a victim-focused approach in their activities rather than one that puts their organisation or profession first. An inclusive attitude that takes account of the work of the third sector and other non-statutory bodies will ensure that a more complete picture of possible or suspected abuse is available.

> The second enabling factor that allowed Savile to offend with impunity for so long was the context and environment in which he was operating that valued celebrity over safeguarding the vulnerable, compounded by the limited awareness and understanding of child sexual exploitation at the time.

This lack of understanding of the issues applied as much to the police as anyone else. It was not until well into the 21st century that our attitudes began to change. Whilst Operation Yewtree has undoubtedly shone a light on this specific form of child sexual exploitation (CSE), other initiatives were running in parallel to this, including an inquiry led by Alexis Jay OBE in Rotherham (Jay, 2014) and studies by the Office of the Children's Commissioner (OCC). In November 2013, the OCC published their report *If Only Someone Had Listened* (Berelowitz *et al.*, 2013), a two-year study into CSE. The lead author, Sue Berelowitz, then Deputy Children's Commissioner for England, said:

> The evidence gathered for this inquiry over the last two years has shown the country the stark and grim reality of child sexual exploitation in gangs and groups. While there has undoubtedly been significant progress in tackling this problem, there is still a very long way to go before we can confidently state that our children are being comprehensively and effectively protected. (Children's Commissioner, 2013)

Savile was clearly not the only sexual predator to have escaped justice for so long. Other men had been exploiting the vulnerable in different contexts, often around the nighttime economy, and new strategies were being developed to tackle the problem. Public awareness of the subject has increased and local authorities across the UK have now put CSE on the agenda of their local safeguarding children boards (LSCBs). Training has been rolled out across the public sector to enhance the awareness of professionals, and police in many areas have started to educate those working in the nighttime economy, such as hotels, mini-cabs and cafes, of the signs and symptoms of CSE. The high profile given to this subject will have heightened understanding too in the entertainment and health sectors where Savile primarily operated.

Kate Lampard QC was appointed by the Department of Health in late October 2012 to coordinate and quality assure the work by the health trusts that had encountered Savile. She joined the Operation Yewtree Stakeholder Forum and worked closely with the investigative team. On 26 February 2015, her report *Themes and Lessons Learnt from NHS Investigations into Matters Relating to Jimmy Savile* (Lampard and Marsden, 2015) was published and made 14 recommendations. The common themes and issues that emerged from the investigations' findings were grouped under the following general headings:

- security and access arrangements, including celebrity and VIP access;
- the role and management of volunteers;
- safeguarding;
- raising complaints and concerns (by staff and patients);
- fundraising and charity governance; and
- observance of due process and good governance.

(para.4.9)

Whilst none of the findings or recommendations made specific mention of the police, what did emerge was the lack of engagement by health services with LSCBs, one of the main mechanisms in place to enable effective information sharing. The police service has often found it difficult to engage with health professionals who face significant staffing challenges, have a strong culture of confidentiality and privacy, and a primary focus on treating patients rather than engaging with other agencies. Nevertheless, the College of Policing has issued all forces with new guidance on tackling CSE in the form of Authorised Professional Practice which states:

> Partner agencies are more likely to involve the police as soon as possible if effective relationships have been established. This ensures that information which may be critical to the investigation is not lost. It also means an early disruption plan can be established against the offender. (College of Policing, 2017)

These initiatives are helping to change the environment inhabited by the modern-day predator and will go some way to reducing the risk that others fall victim to such attacks. However, the online environment provides many other challenges for the safeguarding community as offenders migrate to cyberspace for sexual gratification. The ready availability of hard-core pornography and indecent images of children has been used to desensitise both victims and offenders and can inhibit the young person's understanding of what a healthy sexual relationship should look and feel like. Law enforcement must strike a careful balance with its resources to ensure those who pose the greatest threat are prioritised and develop the technical capabilities to track them down. Through working in partnership with communications service providers, more preventative activity can be focused to ensure our social attitudes to this type of offending do not lead to acceptance of this criminal behaviour.

> British society failed to take those reporting abuse seriously or provide them with effective mechanisms to speak out and be heard.

The police do not operate in a vacuum and rely on both the public and their statutory and third sector partners to provide evidence of criminality to assist in building a case against their suspects. Furthermore, the police service is the outward facing, first step towards criminal justice, and the public need to have confidence in their police and indeed the wider criminal justice system if they are going to come forward and share deeply personal details of horrific crimes. Investigators must be seen to be taking seriously, proportionately and open-mindedly reports of abuse, whether they are allegations of crime or less developed intelligence. It is vital that victims feel that they are being treated with consideration for their needs, compassion and understanding. Otherwise they will walk away from the criminal justice system.

In recent years, the police service has moved from focusing on tackling acquisitive crimes such as theft from motor vehicles to concentrating on reducing threat, risk and harm. Public protection is now an established policing discipline that has attracted more resources and profile. New policies and training have been developed by the College of Policing, which held a debrief of all forces involved in the Savile case to identify best practice and establish 'what worked' as part of the evidence base for developing the response to these crimes. Nevertheless, more work will be required in this area as the evidence base grows.

When Savile was at his most prolific, detectives would have been taught the ABC of investigation: Accept nothing; Believe no-one; Confirm everything. If this approach became apparent to the victims, many would have been dissuaded from progressing reports of abuse. The current approach is much more nuanced and can be found in the College of Policing policy published in March 2016 which states that 'at the point when someone makes an allegation of crime, the police should believe the account given and a crime report should be completed' (Henriques, 2016, p.14).

The whole issue of being believed has been subject to much public debate, arising in the main from one specific Metropolitan Police investigation, Operation Midland (see above). A hard-hitting review into Midland by the retired High Court Judge Sir Richard Henriques was published on 31 October 2016 and is critical of many aspects of the police approach. Henriques was concerned about the concept of 'belief' of victims and indeed recommends that the word 'victim' should be excluded from the investigative process and advocates that the word 'complainant' be used instead (Henriques, 2016). He fails, however, to make any mention of this word being used in the same context throughout documents such as the *Code of Practice for Victims of Crime* (Ministry of Justice, 2015) and other recognised national policies such as the Home Office *Counting Rules* (Home Office, 2013) on the recording of crime.

The second recommendation in Henriques' report (p.24) is that the instruction to believe a victim's account should cease and encourages a more open-minded approach. In the HMIC report on Crime Data Integrity published in November 2014, *Making the Victim Count*, the Chief Inspector of Constabulary Sir Thomas Winsor had proposed, 'The presumption that the victim should always be believed should be institutionalised. The practice of some forces of investigating first and recording later should be abandoned immediately' (HMIC, 2014, para.1.31). This assertion is questioned by Henriques, although he fails to acknowledge that HMIC were stating this in the context of the initial recording of crimes rather than investigation of them and that this presumption is more in keeping with the spirit of the Home Office *Counting Rules* on crime recording.

In summary, the police service has faced numerous challenges in recent times in its approach to the recording and investigation of serious sexual assaults. It has worked closely with other criminal justice partners to improve the service it provides to those who come forward to report such crimes, but it is still widely accepted that rape is under-reported. This is highlighted by the HMIC Rape Monitoring Group in their digest published for 2014/15 where they state:

> ...many more rapes are committed than are reported to and recorded by the police. The 2013/14 Crime Survey for England and Wales (Ch. 4, Crime Statistics, Focus on Violent Crime and Sexual Offences, Office for National Statistics, February 2015) found that, of respondents who had experienced a serious sexual assault (including rape) since the age of 16, two thirds of the victims told somebody about their most recent experience, but only one in six told the police. The data held by the police can, therefore, only provide a partial picture of the prevalence of rape. (HMIC, 2015, p.12)

The picture is improving with many more coming forward as part of the so-called 'Yewtree effect' (see below), but alternative pathways for reporting, such as through Rape Crisis or Women's Aid, require resourcing and their relationships with police must be strengthened to ensure victims do not continue to suffer in silence.

Law enforcement and social/healthcare agencies either failed or were unable to capture, record and share information about his behaviour.

It is widely accepted that those in authority didn't do enough to pursue allegations of sexual abuse by Savile and others in the past. The Independent Police Complaints Commission in November 2016 stated that they had recorded 187 investigations across 18 forces into allegations that the service had failed to properly record and investigate allegations of non-recent sexual abuse (Daily Express, 2016). It is not clear how many of these related directly to Savile but they do involve prominent individuals and have arisen from the clamour from both Operation Yewtree and CSE cases in forces such as South Yorkshire. This has led the National Police Chiefs' Council to reconsider its response to this subject.

The National Police Chiefs' Council established Operation Hydrant as a coordination hub in June 2014 to deliver the national policing response, oversight and coordination of non-recent child abuse investigations concerning persons of public prominence, or in relation to those offences which took place historically within institutional settings. It became apparent that forces around the country were investigating a significant number of non-recent allegations of sexual abuse involving persons of public prominence or within institutions. There was a risk that investigators were looking at the same individuals and institutions and it was also clear that officers dealing with these complex cases required support and guidance. Operation Hydrant is informed by individual Forces of investigations meeting the criteria, and then coordinates the information to prevent duplication, a process known as deconfliction.

Hydrant does not carry out individual investigations – this is done by individual Forces and, by December 2015, there were 2228 suspects under investigation, of whom 302 were classified as of 'public prominence' (including 99 politicians and 147 celebrities from the media), and 1217 operated within institutions (including 86 religious institutions, 39 medical establishments, 25 prisons/young offenders institutes, 22 sports venues, 10 community institutions, 81 other institutions such as guest houses and 6 unknown) (BBC, 2015). More recently, the media focus switched to abuse in football, and one year later, on 21 December 2016, the BBC reported that the total number of suspects being coordinated by Hydrant had risen to 3469, 155 related to football clubs, with a possible 429 victims (BBC, 2016).

This significant increase in demand has required the police service to look long and hard at how it manages its response to this once hidden issue. Undoubtedly, it has put a strain on resources and led to some public debate on the energy and effort into some of these investigations during a period of austerity with year-on-year cuts to the public sector. The police service will need to continue to divert resources away from other more routine enquiries if it is to tackle this area of criminality effectively. Moreover, the likely increase in reporting arising from the work of the Independent Inquiry into Child Sexual Abuse chaired by Professor Jay could generate many new reports of crime (Guardian, 2016).

Finally, we turn to the so-called 'Yewtree effect', a phrase that has been used in various criminal justice circles to describe some of the consequences of the success and profile of this unique investigation. At times it has been used in a negative context when defence lawyers and commentators have accused victims (or complainants, depending on your perspective) of climbing on a bandwagon or only making allegations of sexual assaults to gain attention or compensation. There are, however, some very positive outcomes for those whose lives have been affected by this type of criminality. Perhaps the most significant is the exponential rise in the reporting of rape since October 2012. The HMIC-led Rape Monitoring Group publishes an annual report of the statistics on rape collected from the various criminal justice agencies. In their 2015/16 report published in October 2016, they highlight the 124 per cent increase and state:

> As a consequence of Operation Yewtree, the establishment of the Independent Inquiry into Child Sexual Abuse and associated investigations, there has been a significant increase in reporting of such offences, and numbers of recorded rapes nationally have more than doubled between the 12 months ending December 2012 (the start of Operation Yewtree) and the 12 months ending March 2016. (HMIC, 2016, p.10)

In July 2014, the government announced that a public inquiry would be established to examine how the country's institutions had handled their duty of care to protect children from sexual abuse. In July 2015, the Independent Inquiry into Child Sexual Abuse (IICSA) announced that the inquiry would be undertaking 12 separate investigations into organisations such as churches and local authorities as well as individuals in positions of power and responsibility. The police service support to the inquiry is through Operation Hydrant as a two-way flow of information between the two parties is key to its success. Estimates of the potential number of new victims coming forward to the inquiry have been as high as 20,000 based on extrapolated data from other countries that have undertaken similar work.

It is not just the statutory sector that has experienced such increases in reporting. The NSPCC, in their annual report of October 2016, identified a 40 per cent rise in calls to their helpline that have led to cases being referred to the authorities (NSPCC, 2016). In 2012/13 23,733 cases were referred compared with 33,333 in 2015/16, and NSPCC CEO Peter Wanless commented, 'These figures reveal a nation that is more alive to the issue of child abuse following recent high profile scandals and the on-going investigation into non-recent child abuse.' They have recruited 12 additional permanent staff to their helpline to deal with the increase that will be a direct result of their commitment to support Yewtree from the outset. Overall, Yewtree has been a watershed moment for the reporting and investigating of child sexual exploitation and many will have benefited from the efforts of all of those involved.

References

BBC (2015) *Operation Hydrant: UK Police Identify 2,228 Child Abuse Suspects.* Accessed on 30 March 2017 at www.bbc.co.uk/news/uk-34977255

BBC (2016) *Football Child Abuse Scandal: Police Identify 155 Suspects.* Accessed on 30 March 2017 at www.bbc.co.uk/news/uk-england-38378361

Berelowitz, S., Clifton, J., Firmin, C., Gulyurtlu, S. and Edwards, G. (2013) *'If Only Someone Had Listened': Office of the Children's Commissioner's Inquiry into Child Sexual Exploitation in Gangs and Groups Final Report.* Accessed on 14 August 2017 at www.thebromleytrust.org.uk/files/chidrens-commission.pdf

Bichard, M. (2004) *The Bichard Inquiry Report.* London: TSO. Accessed on 14 August 2017 at http://dera.ioe.ac.uk/6394/1/report.pdf

Children's Commissioner (2013) 'Services continue to fail to protect children from exploitation in gangs and groups.' Press release, 26 November. Accessed on 25 August 2017 at http://5.198.140.47/news/services-continue-fail-protect-children-sexual-exploitation-gangs-and-groups

College of Policing (2017) *Responding to Child Sexual Exploitation.* Accessed on 30 March 2017 at www.app.college.police.uk/app-content/major-investigation-and-public-protection/child-sexual-exploitation/#working-with-partners

Crown Prosecution Service (2013) *Guidelines on Prosecuting Cases of Child Sexual Abuse.* Accessed on 25 July 2017 at www.cps.gov.uk/legal/a_to_c/child_sexual_abuse

Daily Express (2016) *Police Forces Facing 187 Investigations for FAILURE to Investigate Allegations.* Accessed on 30 March 2017 at www.express.co.uk/news/uk/735922/Child-sex-abuse-police-investigation-allegations

Exton, L. and Thandi, K. (2013) *Would They Actually Have Believed Me? A Focus Group Exploration of the Underreporting of Crimes by Jimmy Savile.* London: NSPCC. Accessed on 14 August 2017 at www.nspcc.org.uk/globalassets/documents/research-reports/would-they-actually-believed-me-savile-report.pdf

Gray, P. and Watt, P. (2013) *Giving Victims a Voice: A Joint Report into Sexual Allegations against Jimmy Savile.* London: Metropolitan Police. Accessed on 11 August 2017 at www.nspcc.org.uk/globalassets/documents/research-reports/yewtree-report-giving-victims-voice-jimmy-savile.pdf

Guardian (2016) *Police Expect 30,000 New Child Abuse Reports from Goddard Inquiry.* Accessed on 30 March 2017 at www.theguardian.com/uk-news/2016/may/19/child-sex-abuse-police-expect-30000-goddard-inquiry-cases

Henriques, R. (2016) *An Independent Review of the Metropolitan Police Service's Handling of Non-Recent Sexual Offence Investigations Alleged Against Persons of Public Prominence.* London: Metropolitan Police.

Her Majesty's Inspectorate of Constabulary (HMIC) (2013) *'Mistakes Were Made': HMIC's Review into Allegations and Intelligence Material Concerning Jimmy Savile between 1964 and 2012.* London: HMIC. Accessed on 11 August 2017 at www.justiceinspectorates.gov.uk/hmicfrs/media/review-into-allegations-and-intelligence-material-concerning-jimmy-savile.pdf

Her Majesty's Inspectorate of Constabulary (HMIC) (2014) *Crime-Recording: Making the Victim Count. The Final Report of an Inspection of Crime Data Integrity in Police Forces in England and Wales.* London: HMIC. Accessed on 14 August 2017 at www.justiceinspectorates.gov.uk/hmicfrs/wp-content/uploads/crime-recording-making-the-victim-count.pdf

Her Majesty's Inspectorate of Constabulary (HMIC) (2015) Rape Monitoring Group, Local Area Data, London, HMIC. Accessed on 25 August 2017 at www.justiceinspectorates.gov.uk/hmicfrs/publications/rape-monitoring-group-digests-and-data-2014-15

Her Majesty's Inspectorate of Constabulary (HMIC) (2016) Rape Monitoring Group, Local Area Data, London, HMIC. Accessed on 25 August 2017 at www.justiceinspectorates.gov.uk/hmicfrs/news/news-feed/rape-monitoring-group-digests-and-data-2015-16

HM Government (2015) *Working Together to Safeguard Children: A Guide to Inter-agency Working to Safeguard and Promote the Welfare of Children.* Revised. London: Department for Education. Accessed on 15 August 2017 at www.gov.uk/government/uploads/system/uploads/attachment_data/file/592101/Working_Together_to_Safeguard_Children_20170213.pdf

HM Government (2016) *Reporting and Acting on Child Abuse and Neglect: Government Consultation.* London: Department for Education and Home Office. Accessed on 14 August 2017 at www.gov.uk/government/consultations/reporting-and-acting-on-child-abuse-and-neglect

Home Office (2013, last updated 2017) *Counting Rules for Recorded Crime.* Accessed on 25 August 2017 at www.gov.uk/government/publications/counting-rules-for-recorded-crime

Home Office (2016) *Mandatory Reporting of Female Genital Mutilation – Procedural Information.* London: Home Office. Accessed on 14 August 2017 at www.gov.uk/government/publications/mandatory-reporting-of-female-genital-mutilation-procedural-information

Jay, A. (2014) *Independent Inquiry into Child Sexual Exploitation in Rotherham 1997–2013.* Accessed on 26 July 2017 at www.rotherham.gov.uk/downloads/file/1407/independent_inquiry_cse_in_rotherham

Laming, Lord (2003) *The Victoria Climbié Inquiry: Report of an Inquiry by Lord Laming.* London: TSO. Accessed on 26 July 2017 at www.gov.uk/government/publications/the-victoria-climbie-inquiry-report-of-an-inquiry-by-lord-laming

Lampard, K. and Marsden, E. (2015) *Themes and Lessons Learnt from NHS Investigations into Matters Relating to Jimmy Savile: Independent Report for the Secretary of State for Health.* London: Department of Health. Accessed on 11 August 2017 at www.gov.uk/government/uploads/system/uploads/attachment_data/file/407209/KL_lessons_learned_report_FINAL.pdf

Levitt, A. (2013) *In the Matter of the Late Jimmy Savile: Report to the Director of Public Prosecutions.* London: CPS. Accessed on 11 August 2017 at www.cps.gov.uk/news/assets/uploads/files/savile_report.pdf

Ministry of Justice (2015) *Code of Practice for Victims of Crime.* Accessed on 25 August 2017 at www.cps.gov.uk/legal/assets/uploads/files/OD_000049.pdf

National Society for the Prevention of Cruelty to Children (NSPCC) (2016) *NSPCC Annual Review.* London: NSPCC.

Pollard, N. (2012) *The Pollard Review: Report.* London: BBC. Accessed on 11 August 2017 at http://downloads.bbc.co.uk/bbctrust/assets/files/pdf/our_work/pollard_review/pollard_review.pdf

Smith, J. (2016) *The Independent Review into the BBC's Culture and Practices during the Jimmy Savile and Stuart Hall Years*. London: BBC. Accessed on 11 August 2017 at www.bbc.co.uk/bbctrust/dame_janet_smith

Social Services Inspectorate, Commission for Health Improvement, Her Majesty's Inspectorate of Constabulary, Her Majesty's Crown Prosecution Service Inspectorate, *et al.* (2002) *Safeguarding Children: A Joint Chief Inspectors' Report on Arrangements to Safeguard Children*. London: HMIC. Accessed on 14 August 2017 at www.justiceinspectorates.gov.uk/cjji/inspections/safeguarding-children-a-joint-chief-inspectors-report-on-arrangements-to-safeguard-children

Surrey Police (2016) *FOI Disclosure Logs: Jimmy Savile Interview – Operation Ornament*. Accessed on 10 March 2017 at www.surrey.police.uk/foi-disclosure-logs/jimmy-savile-interview-operation-ornament

10

SAVILE AND THE NATIONAL HEALTH SERVICE

JOANNE DURKIN AND MARCUS EROOGA

Introduction

> 'The NHS Constitution establishes the principles and values of the NHS in England.'
>
> (Department of Health, 2012)

Reviewing the National Health Service (NHS) Constitution from the perspective of this chapter, references to the NHS and protection are surprisingly limited and relate largely to protection of patients' data and the protection offered to employees regarding their employment. The Constitution is not totally silent on the matter of protecting patients from harm and does refer to patients' right to be protected from degrading or inhumane treatment while in the care of health services (Department of Health, 2012).

This chapter focuses on the lessons identified as part of the 44 reviews of Savile's offending in the NHS (see Appendix). It explores the cultural changes within the NHS, which has seen a shift in focus to culture and values becoming an important part of a patient and staff experience of health and putting the patient back at the heart of everything the NHS does (NHS Choices, 2013).

Since the development of Safeguarding Adults Boards encouraged by Department of Health guidance issued in 2000 (Dunn, 2000), the multi-agency responsibilities of safeguarding adults and vulnerable children have further developed and changed the way in which patients are safeguarded. These developments have further supported the changes in culture in how safeguarding concerns are addressed (Braye *et al.*, 2012).

As discussed in previous chapters, offenders are often skilled at understanding how organisations, in this case the NHS, work. Savile's offending within the NHS was not only prolific but devious. From working beside and befriending porter teams (people who have access and in-depth knowledge of the whole hospital and provided a wide range of access [Barlow and Scott, 2014]) in Leeds General Infirmary to cultivating senior management at Broadmoor to enable unrestricted access to vulnerable patients (Kirkup and Marshall, 2014), Savile proved that he could navigate the NHS effectively. His grooming of NHS personnel enabled him to move freely into patient spaces and access his victims. While understanding offending behaviour in the NHS is critical, equally important is a meaningful understanding of the importance of the role of organisational culture in the prevention of abuse, and NHS culture is therefore addressed first.

At the conclusion of the process of 44 NHS individual reviews being undertaken, the Secretary of State for Health tasked Kate Lampard and Ed Marsden with preparing an overview report (2015) with recommendations for the NHS post-Savile, and these will then be discussed with a view to understanding what the NHS as a whole needs to change – with the intention of continuing the 'wider public conversation' that Lampard and Marsden encourage (p.11).

The chapter will then consider another high-profile case of sexual offending from within the NHS to understand what is being learned about the need to create a stronger culture of safeguarding. It goes on to review the factors that allowed this abuse to happen and asks whether it is possible for another prolific offender to abuse the trust of vulnerable adults and children in the NHS.

It concludes by considering preventative tools that could support an organisation in recruiting employees committed to a culture of safeguarding who understand their role in protecting vulnerable adults and children.

NHS culture

Recent years have seen a renewed interest in understanding the culture of the NHS and linking the improvement of culture to better patient outcomes and safety (Darzi, 2008; National Advisory Group on the Safety of Patients in England, 2013; Johnson, Haskell and Barach, 2015). In 2013, Sir Robert Francis' Report of the Mid Staffordshire NHS Foundation Trust Public Inquiry (Francis, 2013) considered substandard treatment of patients, a number of whom died as a result of the treatment they had received at the hospital. Francis detailed a whole-system failure where there was lack of openness to criticism, lack of consideration for patients, secrecy, misplaced assumptions and acceptance of poor standards. The report called on healthcare providers to foster a common culture of 'putting the patient first' and to enhance support for staff providing healthcare (Francis, 2013).

The Francis Report outlined issues relating to the quality of patient care, patient safety, leadership and culture across the NHS. Significantly, the report made 290 recommendations intended to change culture and practice at the Department of Health, the Care Quality Commission (CQC), Monitor (at the time the sector regulator for health services in England), the General Medical Council (GMC) and the Nursing and Midwifery Council (NMC), in addition to local patient and public scrutiny organisations (Thorlby *et al.*, 2014). The CQC redesigned the inspection regime for hospitals, and, in turn, the requirement for achieving Foundation Trust status, which allows them to become semi-autonomous organisational units, went through a complete overhaul.

A central theme from the public inquiries into the failings outlined in the report was the knowledge that learning from mistakes was critical to improving patient safety. To do this it was essential that the culture of the NHS became one that valued the protection of the patient over the protection of 'the system' (DoH, 2015). A further review was set up to review whistle-blowing in the NHS following disquiet about the way those who raise concerns about the NHS were treated. Chaired once again by Sir Robert Francis, the

Freedom to Speak Up report (Francis, 2015) set out 20 overarching principles and actions for the NHS. These principles focused on the culture changes required to move from a 'Who is to blame?' approach to a 'just culture', where those who raise concerns are treated fairly and concerns are acted on and learnt from. Further themes identified were opportunities to improve handling cases, implement measures that support good practice and particularly to support vulnerable groups within the NHS (Francis, 2015).

These reports, alongside those focusing on Savile's abuse, highlight the importance of transparency when dealing with concerns relating to harm. The NHS has long being criticised for being both secretive in its dealings (Craft, 1994) and passive in its approach to acknowledging faults within the system and to learn (Forman and Goodman, 1990). The movement towards an open and just system working to improve conditions for patients, employees and leaders is a long process. That process requires commitment from all parties: government, health leaders and managers who can instil confidence in frontline NHS staff who have concerns and ensure they know that they are not only free to speak but are encouraged to do so. The next section addresses the measures that could support that vision coming to fruition.

Key post-Savile recommendations for the NHS

Possibly one of the most discouraging aspects of reviewing learning from inquiries into cases of organisational abuse is the apparent difficulty of embedding basic good practice in organisations and therefore the repetition of similar issues in inquiry reports and their recommendations. This is echoed by Lampard and Marsden (2015) who, in making observations about the key components of a 'safer NHS', comment:

> The operational and behavioural features of effective safeguarding we set out here are hardly novel or revolutionary. They may seem obvious. But the lack of these features in the hospitals with which

> Savile had a relationship clearly contributed to his acting as he did. NHS hospital trusts need to ask themselves regularly whether their own arrangements are characterised by the specific features of effective safeguarding which we have identified. (para.12.62)

Whilst their observations are therefore not 'novel or revolutionary', the importance of following them should in no way be underestimated. What they identify are the components of a safeguarding culture in the NHS, beginning with leadership that promotes the right culture – that is, leaders who develop cultures and values in a way that encourages the openness, leadership and support that staff need to deliver effective safeguarding. Related is the need for senior staff to be approachable and informed and for there to be visible and widely understood openness and listening when people, including children, raise concerns. Finally, they highlight the central importance of training staff and communicating with them about safeguarding in order to ensure that they are properly aware and are encouraged to raise concerns.

In 2015 all NHS trusts were asked to provide a response to Lampard and Marsden's 'Lessons Learnt' report (2015). They were asked to address any planned action to respond to the nine recommendations specifically directed to NHS trusts (the recommendations are listed in Table 10.1). Chief executives at these trusts were asked to put in place policies to ensure the safe management of celebrity guests, VIPs and other official visitors while on NHS premises. Uncontrolled access without appropriate safeguards in place had allowed Savile to access and abuse people at their most vulnerable moments. The tightening or restricting access was a focus of the recommendations, as were the responsibilities for reporting safeguarding concerns to the appropriate authorities.

Table 10.1 *Lessons Learnt* report recommendations

Recommendation number	Recommendation
R1	All NHS hospital trusts should develop a policy for agreeing to and managing visits by celebrities, VIPs and other official visitors. The policy should apply to all such visits without exception.
R2	All NHS trusts should review their voluntary services arrangements and ensure that: they are fit for purpose; volunteers are properly recruited, selected and trained and are subject to appropriate management and supervision; and all voluntary services managers have development opportunities and are properly supported.
R4	All NHS trusts should ensure that their staff and volunteers undergo formal refresher training in safeguarding at the appropriate level at least every three years.
R5	All NHS hospital trusts should undertake regular reviews of: their safeguarding resources, structures and processes (including their training programmes); and the behaviours and responsiveness of management and staff in relation to safeguarding issues to ensure that their arrangements are robust and operate as effectively as possible.
R7	All NHS hospital trusts should undertake DBS checks (including, where applicable, enhanced DBS and barring list checks) on their staff and volunteers every three years. The implementation of this recommendation should be supported by NHS Employers.
R9	All NHS hospital trusts should devise a robust trust-wide policy setting out how access by patients and visitors to the internet, to social networks and other social media activities such as blogs and Twitter is managed and where necessary restricted. Such policy should be widely publicised to staff, patients and visitors and should be regularly reviewed and updated as necessary.
R10	All NHS hospital trusts should ensure that arrangements and processes for the recruitment, checking, general employment and training of contract and agency staff are consistent with their own internal HR processes and standards and are subject to monitoring and oversight by their own HR managers.
R11	NHS hospital trusts should review their recruitment, checking, training and general employment processes to ensure they operate in a consistent and robust manner across all departments and functions and that overall responsibility for these matters rests with a single executive director.
R12	NHS hospital trusts and their associated NHS charities should consider the adequacy of their policies and procedures in relation to the assessment and management of the risks to their brand and reputation, including as a result of their associations with celebrities and major donors, and whether their risk registers adequately reflect such risks.

Source: Lampard and Marsden, 2015

Lampard and Marsden identify the absence of procedures for *how* concerns could be raised or when concerns should be raised when dealing with concerning behaviour. Not having a trusted conduit to share information of concern appears to have led many NHS staff members to remain silent on key issues that concerned them. At the core of a safeguarding culture is the acknowledgement that vulnerable adults are more susceptible to abuse when poor organisational culture, such as failure to listen and act on concerns, is left unchallenged (Stevens, 2013).

The issues surrounding silo working rather than a multidisciplinary approach to safeguarding and sharing of concerns is a common theme throughout Lampard and Marsden's report and indeed most of the 44 reports into Savile's offending within the NHS. The absence of multidisciplinary working created an unsafe environment for patients as concerns were not shared. As outlined by Erooga (2012), characteristics of safe organisations include working closely with colleagues across disciplines while also accepting advice on safeguarding issues.

Johnstone and Dent (2015) explored this issue in their report into Savile's association with Stoke Mandeville Hospital, with witnesses describing sexualised comments from Savile that were excused as eccentric and flamboyant rather than an indication of more wide-scale issues around his suitability to work with vulnerable patients. Equally, the nature of Savile's celebrity had an influence on how people responded to concerns as hospitals weighed up the benefits of association with a high-profile celebrity and successful fundraiser (Johnstone and Dent, 2015; Lampard and Marsden, 2015).

No formal checks or other measures were used to assess Savile's suitability to have access to vulnerable people. Rather, there was reliance on his public persona as an indication that his presence was desirable. Where he could gain favour, where people liked him and where he understood how best to gain access, supervision was not enforced (Lampard and Marsden, 2015).

Savile understood how the NHS worked and effectively navigated the system. He was celebrated for his networking and influencing skills as they generated significant charitable income for many NHS organisations, with a lack of awareness that he also used his skills to network with, and influence, key gatekeepers whose job it was to offer protection to vulnerable adults and children. Indeed, so effective was he that, in possibly the most startling example of this exercise of influence, in the late 1980s he became Chair of Broadmoor Hospital's Advisory Committee, at that time effectively the management committee of the hospital (Kirkup and Marshall, 2014).

Visits from celebrities and other key stakeholders, including VIPs and donors, play a valuable role in promoting a hospital's services. Positive media coverage of these visits can also be important in building and maintaining public confidence in the NHS. Visits can enhance the experience of patients and raise employee morale while also increasing charitable donations that in turn lead to improved facilities for patients.

Cases like Savile risk jeopardising the viability of any external contact with non-staff, which would be a high price for individual institutions to pay. Such visits can be accommodated safely provided the importance of safeguarding a patient's privacy and dignity is held to be paramount. An appropriate policy providing guidance to those being approached or arranging such visits is a base-level requirement. A basic policy should include action prior to the visit to determine the relevance and suitability of the person requesting access and ensure there are internal communication links between senior management, local managers and departmental employees prior to access.

Once access is determined to be appropriate, a plan and risk assessment should be completed at departmental level to plan for eventualities, which should include detailed planning for supervision throughout access agreed by both employee and the visitor.

Post-event publicity, such as press releases and approved communication, should demonstrate the benefits of the visit.

The relationship between policy and practice

Policy is the fundamental starting point for management to convey what is intended to happen operationally at all levels of the organisation. A policy cannot stand alone and be considered relevant and accessible to those who use it to guide their practice without consultation and discussion conveying the practical meaning of that policy to the workforce. The development of policy should therefore be accomplished in consultation and discussion with a range of stakeholders and then be supported by training for staff. All this should be in the context of creating a larger conversation around organisational safeguarding and protection of those who are vulnerable.

A safeguarding policy should be a living document. Much like a business plan, it should be constantly adapted to meet constantly changing requirements. Policies, procedures and training should be regularly reviewed with stakeholders, and structures and support processes put in place to ensure that they remain fit for purpose. Reviews should include organisational responses to previous issues within the organisation itself, regularly holding the organisation to account and identifying learning. This level of monitoring should be challenging whether the organisation has a strong safeguarding culture and what steps the organisation can take to strengthen that culture.

Training every three years is part of a basis for developing an organisational safeguarding culture. However, it can only be part of a wider programme of putting safeguarding behaviours into action. Safeguarding training and support should ensure that employees are aware that abuse does happen and what preventive action can be taken. Equally important is for employees to understand their roles and responsibilities in identifying and escalating concerns and the support available for them to do so.

Working within Human Resources in the NHS, the first author's experience was that informal arrangements for visitors and helpers within the NHS were a constant challenge to the safeguarding culture. It is human to rationalise the access people are given: 'I know him', 'I can vouch for her', 'My friend's son wants to be a doctor so he is coming in to shadow me', 'She wants some work experience so she is just coming in to do some basic work so that she can be in the right environment.' When statements like this are made, something important is being forgotten, that staff are in a privileged position when working with vulnerable people in the NHS.

To use external visitors as an example, a safeguarding culture in practice surpasses simply following an instruction, 'Don't leave them [external visitors] alone with a patient.' If training and support are in place for staff that supports them in understanding *why* the instruction is so important, then it reinforces the idea that a safeguarding culture can be present in, and inform, all interactions.

The case of Dr Myles Bradbury

Cases of abuse of vulnerable patients are relatively rare in the NHS. However, consideration of another high-profile case is instructive in that the themes identified are similar to those in the reviews of Savile's behaviour.

Background

Dr Myles Bradbury was a paediatric haematologist at Cambridge University Hospitals (CUH) NHS Foundation Trust. In November 2013, the family of a young patient raised a concern about possibly inappropriate behaviour by Dr Bradbury. Following a police investigation he was charged, and in September 2014 he pleaded guilty to 25 sexual offences against 18 children who had been his patients, as well as to charges of voyeurism and possession of indecent images. His victims were adolescent boy patients and the offences took place under the guise of necessary medical genital examination, including using a concealed camera to record images.

He was sentenced to a total of 22 years' imprisonment. On appeal his sentence was restructured to 16 years' imprisonment and six years on licence. Following his conviction, the Trust commissioned an independent investigation into governance arrangements within the paediatric haematology and oncology service where Dr Bradbury had worked.

Inquiry findings

The inquiry (Scott-Moncrieff and Morris, 2015) found evidence of consistent breaches of protocol and guidelines by Dr Bradbury: by seeing children under 14 years unchaperoned and by carrying out intimate examinations during some of those appointments; by giving his mobile phone number to patients and their families; and seeing some patients unnecessarily, and much more frequently than their stage of treatment required. He avoided this being known by other staff by making appointments directly with the families, and out of clinic times or for different clinics. The inquiry established that it was no one's job to monitor any of these practices or policies for unusual behaviour or non-compliance. Patients and families were not given information on the policies or practices, so were not in a position to notice any breaches.

By contrast with findings from a number of Savile inquiries, the inquiry found that the Health Trust had robust and effective safeguarding governance arrangements, going to board level; a safer recruitment policy in accordance with NHS guidance, which was followed in Dr Bradbury's case; and a suitable and robust appraisal policy that was also followed in Dr Bradbury's case.

Given that there appeared to be good governance it might have been assumed that patients would be safe using Trust services. The inquiry also found evidence of a strong safeguarding culture in that there was a wide commitment to safeguarding and the Trust appeared to engage wholeheartedly with the Cambridgeshire LSCB. It notes, however, that the effectiveness of this culture was weakened by the lack of understanding and awareness of the possibility of abuse by a respected colleague (para.4.29).

A repeated theme in inquiries, whether about Savile, Bradbury or in other settings (e.g. William Vahey at Southbank International School – see Chapter 11), is that whilst it is highly unusual for anyone to suspect abuse there are usually indicators of boundary violations at an apparently relatively minor level (as with Bradbury) or more grossly (as with some of Savile's public behaviour) but the possible significance of that behaviour is all too often not understood, an issue explored further in Chapter 4. That foreshadows the answer to the question posed in the next section.

Could it happen again?

The repeated message from the various Savile inquiries is that the failure of NHS employees to understand their duty in protecting children and vulnerable adults could lead to another prolific offender being unchallenged and allowed to offend within an NHS setting.

> It must be noted however that all NHS services should be alert to predatory sexual offenders like Savile who can be placed in a position of trust and authority. Individuals like Savile operate covertly and use their influence to further their own ends in such a manner that may not be immediately obvious to those around them. Policies and safeguards are in place nationally to protect society's children and vulnerable adults. All workers in the NHS have a duty to ensure these are adhered to at all times. The failure to do so could lead to a similar situation happening again. (Johnstone and Dent, 2015, p.iv)

In 2015, following the various Savile inquiries, the child sexual exploitation inquiry in Rotherham and the case of Dr Myles Bradbury in Cambridge, the Home Secretary established the Independent Inquiry into Child Sexual Abuse (IICSA), a statutory inquiry with the aim of conducting an overarching national review of the extent to which institutions in England and Wales have discharged their duty of care to protect children against sexual abuse.

As discussed above, most relevant to Health is the investigation into the management of Myles Bradbury at the Cambridge University Hospitals NHS Foundation Trust. A key recommendation supported the need for a safeguarding lead to deal with concerns relating to staff. Outlined in the Bradbury report is that while the hospital had safeguarding policies and procedures, they should also have been explicit about the risk of abuse by colleagues, and that for this to happen a culture change is needed, centring on the empowerment of staff, patients and their parents and carers. The report stated, 'Safeguarding policies and practices are necessary elements of a safe environment, but are not sufficient. A safe environment also requires a safeguarding culture, in which safeguarding is threaded through everything that everyone does' (Scott-Moncrieff and Morris, 2015, para.10.18).

Further opportunities exist in terms of promoting safeguarding roles, responsibilities and such a culture change. Rather than focusing on preventative measures intended to screen undesirable people out of an organisation, there is far more opportunity to both educate and empower the workforce to understand better their role in protecting children and vulnerable adults. One part of this would be interviewing and assessing for behaviours focused on values that exhibit the commitment to protecting others from harm.

Value Based Interviewing

Since the publication of the Francis Report, there has been increased interest in interviewing processes which integrate values and behaviour into NHS selection methods for staff recruitment:

> Patients must be the first priority in all of what the NHS does by ensuring that, within available resources, they receive effective care from caring, compassionate and committed staff working within a common culture and protected from avoidable harm and deprivation of their basic rights. (Francis, 2013, para.1.122)

Recommendation 185 of the Francis Report specifically focuses on the need for the selection of recruits who evidence appropriate values, attitudes and behaviours. There is evidence that value alignment between employees and employing organisations results in higher levels of staff engagement (MacLeod and Clarke, 2009). In turn, the Department of Health's *Staff Engagement Toolkit* (NHS Employers, 2013) shows that higher engagement scores in NHS providers correlate to higher patient satisfaction and lower standardised hospital mortality rates.

The terms 'Value Based Recruitment' and 'Value Based Interviewing' refer to specific selection and interviewing methods to help select employees whose personal values and behaviours align to NHS values. Whereas traditional recruitment methods could be considered 'competency-based recruitment', a value-based approach to selection focuses on assessing the values and behaviours of an individual. Further resources and information can be found at the end of this chapter.

An interview focusing on values provides additional insight into a candidate's behaviours, attitudes and motivations. As an evidence-based tool it reduces interviewer subjectivity in the recruitment process. While traditionally interviews might focus on questions about hypothetical situations such as 'What would you do if…?', a values interview explores past events and experiences (e.g. 'Can you give an example when you…?') as a predictor of future behaviour.

If an NHS provider has a safeguarding culture where employees understand their role in protecting others, and if it recruits for people who hold a value of 'protect others', then this seems likely to both support and build on a safeguarding culture.

Before a method to assess this value can be designed, it is necessary to establish what behaviours underpin this value. What behaviours, if exhibited, would demonstrate working to protect another person? Equally important, what are the behaviours that, if exhibited, would mean that this is not a person who behaves in a way that will protect others?

The multiple inquiries into Savile's abuse in the NHS, the inquiry into the behaviours of Dr Myles Bradbury at Addenbrookes Hospital and the review of the failings at Winterbourne View Hospital (Flynn, 2012) help us understand what behaviours that protect others look like and what behaviours lead to people not being protected from harm.

Those who demonstrate protective behaviour take the time to understand what concerns them and can then articulate that concern to others to ensure they are understood. The use of organisational processes to escalate concerns is essential, as is resilience in the face of real or perceived barriers that prevent concerns being escalated. Raising safeguarding concerns requires both courage and determination to be heard in some cases, and this cannot be underestimated.

Those who do not protect others don't question the appropriateness of behaviour or ignore poor behaviour in others. They use inappropriate mechanisms, such as gossip, to voice concern. At times, they may escalate concerns to management without ensuring they have been heard and pass responsibility to others to address problems.

Using these examples, a behavioural framework can be developed that may be used to assess the value of 'protect' at an interview (see Table 10.2).

Table 10.2 Value: To protect others

Behaviours that protect others (aligned)	Behaviours that do not protect others (non-aligned)
Understand what concerns them and the source of the concern	Does not take time to understand the concerns or identify the source of their concern
Articulates concerns in a way that can be understood by others	Cannot articulate their concerns and be understood by others, is vague or uncommunicative
Escalates their concerns appropriately to others – e.g. using organisational processes	Keeps concerns to themselves or discusses them inappropriately with others – e.g. gossips
Demonstrates resilience in the face of resistance to escalation of concerns	Fails to demonstrate resilience; does not persist in raising the concern
Shows determination to receive a response they are satisfied with when escalating concerns	Passes responsibility to others to escalate concerns/does not ensure they are satisfied with the response
Can demonstrate learning from the event	Cannot demonstrate learning from the event
Uses this learning to inform their practice in the future, reflecting on the outcome	Does not use any learning to inform practice, and does not reflect on the outcome

In a values interview the interviewer will ask candidates to give examples of real-life situations they have experienced and talk through what they did, how they did it and crucially why they behaved in the way that they did. The technique uses open questions that will engage the candidate and allow the free flow of information that provides insight into the attitudes and beliefs that underpin their behaviour.

Examples of Value Based Interview questions: To protect others

Assessing for behaviours you want to see in the NHS

Q: Tell me about a time when you became uncomfortable with the behaviour of another person.

Q: Tell me about a time when you raised a concern with someone you work with.

Q: Tell me about a time when you had a concern about the personal safety of one of your patients.

Q: Tell me about a time when you had a safeguarding concern about someone.

Value Based Interviewing alone cannot change the culture of an organisation, but as part of a wider values-into-action programme where the values are integrated into training, appraisal, induction, one to ones and day-to-day conversations, it can make a vital contribution to culture change and can support organisations in building a safeguarding culture by recruiting people who exhibit behaviours that lead to the protection of vulnerable people and screening out those whose passive approach contributes to harm.

Conclusion

When reflecting on Jimmy Savile's nearly 30-year association with the NHS and the sheer scale and range of the abuse that he perpetrated, it seems unbelievable to think that so many people were concerned about him and yet felt powerless to act, that so many knew something and did nothing. And yet we must question why we think this is unbelievable. Since the earliest inquiries into the NHS in the late 1960s (Walshe, 2003) common themes have been identified as contributing to the issues under investigation. These include disempowerment of those within the institution that led to concerns not being raised; inadequate leadership; failure to tackle known problems; poor communication; and systems failure (Walshe, 2003). Of the 44 inquiries into Savile's offending in the NHS, all reinforce the learning identified by Walshe. The same issues continue to resonate today.

Repeatedly, reports into Savile's offending identify the importance of transparency when responding to concerns relating to harm and a greater understanding of the role staff have to protect. As Francis (2013) stated, 'A common culture of serving and protecting patients and of rooting out poor practice will not spread throughout the system without insisting on openness, transparency and candour everywhere in it.'

Lampard and Marsden (2015) advise the Secretary of State for Health to view the report into Savile's offending as the start of a wider conversation about how professionals tackle abuse. It is this movement towards an open and just system where NHS staff feel able to speak about what concerns them that will reduce the ability of potential offenders to succeed unchallenged. Without these conversations, those who are vulnerable seem likely to again fall victim to an offender.

As this chapter outlines, the NHS should consider how it can continue to learn from the ways in which Savile was able to abuse and from the reasons for inaction on the part of others. There is a need to continue to build on the safeguarding culture essential to ensure the safety of the vulnerable. Equally, policy and procedure providing guidance to NHS staff on when and how concerns relating to harm are raised are essential. However, policy and procedure are only small components of a safeguarding culture. Ongoing discussion, education and training about how safeguarding issues present themselves in organisations are essential to ensure that staff continue to understand their privileged position and don't become complacent about their duty. That duty is not just to report and escalate concerns but actively to protect.

This chapter also considered Value Based Interviewing, a measure that can contribute to a 'safer' workforce by determining whether an individual has the appropriate values, attitudes and behaviours to work in the NHS. Crucially, the chapter asserts, the value of 'protect others' should be made explicit and potential recruits to the NHS should be asked to evidence behaviours that are essential in ensuring that patients are protected.

To work within the NHS may sometimes be thankless, but nonetheless it is a privilege. To care for those who are vulnerable is a privilege. If that privilege is forgotten and access to vulnerable people is not protected, we should not be surprised when more offenders succeed in exploiting the vulnerable. Managers need to be aware of the importance of engagement with their workforce, staff need to be supported, patients to be empowered. Above all everyone needs to be clear both about what is considered acceptable behaviour and what to do if those boundaries are crossed.

We conclude with the words of Dee Coles, abused by Savile when she was 15 years old: 'This isn't just a product of the [19]70's, something that happened to hundreds of us then, it's still happening' (Lambert, 2016). She is right, we haven't yet found a way to end sexual violence. However, if heeded, the repeated messages for the NHS about what needs to be done can at least maximise the possibility that those in their care will be safeguarded.

Further information on Value Based Recruitment/Interviewing in the NHS

NHS Employers Values Based Recruitment: www.nhsemployers.org/your-workforce/recruit/employer-led-recruitment/values-based-recruitment

Health Education England Values Based Recruitment: www.hee.nhs.uk/our-work/attracting-recruiting/values-based-recruitment

Oxford University Hospitals NHS Foundation Trust Value Based Interviewing: www.ouh.nhs.uk/about/vision-and-values/value-based-interviewing.aspx

References

Barlow, J. and Scott, S. (2014) *A Further Investigation into the Allegations of Abuse by Jimmy Savile at Leeds General Infirmary: A Report by Leeds Teaching Hospitals NHS Trust*. Accessed on 26 July 2017 at www.leedsth.nhs.uk/assets/Uploads/A-Further-Investigation-into-the-Allegations-of-Abuse-by-Jimmy-Savile-at-Leeds-General-Infirmary-A-Report-by-Leeds-Teaching-Hospitals-NHS-Trust.pdf

Braye, S., Orr, D. and Preston-Shoot, M. (2012) 'The governance of adult safeguarding: findings from research.' *The Journal of Adult Protection 14*, 2, 55–72.

Craft, N. (1994) 'Secrecy in the NHS.' *BMJ 309*, 6969, 1640–1643.

Darzi, A. (2008) *High Quality Care for All: NHS Next Stage Review. Final Report.* London: The Stationery Office. Accessed on 14 August 2017 at www.gov.uk/government/uploads/system/uploads/attachment_data/file/228836/7432.pdf

Department of Health (DoH) (2012) *NHS Constitution.* London: DoH. Accessed on 14 August 2017 at https://www.gov.uk/government/publications/the-nhs-constitution-for-england

Department of Health (DoH) (2015) *Culture Change in the NHS: Applying the Lessons of the Francis Inquiries.* London: DoH. Accessed on 14 August 2017 at https://www.gov.uk/government/uploads/system/uploads/attachment_data/file/403010/culture-change-nhs.pdf

Dunn, P. (2000) *No Secrets: Guidance on Developing and Implementing Multi-Agency Policies and Procedures to Protect Vulnerable Adults from Abuse.* London: Department of Health.

Erooga, M. (ed.) (2012) *Creating Safer Organisations: Practical Steps to Prevent the Abuse of Children by Those Working with Them.* Chichester: John Wiley and Sons.

Flynn, M. (2012) *Winterbourne View Hospital: A Serious Case Review.* Gloucester: South Gloucestershire Safeguarding Adults Board. Accessed on 14 August 2017 at http://hosted.southglos.gov.uk/wv/report.pdf

Forman, D. and Goodman, K.J. (1990) 'How the NHS can improve safety and learning.' *Cancer 61*, 575–578.

Francis, R. (2013) *Report of the Mid Staffordshire NHS Foundation Trust Public Inquiry: Executive Summary.* London: The Stationery Office. Accessed on 14 August 2017 at https://www.gov.uk/government/uploads/system/uploads/attachment_data/file/279124/0947.pdf

Francis, R. (2015) *Freedom to Speak Up: An Independent Review into Creating an Open and Honest Reporting Culture in the NHS.* London: Freedom to Speak Up. Accessed on 14 August 2017 at https://www.gov.uk/government/groups/whistleblowing-in-the-nhs-independent-review

Johnson, J.K., Haskell, H.W. and Barach, P.R. (2015) *Case Studies in Patient Safety: Foundations for Core Competencies.* Burlington, MA: Jones and Bartlett Publishers.

Johnstone, A. and Dent, C. (2015) *Investigation into the Association of Jimmy Savile with Stoke Mandeville Hospital: A Report for Buckinghamshire Healthcare NHS Trust.* Amersham: Buckinghamshire Healthcare NHS Trust. Accessed on 12 August 2017 at www.speakingoutinvestigation.com/Downloads/Speaking%20out%20investigation/2902210_Investigation%20into%20the%20Association%20of%20Jimmy%20Savile%20with%20Stoke%20Mandeville%20Hospital.pdf

Kirkup, B. and Marshall, P. (2014) *Jimmy Savile Investigation. Broadmoor Hospital: Report to the West London Mental Health NHS Trust and the Department of Health*. London: West London Mental Health NHS Trust. Accessed on 11 August 2017 at www.gov.uk/government/publications/jimmy-savile-investigation-broadmoor-hospital

Lambert, O. (dir.) (2016) *Abused: The Untold Story*. BBC.

Lampard, K. and Marsden, E. (2015) *Themes and Lessons Learnt from NHS Investigations into Matters Relating to Jimmy Savile: Independent Report for the Secretary of State for Health*. London: Department of Health. Accessed on 11 August 2017 at www.gov.uk/government/uploads/system/uploads/attachment_data/file/407209/KL_lessons_learned_report_FINAL.pdf

MacLeod, D. and Clarke, N. (2009) 'Engaging for success: enhancing performance through employee engagement: a report to government.' London: Department for Business, Innovation and Skills.

National Advisory Group on the Safety of Patients in England (2013) *A Promise to Learn – a Commitment to Act: Improving the Safety of Patients in England*. Accessed on 26 July 2017 at www.gov.uk/government/uploads/system/uploads/attachment_data/file/226703/Berwick_Report.pdf

NHS Choices (2013) *The NHS in England: About the National Health Service*. Accessed on 20 May 2013 at www.nhs.uk/NHSEngland/thenhs/about/Pages/overview.aspx

NHS Employers (2013) *The Staff Engagement Toolkit: An Online Resource, Supporting You to Increase Staff Engagement in Your Organisation*. Accessed on 11 August 2017 at www.nhsemployers.org/~/media/Employers/Documents/SiteCollectionDocuments/staff-engagement-toolkit.pdf

Scott-Moncrieff, L. and Morris, B. (2015) *Independent Investigation into Governance Arrangements in the Paediatric Haematology and Oncology Service at Cambridge University Hospitals NHS Foundation Trust following the Myles Bradbury Case: A Report for Cambridge University Hospitals, NHS Foundation Trust*. London: Verita. Accessed on 14 August 2017 at https://southwestlincolnshireccg.nhs.uk/about-us/key-documents/safeguarding-1/1316-myles-bradbury-report-2015/file

Stevens, E. (2013) 'Safeguarding vulnerable adults: exploring the challenges to best practice across multi-agency settings.' *The Journal of Adult Protection 15*, 2, 85–95.

Thorlby, R., Smith, J., Williams, S. and Dayan, M. (2014) *The Francis Report: One Year On*. London: Nuffield Trust. Accessed on 14 August 2017 at www.nuffieldtrust.org.uk/research/the-francis-report-one-year-on

Walshe, K. (2003) *Inquiries: Learning from Failure in the NHS?* London: Nuffield Trust.

11

AFTER SAVILE

Implications for Education Settings

JANE WONNACOTT, JANE FOSTER AND HILARY SHAW

Compared to Savile's prolific abuse in health and media organisations there is relatively limited evidence of him gaining access to children in schools and other education settings (Scott-Moncrieff, 2015). Most of the alleged incidents took place in healthcare settings and at the BBC, with the notable exception of Duncroft Approved School, a Barnardo's-run boarding school for 'emotionally disturbed' girls whose situation at that school would have made them both more inherently vulnerable and less likely to be believed should they complain.

Given the scale of allegations about assaults by Savile in health settings and the BBC, and the possibility that this was also the case in educational establishments and children's homes he visited, the Minister for Education ordered inquiries to be undertaken in all such establishments where Savile was believed to have had contact. At the same time an independent assurance process (Scott-Moncrieff, 2015) was commissioned to ensure that the inquiries were comprehensive, thorough and recognised relevant lessons for current practice. This overview report identified that none of the investigations had been able to reach firm conclusions about whether abuse had taken place and that today 'the risk of a paedophile having unrestricted access to children, as Savile apparently had, is substantially reduced' (para.4.1), a statement that should be treated with caution given more recent reports of abuse in education settings.

There is no room for complacency. There is accumulating evidence that many of the factors associated with Savile's predatory behaviour are common to abuse known to have taken place in schools more recently and that the lessons about action to better protect children in schools are similar. This chapter, based on published reviews and other information in the public domain, explores five examples of abuse in school settings. The way in which the abuse was perpetrated is discussed in the context of the findings from the literature relating to abuse in schools and to the Savile inquiries, with a focus on the barriers to identification and subsequent lack of action in education settings.

Whilst there are many challenges to those charged with keeping children safe in education (including being able to recognise where children might be being abused by peers or family), the focus of this chapter is to identify measures which can be put in place to protect children from abuse by the adults who are working with them in a school setting, and to see this as a part of the culture of safeguarding children.

Sexual abuse in education settings: What do we know?

The empirical research base in relation to sexual abuse in schools is very limited with little reliable data to draw on (Smallbone, 2013). One review of the international literature by Charol Shakeshaft (US Department of Education, 2004) set out in detail the limitations of current studies but then went on to identify a number of patterns of sexual misconduct with pupils and common responses. Patterns included the context in which the abuse takes place (trusted, respected and hence powerful teachers being among the abusers group) and careful selection of children least likely to complain. The evaluation noted that allegations may take a variety of forms and only about 6 per cent of pupils report abuse to someone who can do something about it, with most students telling a friend. Concerns about false allegations can inhibit responses, students may not be believed and responses will be less effective where the investigative skills of staff are poor.

This evaluation chimes with findings of a thematic review of institutional abuse in a range of sectors (NCA CEOP, 2013) and the findings of recent reviews in the UK into abuse in education, which are also consistent with the Savile inquiries. Key factors are the abuse of trust; powerful and sometimes charismatic personalities who align themselves with those in power and who have the ability to manipulate the school community (including parents); organisational cultures which are hierarchical and disempowering; the failure of managers to recognise abuse or act on it when brought to their attention; failure to listen to children; and systems that provided insufficient safeguards. Sometimes the focus on reputation of organisation or individuals' professional reputation was given priority over openness and transparency – and therefore over safeguarding.

This is explored here further through an analysis of four serious case reviews and one independent report into abuse perpetrated by professionals working in schools in England. The schools cover a range of types of school and ages of children:

- one independent (fee paying) secondary boarding school, taking pupils from age 11 to 18
- one independent (fee paying) international day school, taking pupils from age 11 to 18
- one state-funded secondary school
- one state-funded first school, taking pupils between the ages of 5 and 8
- one state-funded primary school, taking pupils from 5 to 11.

The perpetrators in these cases are:

> *Jonathan Thomson-Glover*, a teacher at an independent boarding school in Bristol. He was a former pupil at the school (as was his father and his grandfather), who had taught at the school for 31 years and was found with 1400 indecent images on 330 tapes. He admitted 36 charges of making, taking and possessing indecent images of children and later also admitted further sex offences against children at a previous school. (Jones, 2016)

> *William Vahey*, a teacher at an independent London secondary-level international school who seriously sexually abused more

> than 50 boys over a period of four years. The boys were drugged and probably not aware of his actions. (Wonnacott and Carmi, 2016)
>
> *Jeremy Forrest*, a teacher at a secondary school in East Sussex who developed an abusive relationship with a female student aged 14–15 years, abducting her and taking her abroad until found by the police. He was convicted after pleading guilty to five counts of sexual activity with a child. (Harrington, 2013)
>
> *Nigel Leat*, a teacher at a primary school in North Somerset who sexually assaulted at least 20 girls between the ages of six and eight. He was also found to be in possession of 30,000 indecent images of children. (Craddock, 2012)
>
> *Robert Stringer*, a teacher at a North London primary school, who was convicted of 25 offences against four children whom he sexually assaulted whilst running a drama club at the school. (Raynes, 2011)

Whilst each of these cases involved a male perpetrator of abuse, it is important to stress that abuse in schools (and other settings) may also be carried out by women. In the UK there have been a number of cases of successful prosecutions of women teachers who have abused pupils; for example, Lauren Cox (The Times, 2016), Kelly Burgess (BBC News, 2014), Anne Lakey (Independent, 2015) and Helen Goddard (Mail Online, 2009). However, there have been no published reviews of abuse by women in schools which could give an insight into the factors which allowed the abuse to take place, and abuse by women appears to be more often discussed in the media in terms of an 'affair' or a 'relationship', an issue which in itself would benefit from further examination in terms of gender bias distorting understanding of the issue. The serious case review into Little Ted's Nursery did explore the abuse perpetrated by Vanessa George (Wonnacott, 2010) and has many similarities to factors found in schools, but is not included here as there were also very specific issues pertinent only to the early years environment.

Whilst the types and circumstances of abuse are different in each case, close analysis demonstrates that there are a number of common factors, including some level of knowledge/understanding by colleagues of inappropriate or potentially abusive behaviours and an acknowledgement of missed opportunities for intervention. The key features of the five settings that are discussed in this chapter are set out in Table 11.1.

Common themes

It is clearly possible to identify a number of common themes across the five education settings and to recognise that these in many cases reinforce what is known about abusive behaviour in other institutions as well as the behaviour of Jimmy Savile and those in contact with him.

GROOMING THE COMMUNITY

Grooming is a term commonly used to describe the way in which perpetrators of abuse prepare their victims for abuse, so McAlinden describes it as:

> (1) the use of a variety of manipulative and controlling techniques (2) with a vulnerable subject (3) in a range of inter-personal and social settings (4) in order to establish trust or normalise sexually harmful behaviour (5) with the overall aim of facilitating exploitation and/or prohibiting exposure. (2012, p.11)

The perpetrators in this sample not only groomed the pupils they abused but also obtained and maintained power through grooming (in fact, manipulating) the whole school community. In some cases they used personal relationships to assist this process: Jonathan Thomson-Glover was a former pupil of the school whose family were friends with at least one head teacher and whose behaviour was unchallenged as staff feared they could lose their jobs; William Vahey's wife was prominent in the international school community and he was explicit with staff that he could negatively influence their career progression.

Table 11.1 Summary of key features

	The perpetrator	Pupils	Colleagues
Jeremy Forrest State secondary	Male age 35 'Relationship' with a teenage girl Set up additional lessons and contacted via social media Convicted 2013	One pupil age 14–15 who was already known to have been vulnerable from contact with a previous predator when aged 12	Accumulating concerns, aware of 'inappropriate relationship', used Twitter to communicate with pupil Colleagues supportive and reluctant to believe JF may be an abuser JF seen as the victim of pupil's infatuation
Robert Stringer State primary	Male, 56, joined school as a newly qualified teacher Abused girls Charged with 25 offences against four children, 2000–2007 Set up and led prestigious drama club and used this to test out the likely resistance of children he targeted for abuse Difficult to manage, flouted school rules and his lessons were known to lack structure	Known to have favourites Pupils aware RS had access to a large knife used in drama productions Pupils sought status through selection for roles in the drama club Pupils were told he would go to prison if they disclosed and no one would then be able to look after his disabled wife	Head and colleagues found him 'difficult' Instilled fear in staff through his behaviour – e.g. shouting at them Staff expressed concerns about RS's relationship with pupils in the drama club Anonymous referral made to the head teacher Reported concerns included suspicious photos on his computer and showing 15-rated DVD with explicit sex scenes to Year 5 (9-year-old) pupils Two teachers who attended safer recruitment training informed the head teacher that Stringer 'ticks all the boxes of the exercise "profile of an abuser"'
Nigel Leat State primary	Male – previously musician and music teacher Female victims – youngest aged six Pleaded guilty to 36 sexual offences including eight counts of penetration of a child under 13. Possessed 30,500 indecent photographs and 720 indecent films Known to have a lax approach to teaching and classroom discipline	Had favourite pupils and targeted those academically less able, vulnerable and 'pretty' Gave his favourite pupils presents Two pupils did report to the school that he kissed them and touched their legs but the abuse only came to light after a pupil made a disclosure to her mother	Thirty incidents of inappropriate behaviour reported, ranging from low-level issues around content of lessons to touching pupils inappropriately. It was 'common knowledge' that he made inappropriate jokes Staff were unaware of safeguarding procedures, and internal training had not enabled them to identify Leat as an abuser Non-professional staff made complaints – e.g. having a child on his knee, having an erection whilst holding a child
William Vahey Secondary private/international	Male, 60 Known to have abused 54 boys between 2009 and 2013 Previous history in the USA (1969) of abusing children not picked up in pre-employment checks Ran prestigious 'travel club' involving residential trips abroad Drugged victims, many of whom were not aware that they had been abused Aligned himself with those in power, making it difficult to challenge behaviour that may have caused concern Abuse came to light after he had left the school and was working abroad – a maid stole a data stick containing images of abuse	Abused boys – either very popular pupils or those with some vulnerability Pupils were 'chosen' or selected to go on trips, which were used as a reason to be alone with pupils Pupils joked that Vahey was a 'paedo', but his popularity and mechanism for abusing boys when they were drugged meant that no formal allegations were made	Some staff were uneasy about the perpetrator's behaviour but put it down to 'informal style' Not universally popular with staff but difficult to challenge as aligned with those in power Staff were overtly threatened that Vahey could use his wife's influence (she held a high-profile position in the professional community) to damage their careers Training on safeguarding had focused mainly on abuse within the family and had not equipped staff to understand indicators of abuse in their own organisation or how to report them
Jonathan Thomson-Glover Independent boys' day and boarding school	Housemaster and former pupil Convicted of taking indecent images from 1998 to 2004. 330 tapes recovered by police. Secretly installed cameras Groomed pupils by providing friendship, beer, pizza, socialising and encouraging them to break school rules. Sexualised relationships through 'banter' and discussing his own sexual relationships Befriended adult carers and head teachers Described by boys as behaving like a friend rather than a teacher	Boys – 'good looking, naughty, sporty' boys would be favourites 'Chosen' to go and stay at holiday cottage owned by the perpetrator Also chosen to socialise with him in his study where alcohol was consumed In 2003 pupils complained about the perpetrator sleeping in the house, locking the kitchen and drinking alcohol	Colleagues noticed blurred boundaries between pupils and the perpetrator An educational psychologist was concerned about favourites and Thomson-Glover fitting the profile of an abuser Several allegations were made about the perpetrator being tied up in his study by pupils in a state of undress. A cleaner reported him wrapping a boy in cellophane as a prank Concerns were expressed by non-teaching staff who could see his behaviour was different Complaints were diluted, lost or disbelieved as they went up the management chain

Leadership and management	Organisational culture	Family and community
Ineffective – procedures not followed and accumulating concerns not recorded No record of, or agreement to, supplementary lessons No supervision of staff with safeguarding responsibilities JF's denial when asked about the relationship taken at face value	Safeguarding not high on the agenda in spite of recent case of abuse in the school which resulted in staff member going to prison 'Head in the sand' approach to safeguarding and assumption of false allegations Adult-focused culture where pupils' voices not heard Victim seen as the problem	Spoke directly to parents of the pupil to reassure them there was no relationship Parents accepted daughter had a 'crush'
Direct complaints from parents and staff were not formally investigated Conduct issues were not dealt with. First head teacher made excuses, described his behaviour as 'fatherly' and 'touchy-feely' First head teacher failed to take or keep accurate records or refer to the local authority or police Staff did not know where to take concerns Almost all abuse took place under the first head teacher's regime Second head teacher was warned about RS but was diverted from a focus on the school by home issues Under second head teacher disciplinary procedures started but stopped when Stringer resigned – contrary to official guidance at the time Rejoined the workforce via teaching supply agency	Weak leadership of the first head teacher and personal distractions of the second head teacher fostered a culture where safeguarding was not taken seriously Lack of record-keeping meant patterns of behaviour were not identified	Parents were desperate for their children to get into the drama club, and through this Stringer fostered strong relationships with parents Parents petitioned for RS to return to the school when he was suspended Had strong backing from the governing body, making it difficult for the second head teacher to challenge him
Staff were told (by?) not to insinuate things about him No evidence of formal recording of incidents or of them being viewed cumulatively Disciplinary procedures not followed and no referral to outside agencies. External regulators did not identify poor leadership and unhealthy aspects of school culture The head teacher of the school at the time was subsequently barred for life from working with children due to his lack of action in response to the concerns	Evidence of poor relationships in school. Not all staff felt they were treated equally The school culture did not put children first and discouraged open communication There was evidence of a hierarchical culture where junior staff did not feel they would be taken seriously	School community not particularly local – parents may not have shared concerns with each other School not seen by external agencies as being in need of support, leading to false sense of security in the parent group
For much of Vahey's time at the school informal processes prevailed and there was no consideration of cumulative concerns Status and accountability of Vahey's travel club were blurred There was no debrief after residential trips, which would have highlighted patterns of sickness for some of the pupils Little scrutiny of safeguarding by the school management board. Procedures set by the owners of the school were generally not followed, particularly in relation to residential activities Emphasis was given to acceding to the wishes of parents not to take action in individual cases rather than consideration of safeguarding for whole school community Designated safeguarding leads were inadequately trained and there was no central point for concerns to be raised Management style changed with a new principal, moving from laissez faire to hierarchical	Laissez faire and relaxed under first head Changes in leadership, management and proprietors caused uncertainty and rifts in staff group. This diverted attention from any concerns about Vahey Over-reliance on external inspection regimes rather than reflective practice with clear lines of accountability concerning governance to scrutinise effectiveness of safeguarding practice	Quickly normalised behaviours such as being alone with children and manipulating staff ratios for trips Popular with parents and students – came second in popularity ratings Families from abroad may not have been familiar with child protection expectations and procedures in the UK and were provided with very limited information The school was a strong social hub for families from abroad where school perceived as 'part of the family'
Head teacher 1 – informal style Lack of recording of any concerns or action taken *Head teacher 2* – focused on improving finances and processes (including safeguarding policy). This was unpopular with staff (e.g. strict no alcohol policy) Staff ratios for school trips not adhered to. Unauthorised trips took place and others with no risk assessment Training content focused on familial abuse and did not include allegations against staff *Head teacher 3* – focus was on improving finance and academic performance. Disliked formality. Little interest by head teacher or school management board in safeguarding Defensive management decisions and keeping things in house	Liberal ethos in school had developed from its early days and this deterred people from reporting concerns when rules were broken Favouritism was part of the school culture Culture of 'informally socialising' Culture of 'pranks' in the school Lack of curiosity or consideration that it could happen here	Permeable boundaries with families, some of whom would make private visits to the perpetrator's holiday cottage Some parents complained that trips were only for favourites Lack of confidence in the complaints system by families in late 2000s – did not want to 'rock the boat' in case it was taken out on the pupil Head teacher and perpetrator seemed to be friends

There is a clear parallel with Savile, with perpetrators in schools aligning themselves to those in power and often being seen as a useful and positive ally to head teachers who did not recognise the risks associated with their behaviour. For example, Robert Stringer had not only demonstrated that he was difficult to manage early on in his teaching career but had also swiftly sought the backing of school governors and the parent body in regard to his drama club. Whatever the reasons behind the failure to identify behaviours or to take action, it is significant that reviews (on Vahey and Leat) have noted a lack of external challenge or scrutiny of safeguarding practice from governing bodies, proprietors and external regulators. It would appear that where the focus of inspection or scrutiny is predominantly on educational attainment and standards and schools are performing well in other aspects of school life, safeguarding may attract less attention from the regulators and less support from the local authority. For example, Anne Lakey, a head teacher who was jailed for sex with students, was described as a visionary for 'turning around' a failing school and making it one of the most improved in the country (Independent, 2015).

Parents are, of course, a key protective factor for children and are often a powerful force in the school community. Where perpetrators engaged pupils in extracurricular activities they had also successfully gained the support of parents, pupils and senior leaders. Stringer's drama club, Vahey's travel club and Thomson-Glover's trips to his holiday cottage were all popular in the school community and were seen as an asset to the school whilst providing the prima facie reason for removing children from other protective factors and giving the abuser the opportunity to abuse.

It is clear that grooming or manipulating the school community was easier in situations where staff had not been equipped to recognise possible inappropriate conduct and unacceptable behaviours in colleagues. The reviews relating to Vahey, Thomson-Glover and Leat all found that child protection training had focused mainly on abuse within the family, leaving staff unaware of the type of behaviours that should worry them or indeed what to do if they had suspicions about a colleague. Where staff had effective training it seems they were confident to speak out; two members of staff returned from accredited safer recruitment training to report the concern that Stringer's behaviour fitted the profile of an abuser, and an education psychologist had noted that Thomson-Glover's behaviour was in line with an abuser's profile.

THE INFLUENCE OF ORGANISATIONAL CULTURE ON INTER-PROFESSIONAL RELATIONSHIPS

The powerful influence of organisational culture on the perpetrators' capacity to abuse is notable. This is not as simple as an organisational 'type' supporting abusive behaviour but rather the vulnerabilities which are exposed when organisational culture adopts an extreme position – for example, liberal/laissez faire cultures where inappropriate behaviours were normalised and boundaries between staff and pupils became blurred, or cultures where a focus on procedures, processes and targets meant that safeguarding was not a priority. Organisations appeared to be particularly vulnerable during periods of cultural instability; senior leaders are a key influence on organisational culture, and situations such as a change of head, proprietor, management or governance can result in the school culture swinging from one end of the spectrum to the other. During such times it seems that those intent on abuse are able to either exploit rifts and weaknesses in the staff body to their advantage (Vahey) or to use the opportunity to abuse undetected whilst the focus of management is elsewhere (Vahey and Stringer). A feature of Savile's individual relationships within organisations was often a contrast between those who felt he was charming and likeable and those who (for a variety of reasons) did not like him (Lampard and Marsden, 2015). At such times it is very difficult for those who want to challenge to be able to do so without their motives being questioned.

INEFFECTIVE MULTI-AGENCY WORKING

Multi-agency working is an underlying principle of safeguarding children in the UK – see, for example, the Children Act 2004, *Working Together to Safeguard Children* (HM Government, 2015), local child protection arrangements and *Keeping Children Safe in*

Education (Department for Education, 2016). In England and Wales safeguarding procedures are designed to support a system where schools are part of a wider safeguarding community; advice can be sought from the local authority, and where there are any concerns these are investigated swiftly and fairly. Schools in these cases did not consult properly with the local authority or other statutory agencies, appeared to be isolated and preferred to manage issues internally rather than by multi-agency safeguarding systems which could have offered advice and support. In effect these schools were, in some ways, 'invisible' to the system – a position which may reflect the local community perception of the schools as 'good' or 'excellent' based on reports of academic attainment alone; that is, that nothing prior to discovery of abuse had brought these schools to the attention of any outside body in anything other than a positive light.

EXTERNAL REGULATION AND RECOGNISING ABUSE

All the schools in these cases were subject to a regime of inspections from external regulators in the same way in which hospitals and health settings where Savile perpetrated abuse are regulated by their external bodies. However, in each of these sectors, the regulatory inspection did not identify gaps in the safeguarding system; in fact, the safeguarding arrangements at the schools where Jonathan Thomson-Glover, Nigel Leat and William Vahey taught were all previously variously described in official inspection reports as 'excellent' or 'well managed', and pupils at Jeremy Forrest's school were described by inspectors as 'feeling safe'. By contrast, the specific inspections carried out *after* the abuse had been uncovered found numerous deficits in safeguarding practice in each of these schools. It therefore seems likely that unless inspections are focusing specifically on safeguarding, the wide range of areas to be covered does not allow for the in-depth interrogation of safeguarding practice in a culture where academic achievement has been used to measure a school's success. Where this is underwritten by confirmation that the school has the appropriate policies and procedures in place to deal with other safeguarding issues (bullying, use of social media, etc.), a superficial impression of child safety may be given. The danger of this is that school management, staff and parents are lulled into a false sense of security about these aspects of the school, relying on the commendations of the inspectorate in regard to academic outcomes for children rather than being open to the possibility that 'abuse could happen here'.

INEFFECTIVE RECRUITMENT PRACTICES

The reports into abuse by Savile identified that his fame and celebrity resulted in the usual checks and balances in the recruitment of volunteers being bypassed (Kirkup and Marshall, 2014). In the schools in the cases reviewed here there were also examples of poor recruitment procedures. In some instances, application of more robust procedures could have prevented the perpetrator from having contact with children or carrying out further abuse. Robert Stringer, for example, moved schools after disciplinary processes had been instigated but was still able to get teaching posts through a teaching supply agency. Vahey's situation (although unusual) highlights not only the additional risks associated with teachers who move through the international job market but also the weaknesses of an international criminal records enquiry system; as a young man he was convicted of child abuse in the USA but, due to frequent moves within his home country and across the world, as well as the challenges associated with gaining criminal records information internationally, this information became lost in the system, and the other warning signs, such as his behaviour and conduct once he was employed, were not recognised as indicators of his potential to abuse.

Warning signs

As with Savile, a common feature across all these settings was the presence of emerging warning signs over time. Once abuse came to light it is apparent that, whilst the reality of the abuse having happened was a shock, concerns about the perpetrator rarely came 'out of the blue'. In all cases in this sample there had been times where a range of concerns on a scale from hunches, niggles of doubt and low-level concerns about conduct and behaviour (see Table 11.2) through to clear suspicions or direct knowledge (a member of staff had reported seeing Nigel Leat with an erection when he had a child on his knee) had come to light and had either been discussed amongst staff, recognised by parents or directly reported to head teachers. If we are to have any clear proposals for what we need to do in the future we need to understand what stopped people from reporting, or where concerns were reported, what stopped those higher up the hierarchy of management from taking action.

The report into events relating to Stuart Hall (Dobbs, 2016) clarifies the difference between 'direct personal knowledge' and 'awareness'.

> Awareness covers a range of situations from suspicion to actual knowledge. It is not easy precisely to analyse the extent of a person's awareness because it depends on a number of factors including a person's perception of events. However, if someone has knowledge of something, he or she is clearly aware of it, but actual knowledge of something is not required for an individual to be 'aware' of it. This is important because many members of the BBC staff who have given evidence to the Hall investigation laid heavy emphasis on the distinction between 'direct personal knowledge' on the one hand and something less certain and specific, awareness without direct personal knowledge on the other. It was of particular relevance to some when explaining why no action was taken to stop Hall's sexually inappropriate conduct. (para.2.18)

This is a useful distinction and provides a framework for exploring why, in so many instances, colleagues and pupils of teachers who were abusing children either were not heard or did not feel able to make a strong case to those with the power to intervene. In many instances there was 'awareness' as opposed to 'direct personal knowledge', leaving the person(s) concerned unsure what to do next. In addition, there is a middle category that we refer to as 'accumulating concerns'. In this category there is still no specific knowledge but the accumulation of less tangible concerns should prompt action. The eventual decision as to how to respond will be set within the context of the organisational culture that will have a particularly powerful influence.

Table 11.2 Warning signs: What do the reviews tell us?

Awareness	Accumulating concerns	Direct personal knowledge
←	What might happen?	→
Discomfort with the behaviour of the perpetrator Perpetrator viewed as 'maverick' or pushing the boundaries by some but seen by others as popular and innovative	Lower level concerns may accumulate over time Inadequate reporting processes mean concerns sit with individuals who are unaware of the concerns of others and assumptions may be made that others know and are taking action	Behaviour may be noticed which clearly fits the definition of abuse
←	What might influence responses?	→
Reactions determined by both the school culture as to boundaries of acceptable behaviour and wider society including the expectations of the parent group	Status may influence the degree to which people feel confident to raise concerns Support and non-teaching staff may accumulate a great deal of 'soft' information but feel unsure how this should be interpreted or whether they will be believed	Whether the behaviour is reported will depend upon relationships and hierarchy within the staff team Powerful perpetrators may make threats that careers may be damaged. Staff and pupils will need to feel confident that they will be listened to, taken seriously and not penalised for reporting Fear of damaging relationships with colleagues Taking formal action may highlight tensions between employment legislation and safeguarding procedures with concerns about what will happen if the allegation is found to be false Fear of employee deciding to appeal a disciplinary sanction, including dismissal

In all five cases there is evidence of the full range of warning signs, from awareness that something was not right through to direct observation of behaviour that by any definition would be classed as abusive. Colleagues were 'aware' of Jeremy Forrest's inappropriate relationship with a pupil, it was 'common knowledge' that Nigel Leat made inappropriate jokes, and both Vahey's and Thomson-Glover's informality and lack of boundaries with pupils and parents worried some staff. Whether staff and pupils spoke to others about their worries depended to a large extent on the existence of explicit norms of acceptable behaviour within the school. In very informal cultures, behaviours that with hindsight appear very worrying were at times seen as positive examples of good pupil–teacher relationships and praised by some parents.

Sometimes more concrete concerns began to accumulate, such as Vahey having favourite pupils, staffing ratios on school trips being outside the norm and Vahey being seen coming out of pupils' accommodation on residential activities. Whether these accumulating concerns were identified as worrying depended upon the recording, reporting and reviewing systems in the school and how far these helped a joined-up analysis of what was happening.

As with Savile, there were times when with hindsight it is difficult to understand why positive action was not taken when colleagues noticed behaviour that was unacceptable and needed to be formally investigated. Leat was known to have projected an image of a naked adult in a primary school class and have an erection whilst holding a child. A caretaker found suspicious photos on Stringer's computer and there had been a previous complaint by a parent that he had inappropriately touched her daughter. Thomson-Glover was found tied to a chair in a state of undress and to have locked the boarding accommodation at night against procedures. Most shockingly, Forrest's victim was advised to 'get a boyfriend of her own age' by a schoolteacher responsible for safeguarding. All these incidents warranted action under safeguarding procedures but none was taken. Reasons varied from reframing activities such as the chair-tying episode as a 'prank', using disciplinary procedures alone rather than safeguarding procedures and concerns about damaging the reputation of a colleague without firm 'evidence'.

What do we need to do? Implications for protection and prevention

Smallbone (2013) identifies a three-pronged approach to reducing the likelihood of abuse.

1. Increasing the effort needed to commit the crime by controlling access to the school through effective staff recruitment as well as day-to-day procedures such as procedures for visitors' entry, and building pupils' self-confidence through resilience-building activities and self-protective behaviour to provide an additional barrier.

2. Increasing risk of detection through controlling the physical space and encouraging pupils to raise even apparently trivial concerns.

3. Removing excuses for inappropriate behaviour by providing staff with high-quality training, mentoring for staff with personal problems and clear rules about staff–student relationships.

A thread that must run through all of these approaches is acknowledgement that there are many barriers to recognising abusive behaviour and taking action. This is a key lesson from Savile and the reviews that have been explored in this chapter – that is, that abusers often hide in 'plain sight' and with hindsight it appears inconceivable that the abuse was not recognised and reported.

Using the idea that abuse may be identified from recognition of warning signs from awareness through to direct personal knowledge, it becomes clear that, to be safer, schools need to address issues along the whole continuum (see Table 11.3). Schools should focus on overcoming the barriers to reporting less tangible concerns, properly document accumulating concerns and consider how information is analysed and acted upon, implementing clear procedures where behaviour meets the threshold for formal investigation by statutory agencies. Underpinning all of this is the need to put safeguarding at the heart of a school, explicitly acknowledging and believing that abuse can happen and having a strong commitment to listen to pupils, staff and parents in a context which promotes a transparent and open culture.

Table 11.3 A framework for protection and prevention

Awareness	Accumulating concerns	Direct personal knowledge
← What needs to happen? →		
A culture where expectations around behaviour and conduct are explicit A culture that values and trusts intuitive responses and the gut feelings of staff and pupils alike Opportunities for staff and pupils to discuss low-level concerns in a non-judgemental trusting environment through children being able to identify key staff they feel comfortable to talk to and for staff through supervision, for example Attention paid to the health of the dynamics in the staff team. Splits and factions recognised and addressed	A school leadership style which balances openness, flexibility and approachability with adherence to effective management systems and processes for recording and reviewing safeguarding concerns, including consultation with local authority safeguarding teams as a feature in addition to referrals Maintenance of a culture where safeguarding is the golden thread throughout the organisation – in staff meetings, performance management and governance	Development of clear and well-understood policies and procedures in line with national guidance Sound legal advice and HR support for schools in order to provide a clear direction when potentially abusive behaviour is identified Development of good working relationships with specialist professionals in local authorities to support effective safeguarding practice
← A listening organisation →		
A code of conduct for pupils that sets out behaviour that they should expect from adults and each other Safeguarding training which includes recognising abuse in institutions		

Protection and prevention: Managing the aftermath

The organisational response to the management of the aftermath of children having been abused is likely to have a critical impact on the continuing safety of pupils. It would be tempting to fall back on the notion that once the abuse has been uncovered and the perpetrator brought to justice the organisation is now 'safe' and all those involved need to 'move on' and put the situation behind them. This approach fails to recognise the traumatic nature of the event and the emotional impact, both on pupils who may have been abused and on the whole-school community (including parents) who may feel that they have been not only manipulated but also have a personal sense of responsibility for not having recognised the abuse at the time. William Vahey was extremely popular with many staff and pupils, as was Thomson-Glover, and a range of feelings would have been experienced by those who not only failed to recognise the abuse but also actively encouraged some of the behaviours that allowed it to take place. The serious case review into the abuse by Vahey notes that the initial response from the school's management, and to a certain degree parents, was to recognise that the education of pupils needed to continue and to focus on 'moving on'. This failed to account for the traumatic nature of the revelations and the range of feelings in the school, including those of pupils and staff who felt that they had been groomed, and for pupils who felt that they had failed to protect their siblings and peers. In addition, those same staff were then responsible for developing a protective environment in the school whilst also needing time both to acknowledge and process what had happened to them personally. If the nature of the events is not acknowledged and discussed, the message that feelings need to be kept under wraps may simply perpetuate the lack of openness that allowed the abuse to happen in the first place and will almost certainly result in low morale amongst staff.

Protecting children in education: Final thoughts

A thread running through the five cases in this chapter is the complexity of the systems and relationships that need to be navigated by those charged with protecting pupils from harm and with managing adults who work with children. Staff members (both teaching and non-teaching) throughout the school are juggling often apparently competing demands: being required to improve educational attainment whilst attending to the welfare of pupils, develop good relationships with parents whilst maintaining professional boundaries, and fostering a good working relationship with colleagues. Whilst safeguarding policies and procedures are essential, so too are clear lines of accountability and governance structures which include working in cooperation with outside agencies. Within schools, a code of conduct for staff (which is implemented and where the consequences of failure to adhere are understood by all) is essential. Furthermore, pupils and their parents need to understand what is acceptable behaviour from the adults who work with them and be listened to when they identify and report behaviour that makes them feel uncomfortable.

There is no room for complacency; safeguarding in education is challenging for all involved, and people intent on abusing children will exploit any weaknesses or loopholes in the system, just as Savile did in the institutions where he gained the power and control that allowed his prolific abuse to take place. Equally it should be recognised that some children may be inherently more vulnerable to abuse – for example, those with special education needs, where they are already recognised as in need of protection or support. It is also clear from this sample that children and families who are more wealthy and privileged are not immune from exploitation by abusers. All staff working in schools and particularly those with senior leadership roles need the support and challenge that will help them to manage the complexity of the safeguarding system and maintain an environment where a strong, positive culture keeps the safeguarding of the children as a priority and which is both unattractive and a deterrent to those who are intent on abusing children. Moreover, all those working with children need to be equipped to identify potentially abusive behaviours, and to be empowered to report such concerns in an open and supportive environment where boundaries are explicit and adhered to.

References

BBC News (2014) *Teacher Kelly Burgess Sentenced for Pupil Sex.* 7 April. Accessed on 22 December 2016 at www.bbc.co.uk/news/uk-england-bristol-26927378

Craddock, M. (2012) *The Sexual Abuse of Pupils in a First School: Serious Case Review.* North Somerset Safeguarding Children Board. Accessed on 26 July 2017 at www.northsomersetlscb.org.uk/serious-case-reviews.htm

Department for Education (DfE) (2016) *Keeping Children Safe in Education.* London: DfE. Accessed on 14 August 2017 at www.gov.uk/government/publications/keeping-children-safe-in-education--2

Dobbs, L. (2016) *The Stuart Hall Investigation Report.* Volume 3 of The Dame Janet Smith Review Report. London: BBC. Accessed on 14 August 2017 at http://downloads.bbci.co.uk/bbctrust/assets/files/pdf/our_work/dame_janet_smith_review/hall/stuart_hall_investigation.pdf

Harrington, K. (2013) *Child G: A Serious Case Review.* East Sussex Local Safeguarding Children Board. Accessed on 26 July 2017 at www.eastsussexlscb.org.uk/wp-content/uploads/pdf/SCR%20Child%20G%20December%202013%20PUBLISHED.pdf

HM Government (2015) *Working Together to Safeguard Children: A Guide to Inter-Agency Working to Safeguard and Promote the Welfare of Children.* London: DfE. Accessed on 14 August 2017 at www.gov.uk/government/publications/working-together-to-safeguard-children--2

Independent (2015) *Headteacher Anne Lakey Jailed for Eight Years for Sex with Underage Male Pupils.* Accessed on 22 December 2016 at www.independent.co.uk/news/uk/crime/headteacher-anne-lakey-jailed-for-eight-years-for-sex-with-underage-male-pupils-10341544.html

Jones, P. (2016) *Investigation into Safeguarding Issues at Clifton College Arising from Prosecution of X.* Bristol: Clifton College.

Kirkup, B. and Marshall, P. (2014) *Jimmy Savile Investigation: Broadmoor Hospital – Report to West London Mental Health NHS Trust and the Department of Health.* West London Mental Health NHS Trust. Accessed on 11 August 2017 at www.gov.uk/government/publications/jimmy-savile-investigation-broadmoor-hospital

Lampard, K. and Marsden, E. (2015) *Themes and Lessons Learnt from NHS Investigations into Matters Relating to Jimmy Savile: Independent Report for the Secretary of State for Health.* London: Department of Health. Accessed on 11 August 2017 at www.gov.uk/government/uploads/system/uploads/attachment_data/file/407209/KL_lessons_learned_report_FINAL.pdf

Mail Online (2009) *A Devout Christian with a Glittering Career Ahead, so Why Did Helen Goddard Throw It Away with a Lesbian Affair with a Pupil?* 22 August. Accessed on 26 July 2017 at www.dailymail.co.uk/news/article-1208286/A-devout-Christian-glittering-career-ahead-did-Helen-Goddard-throw-away-lesbian-affair-pupil.html

McAlinden, A. (2012) *'Grooming' and the Sexual Abuse of Children: Institutional, Internet and Familial Dimensions*. Oxford: Oxford University Press.

National Crime Agency (NCA) CEOP (2013) *CEOP Thematic Assessment. The Foundations of Abuse: A Thematic Assessment of the Risk of Child Sexual Abuse by Adults in Institutions*. Accessed on 26 July 2017 at www.nationalcrimeagency.gov.uk/publications/49-ceop-institutions-thematic-assessment/file

Raynes, B. (2011) *Executive Summary of the Serious Case Review Written about Teacher Mr X.* Hillingdon Local Safeguarding Children Board. Accessed on 26 July 2017 at http://ineqe.com/chscb/wp-content/uploads/2015/02/CDM_n5002617_v1_Serious_case_review_Hillingdon_May_2011.pdf

Scott-Moncrieff, L. (2015) *Independent Oversight of Investigations into Matters Relating to Jimmy Savile at Schools and Children's Homes.* London: Department for Education. Accessed on 15 August 2017 at www.gov.uk/government/uploads/system/uploads/attachment_data/file/407429/Independent_oversight_report_relating_to_JS_at_schools_and_childrens_homes_26_feb_2015.pdf

Smallbone, S. (2013) *Sexual Abuse in Schools*. JDiBrief Series. London: UCL Jill Dando Institute of Security and Crime Science. Accessed on 26 July 2017 at www.ucl.ac.uk/jdibrief/crime/sexual-abuse-in-schools

The Times (2016) *Arrogant Teacher Has Sex with Boy 16 after School.* 21 April. Accessed on 22 December 2016 at www.thetimes.co.uk/article/arrogant-teacher-had-sex-with-boy-16-after-school-6g5jdfbtx

US Department of Education (2004) *Educator Sexual Misconduct: A Synthesis of Existing Literature.* Washington, DC: US Department of Education.

Wonnacott, J. (2010) *Nursery Z Serious Case Review.* Plymouth Safeguarding Children Board. Accessed on 15 August 2017 at www.cscb-new.co.uk/downloads/Serious%20Case%20Reviews%20-%20exec.%20summaries/SCR_Archive/Plymouth%20SCR%20-%20Nursery%20Z%20(2010).pdf

Wonnacott, J. and Carmi, E. (2016) *Southbank International School Serious Case Review.* Hammersmith and Fulham, Kensington and Chelsea and Westminster Local Safeguarding Children Board. Accessed on 26 July 2017 at www.rbkc.gov.uk/pdf/Southbank%20SCR%20REPORT%2012%201%2016.pdf

12

SAFEGUARDING IN SPORTS

JANE FOSTER, ALICE CAVE, ADELE EASTMAN, DAVID SMELLIE AND MARIA STRAUSS

Introduction

Whilst Jimmy Savile was known to some extent as a 'sportsman', in that he was a keen runner who was often photographed undertaking charity running events, there is no particular suggestion that he used his sporting activity to facilitate abuse. However, as we have come to understand more about the way in which he exploited his position and the vulnerabilities of organisations, there are striking similarities to what is increasingly coming to be understood about abuse perpetrated by prominent figures in sports.

Recent revelations about sport were triggered by the public disclosure in late 2016 by former professional footballer Andy Woodward, followed by a number of other prominent current and former football players, of significant racial abuse and of sexual abuse of the most severe nature. All of them took the brave step of waiving their right to anonymity in order to bring to the attention of the police, the public and the regulators the extent to which young players had been abused by adults who were ostensibly promoting them in their game.

The response by the media, from other former players and the public to these initial disclosures has been far reaching, with the National Police Chiefs' Council reporting in April 2017 that the police investigation (Operation Hydrant) had been made aware of 560 potential victims (96% of whom are male and were aged between 4 and 20 years at the time of the abuse), and 252 named suspects relating to 311 sports clubs ranging from amateur and grass roots to Premier League football teams (National Police Chiefs' Council, 2017).

The public and victim/survivor reactions to Andy Woodward's initial disclosure have been very similar to the disclosures made by those coming forward after the disclosures about the abuse by Savile (referred to by Peter Spindler in Chapter 9 as 'the Yewtree effect'), where, once victims became aware that they were 'not the only one', they felt empowered to come forward. It is more than probable that the public response to the disclosures about Savile had an impact on those who have come forward more recently to disclose abuse by adults working in other fields. Indeed, Andy Woodward was quoted as saying, 'Because of the Jimmy Savile situation, I think people in this country have just said "enough is enough" – people want to do something about this' (Dickinson, 2016).

However, whilst in the UK the media focus has been on (and subsequent disclosures are largely related to) football, it is unlikely that such abuse will be unique to that sport or that lessons learned as a result of the current investigations will be solely relevant to football. Furthermore, whilst the initial media focus was on whether those engaged in leading sport had and continue to have adequate criminal background checks prior to engagement, and on encouraging parents to check club practice before sending their child to participate in sporting activity, it is much more likely that the outcome of the current investigations will not be restricted to those issues. Rather, as borne out by the Savile inquiries, the case of Jerry Sandusky in the US and previous investigations into sexual abuse in sport (e.g. the NSPCC report *In at the Deep End* into abuse in UK swimming in the 1990s (Myers and Barrett, 2002)), it seems likely that it will be the *culture* of the organisations and settings managing contact with children in sport which is the characteristic that contributes most towards keeping them safe.

This chapter will examine the systems and the culture in sport which have facilitated the actions of those who have wanted to and succeeded in abusing children in their care – factors which in many ways are demonstrably similar to those which facilitated Savile and others to abuse at the BBC, and which enabled abuse by adults working in other institutions such as schools and residential settings. For this purpose, it is always worth considering the point made by Peter Davies (then CEO of the Child Exploitation and Online Protection Centre, CEOP): 'Children in institutional settings are not only at risk from adults who are inclined to abuse them sexually; but also from adults who either fail to notice abuse or, if they do, fail to report it' (NCA CEOP, 2013).

Children and adults (including those of all ages with disabilities and other adults at risk) are encouraged to engage in sport at every level – from amateur community groups to the Olympics. Sport is increasingly promoted as a method of social inclusion for the most disadvantaged, as well as a way in which to improve health and wellbeing. Added to this, the fact that most talented sportsmen and women are seen and promoted as role models puts them in a position to exert influence in terms of the behaviour and aspirations of children and young people. The wealth and iconic status of some players also adds to their power, with young people not only aspiring to succeed in their chosen sport but also to achieve for themselves that same celebrity status and the glamorous lifestyle which goes alongside it. At an elite level the skills and prowess of sportsmen and women (and those who select and coach them at that level) are very often used to the benefit of sporting participants lower in the hierarchy. This beneficial influence should not be underestimated, but such authority and status can and has been exploited in the past. At the other end of the spectrum there are the volunteers (in the UK over a million per week, many of whom are parents or fans) who support the system from grass roots to professional levels and have unprecedented access to children as coaches, drivers and scouts.

Therefore, at the same time as acknowledging the tangible benefits for the thousands of children playing sport each week, there is increasing awareness of the risks of abuse to some children by those professionals and volunteers who work alongside them.

What is known from research

The 2011 University of Edinburgh and NSPCC study of the experiences of children participating in organised sport in the UK (Alexander, Stafford and Lewis, 2011) found that, overall, participating in organised sport is a positive experience for most children and young people. However, it also found that a negative sporting culture can also exist and be accepted as 'the norm', thus allowing it to be perpetuated by peers, coaches and other adults.

Young people in the study (an online survey of 6000 young people followed by 89 in-depth telephone interviews) reported widespread emotionally harmful treatment (75%) and unacceptable levels of sexual harassment (29%). Self-harm was reported equally by both boys and girls (10%). Reports of sexual harm featured at a low level (3%). Peers were the most common perpetrators of all forms of harm reported in the research, with coaches sometimes failing to challenge it effectively. Coaches were the second most common perpetrators of harm, with their role in harm increasing as young athletes advanced through the competitive ranks. The authors observed:

> Disrespectful and emotionally harmful treatment of young people was common in children's experiences of sport in the UK. For some this included being criticised about performance in ways that could be disproportionate or unhelpful, being humiliated, teased, sworn at or bullied. While it occurred mainly between team mates and peers, a third of those reporting it said coaches were involved, either participating directly, or indirectly by creating an ethos where such behaviour was condoned or not effectively dealt with. (p.94)

Most of the sexual harm reported in the survey took place in the form of sexualised behaviour between boys, mainly involving exposing and flashing between peers. While this was shrugged off by young people at the time as 'boys being boys', on reflection it could be viewed differently (and would certainly now be classified as 'peer on peer abuse'), with young people expressing the view that more could have been done by adults involved in their sports to prevent it happening.

The risk of abuse, it seems, appears to increase just before young athletes reach their best performance level, when they have the most to lose and may therefore be most open to manipulation.

Reports of abuse of children participating in sport is not new; in 1995 Paul Hickson, former UK Olympic swimming coach, was jailed for 17 years for sexual abuse, over a period of 15 years, of teenagers in his elite squads (Independent, 1995).

The subsequent disclosure of the abuse of other young swimmers impacted on almost a hundred UK swimming clubs at the time, and the NSPCC's *In at the Deep End* report examining the culture of clubs and risk factors (Myers and Barrett, 2002) used case files from the Amateur Swimming Association (ASA) on the 78 coaches accused by children of abuse between January 1997 and February 2001.

The report, the first of its kind, identified that 'abusers' spend time 'grooming' young swimmers, as well as their parents, often singling the child out for one-to-one training to make sure the swimmer felt special and their parents privileged. It recommended that information on individuals who pose a risk should be shared by local sports organisations and with national sporting bodies, governing bodies must make it their priority to protect children, and coaching licences in all sports should be considered.

A co-author of the report commented that 'whilst the vast majority of coaches and teachers are neither abusers or potential abusers, it must be recognised that this relationship between the young sports person and their coach can create the potential for abuse' and that 'all types of abuse happen in swimming and lessons can be learnt that are applicable to all sports' (Daily Mail, 2011).

The NSPCC Child Protection in Sport Unit (CPSU), which developed mandatory safeguarding structures for all of the UK's main sports, was established in 2001 following the disclosure of abuse scandals in swimming, convictions from the 1990s and joint discussion with the governing bodies of swimming, diving, athletics and gymnastics who met with the then Sports Council (since renamed

Sport England), the NSPCC and the National Coaching Foundation to discuss the need for regulation of child protection in sport.

In 2001 the Football Association (FA) commissioned a five-year research project to map out child protection across all clubs and to monitor a new strategy of child protection for under-18s. However, two or so years into the project, funding was withdrawn, much to the concern of the lead researcher, expert on abuse in sports settings Professor Celia Brackenridge (BBC News, 2016).

Almost 20 years later there are still common themes in the reports of the abuse of young players in sport, and repeated lessons from investigations both in the UK and elsewhere do not seem to have been learned. The examples below, taken from the Freeh Report (Freeh, 2012) into the abuse committed by assistant coach Jerry Sandusky in the USA and current cases in the UK, bear this out.

The Sandusky case

In 2012 in the USA, Gerald Sandusky, a former assistant coach for the nationally famous Penn State Nittany Lions American football team, was convicted of 45 counts of sexual abuse of children during the period 1994–2009 and was sentenced to 60 years' imprisonment. The subsequent inquiry report (Freeh, 2012) notes that it is likely that the abuse may have started as early as the 1970s. Criminal charges were also filed against the athletic director and several other senior university leaders who had had knowledge of the allegations and who had not only failed to report the issues, but who had also in some cases obstructed the course of justice. In June 2017, a former president of Penn State and two other former university administrators were each sentenced to at least two months in jail for failing to alert authorities to a 2001 allegation against Sandusky.

Following this scandal, the Board of Directors commissioned an investigation from ex-Director of the FBI Louis Freeh and his legal firm, who made 120 recommendations to improve safeguarding for children and vulnerable adults. The executive summary of the Freeh Report states, 'The most saddening finding by the special investigative Counsel is the total and consistent disregard by the most senior leaders at Penn State for the safety and welfare of Sandusky's child victims' (p.14).

The officials concealed Sandusky's activities from the Board of Trustees; they had caused additional harm by alerting Sandusky of what they knew; and they empowered Sandusky to attract potential victims to the campus and football events by allowing him to have continued, unrestricted and unsupervised access to the University's facilities and affiliation with the University's prominent football programme. Indeed, that continued access provided Sandusky with the very currency that enabled him to attract his victims. Some coaches, administrators and football programme staff members ignored the red flags of Sandusky's behaviour and no one warned the public about him.

In addition, there was a university president who discouraged dissent and discussion, there was a lack of awareness of whistle-blowing policies and child abuse issues, and a culture of reverence for the (financially very valuable) football programme. The handling of the matter did not comply with the Clery Act which, in effect, places a duty on US colleges to report crime on campus, demonstrated by the fact that the report describes how a janitor had seen concerning events but did not report for fear of reprisals, and another janitor had concluded that the University would close ranks to protect the football programme rather than act.

In terms of the response of officials when the allegations did come to light, no one had notified their superiors of concerns even though Sandusky was known to have showered with boys and had been seen doing so. In fact the official response was to advise Sandusky not to shower with children rather than to explore any further impact. The Board were not advised of what senior members of staff knew.

Equally it was noted that the Board of Trustees did not have oversight of safeguarding and that staff did not feel accountable to their seniors. This meant that there was not regular reporting of risk and that the college therefore did not comply with the reporting requirements of the Clery Act.

Further findings in regard to child protection in university programmes was that background checks had been inadequate, policies were applied inconsistently across departments and there was a lack of training. There was no oversight of compliance with what policies and procedures were in place – some departments had relaxed HR arrangements and overall the department was under-staffed and under-resourced.

A further conclusion was that, in order to avoid bad publicity, the most powerful leaders at the University had repeatedly concealed critical facts relating to Sandusky from the authorities.

UK cases

In the UK there has not, as yet, been an outcome of any formal inquiry into historical abuse in football and, apart from the figures relating to the number of victims, alleged abusers and clubs impacted, the information in the public domain comes largely from media reports. What is known from the media is that historically there has been significant abuse of boys by coaches, drivers and scouts and it is alleged that issues of concern were drawn to the attention of some managers at the time and not acted upon. There appears to have been a commonality in the form that abuse took in different clubs (e.g. 'routine' penis flicking and 'balming'), some perpetrators and managers operated in more than one club and that organised abuse cannot be ruled out. In addition to the alleged perpetrators a number of managers are, at the time of writing (June 2017), suspended and under investigation.

All of this suggests that there was a culture at the time where boundaries were undefined, where people knew of behaviours that were at least bullying and targeted, and at worst sexually motivated and abusive.

The links between those working in coaching and scouting in football and higher management of the clubs is yet to be established, but it is likely that lack of information sharing, coupled with the lack of independence of those with whom information was shared (who often had the closest links to the community under investigation), may have contributed to creating a system where investigators were less likely to take challenging and unpopular action.

How does this accord with what we have learned from Savile?

For the most part we do not know whether children or parents of children abused in sporting organisations complained at the time of the alleged abuse; it is often the case that parents were not aware (and may not even be aware now) of abuse perpetrated against their children.

Reflecting back to Chapter 2 of this book we can, however, see significant similarities with the BBC in the way in which sporting organisations were governed and managed, and the way in which policies and procedures were devised and implemented – there are also significant similarities in the way in which celebrity status or power was managed.

Taking these similarities in the order in which they are addressed in Chapter 2, the following probably contributed to abusers in sport being able to offend either undetected or unreported.

Lack of clarity about expectations of behaviour and conduct and lack of clarity around organisational values and process in response to complaints and allegations

As seen above in relation to the Sandusky case, codes of conduct, their implementation and a lack of understanding of how to challenge inappropriate behaviour observed by colleagues can have a significant effect in facilitating abuse. In June 2014, speaking in the House of Commons (and quoted in Lampard and Marsden, 2015, para.2.11) about the publication of the first tranche of reports into Savile and the NHS, the Secretary of State for Health, Jeremy Hunt, said:

> ...where patients report abuse, they need to be listened to, whatever their age, whatever their condition, and there needs to be proper investigation of what they report. It is deeply shocking

> that so few people felt that they could speak up and even more shocking that no one listened to those who did speak up.

Furthermore, the lack of appropriate action taken when abuse *had* been reported and recognised was shocking. Even more significant than Savile's behaviour, which, although it was known to have caused annoyance and distress in terms of constant sexual innuendo and behaviour towards junior staff, was left largely unchallenged, it has transpired that in several of the publicly disclosed cases from 2016 to date senior management in the organisations concerned had failed to take appropriate action. A significant number of the alleged abusers in football (Bennell, Ormond, Langford and Torbett) *had* previously been known and convicted for sexual offences against children but had been allowed to continue in, or resume, their roles. For example, it has been alleged that high-level meetings were held within the club in relation to Bennell's behaviours and his relationship with young boys but that these had only resulted in an agreement that he should not be alone with boys and should not arrange overnight stays. One explanation given was that it was difficult for the club to act on the word of an individual who had not made a formal complaint. However, it was clear that other staff had also noticed untoward behaviour and had expressed their concerns. The FA had been contacted at the time but had found no case to answer (Taylor, 2016). It has also been separately alleged that managers at the time had been alerted to the concerns by an anonymous letter of complaint.

In the case of football abusers, many were probably protected by lack of procedure around conduct and, in the case of scouts, some coaches and volunteers by employment/volunteer arrangements such as zero-hour and sessional contracts which make it harder to hold an individual to account but simpler to dismiss/or cease to use them if there are issues around competence. There are also similarities to the Stoke Mandeville (Johnstone and Dent, 2015) and Leeds Teaching Hospitals (Proctor *et al.*, 2014) investigation reports' revelations of the disconnection of senior managers from the 'frontline' of their organisations, which meant that they did not know about widespread rumours and concerns about Savile's general behaviour or of the individual complaints made by victims of his abuse (Lampard and Marsden, 2015). A lack of structure around accountability in sports organisations (and in the case of football at least) can mean that conduct issues relating to sessional or temporary staff do not come to the attention of senior management and so are not dealt with appropriately.

Effect of celebrity and status

In Chapter 2 it is observed that the Savile inquiries illustrate the way in which the personal characteristics of, and perceptions about, an abuser can influence colleagues and organisational responses in ways that impede what might otherwise have been protective factors for potential victims. What is common to all is the effect their status had on the way they were regarded by bystanders and on organisational processes, which they were then able to exploit, consciously or otherwise, to behave as they wished.

Reference has been made above to systems where investigators were more likely to wish to preserve appearances and reputation than take challenging, and very probably unpopular, action. Where elite and celebrity players in sport are involved this seems to particularly be the case. In March 2016, some eight months before the current scandal regarding abuse came to light, the NSPCC issued strong criticism of then Premier League Football Club Sunderland FC over their handling of the case involving Sunderland player Adam Johnson. Johnson, also an England national team member, continued to play for Sunderland whilst on bail for sexual offences against a 15-year-old female fan, and was subsequently convicted of three sexual offences against a child and sentenced to six years' imprisonment. Commenting on the club's decision to allow him to continue to play, in a letter to the FA chairman, Greg Dyke, the NSPCC chief executive, Peter Wanless, described it as illustrating 'a perverse sense of priorities at the top of the Club' and went on to say that:

> we are worried that this could be a cultural problem in football as a whole…this is not about one rogue player who behaved badly,

> but a club that seemingly did not have child protection policies embedded into their culture. It was not equipped to handle these allegations and seemingly did not deal with them appropriately, or indeed seriously. (Halliday, 2016)

In terms of status, it is without doubt that coaches and scouts for elite players in sport wield considerable power, not least in their ability to 'make or break' a successful sporting career. It is clear that the alleged abusers in football groomed parents, children and the wider sporting community, and that their power was almost absolute, demonstrated in the words of survivors below:

> I was saying, 'Mum, Mum, which man was it that spotted me? What did he say?' It was so exciting. Because when you've been playing in local leagues and you're desperate for someone to spot you, and then someone does, it is amazing. (Phillips, 2016)

> These boys were at an age when all they wanted in the world was to be a footballer. If they were abused, maybe they were simply too scared to tell someone or they were terrified it was their football career over. (BBC, 2016)

> I didn't know what was going on to be fair – I knew what I wanted to get, and I thought this is what I had to go through. I knew it was wrong but I just went with it. (Masters, 2016a)

> His coaching ability was the best in the country so he had that tool, but then alongside that he also had the power in football and as person to manipulate as many people as he wanted because it's your inspiring dream to be a footballer. (Masters, 2016b)

> Every kid is feeling that. The feeling of that drive and then having someone in control of you, they go hand in hand. He had the power to do what he wanted, when he wanted, where he wanted. (Masters, 2016b)

Access to buildings, grounds and facilities

It is now known that Savile was a frequent visitor to a number of settings and was given significant unrestricted and largely unsupervised access to grounds and buildings, and this contributed to his ability to perpetrate abuse to an unprecedented degree. What is becoming apparent from the disclosures made in the UK in 2016 is that lone contact with children participating in sport has not been unusual in the past. Coaches, scouts and kit men have all had access to children in settings where access is not strictly monitored. In addition, there have been other opportunities for one-to-one access – for example, driving children between events, to and from away matches and on tours, meaning that children are away from other protective adults and personal coaching. In some ways the culture of football in the past was that coaches and other club staff were the players' friends and it would not have been unusual for players to be invited to their homes, or even to stay with them whilst taking part in trials. Whilst it would be comforting to think that this would not happen now, there are still causes for concern about the way in which trips are staffed and run, and about parents' and children's understanding of what is acceptable behaviour.

Conclusions and recommendations

Professor Richard Wortley, Director of the Jill Dando Institute of Security and Crime Science at University College London, is quoted in the Lampard and Marsden (2015) review into lessons arising from Savile's actions in the NHS:

> I actually don't think much can be learned by looking at the motivations and dispositions of Jimmy Savile. If you want my opinion the reason he did it was because he could, and we could debate whether he was a paedophile…or we could debate whether he was after power or whatever it is. At the end of the day, he did it because he could get away with it… I think there is a real danger if we start thinking about Savile as a special case and how he can be explained by his unique motivations and dispositions

> and we think we can identify people like him we will solve the problem; I just think that is misguided. (para.8.13)

If we take this to be true then what can be learned from the extensive abuse perpetrated by Savile is that organisational culture and governance, coupled with knowledge of how offenders operate and empowerment of children, parents, managers and peers to recognise and feel confident to report potentially abusive behaviour, are key to the prevention of abuse. To do this effectively will require systemic change directed at prevention rather than reacting to 'rogue individuals' who have already committed abuse.

As is the case in education, sports clubs from local grass roots to elite sport should give guidance to staff, volunteers, coaches and scouts about the kind of behaviour which is acceptable and that which is not. Clear sanctions need to be in place and applied. Sports players also need to know what to expect of the adults around them and how to report concerns. To achieve this, adults working with children, whatever their status (employed, sessional, volunteer), must be subject to and fully understand the club's safeguarding policy and practice. This should be extended to include contractual arrangements which ensure that those occupations – for example, scouting and personal coaching, which have traditionally been viewed as being outside the umbrella of core corporate identity embraced by the organisation as a part of their brand – are included. In addition, HR procedures relating to conduct and disciplinary matters should be consistent across all departments of the organisation and supported by clear guidance on the application of employment decisions.

As referred to in Chapter 2, publicised whistle-blowing policies and procedures, when followed, also support appropriate responses to issues of concern and help to communicate to both service-users and staff the organisational commitment to openness and addressing difficult issues when necessary. The Huston Inquiry (Social Services Inspectorate, 1994) recommends that agencies providing services to children or vulnerable adults should ensure that a culture of openness and trust is fostered within the organisation, in which staff can share any concerns about the conduct of colleagues and be assured that these will be received in a sensitive manner. Staff should also be encouraged, through formal and informal channels of communication, to question, express concerns or pass on significant information.

Listening to children and their parents is equally important. There should be an understanding from the highest level of any organisation that 'anonymous' does not mean 'malicious', and that if concerns are raised in this way or if individuals are the subject of rumour or gossip they should be treated just as seriously as they would be if they were formal complaints. Without doubt, looking back there were a number of people in sport whose conduct and behaviour had been subject to discussion and conjecture for some time, and the exposure of these people did not come as a surprise to those who knew them. It is also clear that in many cases, before public exposure, the concerns had not been treated with the degree of seriousness required. Where safeguarding concerns are identified it is important that the alleged abuser is subject to the appropriate process, that referrals are made to the police, social care and the regulators and that the individual is not permitted merely to leave the organisation without the matter being properly investigated and reported. Risk to reputation or the potential for loss of key talented players cannot be allowed to take precedence over safeguarding.

To realise these ambitions, sports organisations must also adopt clear reporting structures and record management systems which identify what concerns have been raised, how concerns were investigated (and by whom), the outcome and any required actions such as training or risk assessment.

The implementation and effectiveness of the practice and systems recommended above should all be subject to oversight and challenge by sports regulatory bodies and inspectorates. It would be premature to conclude that a lack of regulation or inspection may have contributed to abuse in football or other sports. That is something which the current reviews (e.g. the review into non-recent abuse to be conducted by Clive Sheldon QC, commissioned by the FA in December 2016) will consider and report on. The reported cases from the 1990s and earlier will have taken place in an environment where there was little or no regulation of safeguarding in the sports sector. A glance across at the schools sector illustrates very clearly the transformation in the safeguarding of children in schools over the last 20 years, and the rigorous inspection of schools by the Office for Standards in Education, Children's Services and Skills (Ofsted), whereby schools cannot be rated higher in their overall inspection than their rating for safeguarding. This leaves two possible conclusions for the sports sector – that the absence of regulation and inspection has been a contributory factor to abuse and that there may still be a case today for strengthening regulation and inspection in the future.

Finally, as noted in Chapter 2, it is tempting to view Savile's offending as a feature of outdated systems that could never occur now. It is possibly worth reflecting that in 2010, prior to Savile's death, the suggestion that anyone could have behaved as he did would have been met with a similarly incredulous response. In UK football, whilst the majority of cases are historical in nature, a significant proportion, we understand, reflect cases of abuse dating from 2011 to the present day, with almost three times more potential victims coming forward to allege abuse than in the case of Savile. This appears to demonstrate that the environment in which abuse takes place has existed even recently and probably still does today.

This does not mean that there has not been progress. The NSPCC Child Protection in Sport Unit (CPSU) has consistently pushed for the regulation and inspection of safeguarding in sport, albeit at sector rather than governmental level. Research carried out by Rhind and colleagues at Brunel University London formed the basis of the Unicef international safeguards for children in sport (International Safeguarding Children in Sport Working Group, 2016), now seen as the best practice model other countries could follow. However, what we have learned from research and regulation can only succeed in supporting safeguarding if its intent is comprehensively embraced by those with the power to make change happen. Football has provided all sport with a graphic illustration of the consequences of not making those changes. There can be no excuse for not learning those lessons for sports in all settings.

References

Alexander, A., Stafford, A. and Lewis, R. (2011) *The Experiences of Children Participating in Organised Sport in the UK.* The University of Edinburgh/NSPCC Child Protection Research Centre. Accessed on 14 August 2017 at www.nspcc.org.uk/globalassets/documents/research-reports/experiences-children-participating-organised-sport-uk-main-report.pdf

BBC News (2016) 'Football Sex Abuse: Crewe Launch Child Abuse Investigation.' Accessed on 26 July 2017 at www.bbc.co.uk/news/uk-38118429

Daily Mail (2011) 'Abuse Risk for Swimming Youngsters.' Accessed on 26 July 2017 at www.dailymail.co.uk/news/article-136710/Abuse-risk-swimming-youngsters.html

Dickinson, M. (2016) 'The Week Football Was Left Distraught by the Horror of Paedophilia.' *The Times*, 26 November. Accessed on 14 August 2017 at www.thetimes.co.uk/edition/sport/the-week-football-was-left-distraught-by-the-horror-of-paedophilia-wwrsl3c77

Freeh, L. (2012) *Report of the Special Investigative Council Regarding the Actions of the Pennsylvania State University Related to Child Sexual Abuse Committed by Gerald A. Sandusky.* Washington, DC: Freeh, Sporkin and Sullivan. Accessed on 17 August 2017 at http://media.pennlive.com/midstate_impact/other/REPORT_FINAL_071212.pdf

Halliday, J. (2016) 'NSPCC: Football Clubs Not Taking Child Protection Seriously Enough.' *Guardian*, 24 March. Accessed on 17 August 2017 at www.theguardian.com/uk-news/2016/mar/24/nspcc-football-clubs-not-taking-child-protection-seriously-enough

Independent (1995) 'Former Olympic Coach Gets 17 Years for Sex Attacks.' 27 September. Accessed on 26 July 2017 at www.independent.co.uk/news/former-olympic-coach-gets-17-years-for-sex-attacks-1603214.html

International Safeguarding Children in Sport Working Group (2016) *International Safeguards for Children in Sport.* Accessed on 14 August 2017 at https://downloads.unicef.org.uk/wp-content/uploads/2014/10/International-Safeguards-for-Children-in-Sport-version-to-view-online.pdf?_ga=2.218624985.1394161336.1502732046-507908007.1502732046

Johnstone, A. and Dent, C. (2015) *Investigation into the Association of Jimmy Savile with Stoke Mandeville Hospital: A Report for Buckinghamshire Healthcare NHS Trust.* Amersham: Buckinghamshire Healthcare NHS Trust. Accessed on 12 August 2017 at www.speakingoutinvestigation.com/Downloads/Speaking%20out%20investigation/2902210_Investigation%20into%20the%20Association%20of%20Jimmy%20Savile%20with%20Stoke%20Mandeville%20Hospital.pdf

Lampard, K. and Marsden, E. (2015) *Themes and Lessons Learnt from NHS Investigations into Matters Relating to Jimmy Savile: Independent Report for the Secretary of State for Health*. London: Department of Health. Accessed on 11 August 2017 at www.gov.uk/government/uploads/system/uploads/attachment_data/file/407209/KL_lessons_learned_report_FINAL.pdf

Masters, J. (2016a) *UK Football Child Abuse: Wayne Rooney Offers Support.* Accessed on 26 July 2017 at http://edition.cnn.com/2016/11/25/football/uk-football-child-sexual-abuse

Masters, J. (2016b) *Andy Woodward: Paedophile Football Coach Could 'Do What He Wanted'.* Accessed on 26 July 2017 at http://edition.cnn.com/2016/11/28/football/andy-woodward-sexual-abuse-football/index.html

Myers, J. and Barrett, B. (2002) *In at the Deep End: A New Insight for All Sports from Analysis of Child Abuse.* London: NSPCC.

National Crime Agency (NCA) CEOP (2013) *CEOP Thematic Assessment. The Foundations of Abuse: A Thematic Assessment of the Risk of Child Sexual Abuse by Adults in Institutions.* Accessed on 26 July 2017 at www.nationalcrimeagency.gov.uk/publications/49-ceop-institutions-thematic-assessment/file

National Police Chiefs' Council (2017) *Operation Hydrant – Football Abuse Statistics up to and Including 30 June 2017.* Accessed on 26 July 2017 at www.npcc.police.uk/NPCCBusinessAreas/OtherWorkAreas/OpHydrant/FootballAbuseStats.aspx

Phillips, A. (2016) *Robbie Savage Fears There are Hundreds of Football Child Abuse Victims as He Demands Full Investigation.* Accessed on 26 July 2017 at www.mirror.co.uk/sport/football/news/robbie-savage-fears-hundreds-football-9337323

Proctor, S., Galloway, R., Chaloner, R., Jones, C. and Thompson, D. (2014) *The Report of the Investigation into Matters Relating to Savile at Leeds Teaching Hospitals NHS Trust.* Leeds: Leeds Teaching Hospitals NHS Trust. Accessed on 11 August 2017 at www.leedsth.nhs.uk/assets/Uploads/40482-LIBRA-main-accessible-v2.3.pdf

Social Services Inspectorate (1994) 'An Abuse of Trust': The Report of the Social Services Inspectorate Investigation into the case of Martin Huston, January, Belfast, DHSSNI.

Taylor, D. (2016) 'Crewe Were Warned about Barry Bennell but He Stayed On, Says Former Board Member.' *Guardian*, 25 November. Accessed on 14 August 2017 at www.theguardian.com/football/2016/nov/25/crewe-barry-bennell-former-board-member

Appendix

SAVILE-RELATED REPORTS

MARCUS EROOGA

Introduction

These are the institution-/organisation-based reports published between 2013 and 2016, organised by setting. It is a common feature that given the length of time since the events described a number of the inquiries had difficulty verifying the facts of some of the allegations.

However, it should be noted that not all the allegations against Savile relate to individual institutions or organisations and the most comprehensive overview of the offending believed to have been perpetrated by him can be found in *Giving Victims a Voice*, the report of Operation Yewtree (see the Gray and Watt, 2013 entry below).

What the individual reports do provide is a vivid account of the behaviour of a prolific sex offender whose behaviour ranged from the brazenly opportunistic to deliberate and purposeful grooming. More importantly in the context of this book, they also provide a detailed insight into the shortcomings of the culture, processes and procedures in so many institutions and organisations that manifestly failed to prevent his abusive behaviour.

Relating to the BBC

Pollard, N. (2012) *The Pollard Review: Report.* London: BBC. Accessed on 11 August 2017 at http://downloads.bbc.co.uk/bbctrust/assets/files/pdf/our_work/pollard_review/pollard_review.pdf

An independent review into the management by the BBC of a Newsnight investigation relating to allegations of sexual abuse of children by Savile. Published 18 December 2012.

Smith, J. (2016) *The Independent Review into the BBC's Culture and Practices during the Jimmy Savile and Stuart Hall Years*. London: BBC. Accessed on 11 August 2017 at www.bbc.co.uk/bbctrust/dame_janet_smith

This three-volume report was published after multiple delays to avoid prejudicing the trial of Stuart Hall. Because of a potential conflict of interest in relation to Stuart Hall, who had also been an active abuser, the parallel inquiry relating to Stuart Hall at the BBC was conducted by former High Court Judge Dame Linda Dobbs but published as part of the Dame Janet Smith Inquiry report. Published 25 February 2016.

Relating to the criminal justice system

Gray, P. and Watt, P. (2013) *Giving Victims a Voice: A Joint Report into Sexual Allegations against Jimmy Savile*. London: Metropolitan Police. Accessed on 11 August 2017 at www.nspcc.org.uk/globalassets/documents/research-reports/yewtree-report-giving-victims-voice-jimmy-savile.pdf

The joint Metropolitan Police Service and NSPCC inquiry into allegations of sexual abuse against Savile under Operation Yewtree was established following the broadcast of an ITV programme on 4 October 2012 alleging abuse by Savile. The police indicated that from those allegations they considered there to be 214 substantive crimes that would have been investigated were Savile alive. Published 11 January 2013.

Her Majesty's Inspectorate of Constabulary (HMIC) (2013) *'Mistakes Were Made': HMIC's Review into Allegations and Intelligence Material Concerning Jimmy Savile between 1964 and 2012*. London: HMIC. Accessed 11 August 2017 at www.justiceinspectorates.gov.uk/hmicfrs/media/review-into-allegations-and-intelligence-material-concerning-jimmy-savile.pdf

Her Majesty's Inspectorate of Police review into allegations and police intelligence material concerning Jimmy Savile between 1964 and 2012. Published 12 March 2013.

Levitt, A. (2013) *In the Matter of the Late Jimmy Savile: Report to the Director of Public Prosecutions*. London: CPS. Accessed on 11 August 2017 at www.cps.gov.uk/news/assets/uploads/files/savile_report.pdf

Report by Alison Levitt QC, Principal Legal Advisor to the Director of Public Prosecutions, into Crown Prosecution Service (CPS) decision-making in relation to allegations arising out of Operation Ornament (see Savell, 2013 below). Published 11 January 2013.

Operation Hibiscus. Accessed on 16 August 2017 at https://northyorkshire.police.uk/news/north-yorkshire-police-statement-regarding-late-scarborough-mayor-peter-jaconelli-record-1972-released-freedom-information-act-crown-prosecution-service

North Yorkshire Police publicised the results of Operation Hibiscus, an investigation into allegations of historic sexual abuse made against the late Scarborough mayor Peter

Jaconelli (who died in 1999) and Jimmy Savile. Thirty-two cases related to Jaconelli, ranging from indecent assault, inciting a child to engage in sexual activity and gross indecency to rape, all incidents occurring between 1958 and 1998. The remaining five, ranging from sexual assault (or indecent assault under current law) to rape, related to Savile between 1979 and 1988. No report was published, but Operation Hibiscus was publicised by North Yorkshire Police on 18 December 2014.

Savell, J. (2013) *Report into Operation Ornament.* Guildford: Surrey Police.

Report by Detective Chief Superintendent Savell for Surrey Police on the 2007–2009 Operation Ornament investigation of allegations of abuse by Savile at Duncroft Residential School and elsewhere in the 1970s. Published 11 January 2013.

Savell, J. (2015) *Operation Outreach Report.* Guildford: Surrey Police. Accessed on 11 August 2017 at http://mandatenow.org.uk/wp-content/uploads/2015/04/Operation-Outreach-29-4-2015-11186-link.pdf

Report by Detective Chief Superintendent Savell on Operation Outreach, an investigation of allegations made after his death of sexual abuse by Jimmy Savile at Duncroft Approved School during the 1970s when Surrey Police said that he carried out 46 sexual assaults on 22 pupils and one visitor and to consider whether any school staff or other visitors had committed a criminal offence. Published 29 April 2015.

Relating to the Department of Health

In total, 45 NHS investigations were conducted, into 35 hospitals, five mental health units, two children's hospitals, one ambulance service, one hospice and one children's convalescent home. They were published in two tranches, in 2014 and 2015. Further reports from the Hull and East Yorkshire Hospitals Trust and Guy's and St Thomas' NHS Trust, London, were published subsequently.

26 June 2014 reports

On 26 June 2014 a series of reports of inquiries into sexual abuse and inappropriate treatment by Jimmy Savile in 27 NHS hospitals and one hospice were published. The Department of Health had asked Kate Lampard QC, former deputy chair of the Financial Ombudsman Service, to provide independent oversight of the 28 reports published in June 2014 and the 17 published in February 2015. Her initial oversight report was also published on that date. The NHS Savile Legacy Unit provided independent oversight of other reports published in 2015.

In a number of cases no evidence of abuse was found (often due to the length of time since the alleged incident and the consequent difficulty in gathering evidence), but the majority of the reports detail the organisations' use of the inquiry process to review their policies and procedures to ensure they are as robust as possible to meet current expectations.

Links to all the reports are listed on the Department of Health website, although not all are still 'live'. Where possible alternative links have been provided. Accessed on 11 August 2017 at www.gov.uk/government/collections/nhs-and-department-of-health-investigations-into-jimmy-savile

Aitkenhead, S. with Hale, L. (2014) *The Royal Marsden NHS Foundation Trust Investigation into Matters Relating to Jimmy Savile*. London: Royal Marsden NHS Foundation Trust.

Review of an allegation that Savile may have been involved in an incident at the Royal Marsden Hospital, London, in the mid-1980s. No evidence was found.

Bean, S. (2014) *Investigation into the Contact that Jimmy Savile Had with the Bethlem Royal and Maudsley Hospitals*. Accessed on 11 August 2017 at www.slam.nhs.uk/media/272480/js_investigation_slam_final_report.pdf

Review of an allegation that Savile may have visited the Maudsley Hospital, London, in 1964–1965. No evidence was found for this.

Carter, C. (2014) *Report of the Investigation into Matters Relating to Jimmy Savile and Leavesden Hospital*. Hatfield: Hertfordshire NHS Trust.

Review of an allegation that Savile may have visited Leavesden Hospital, Hatfield, in the 1970s, but this could not be verified.

Cobham, G. (2014) *Investigation into the Association of Jimmy Savile with Odstock Hospital, Salisbury*. Salisbury NHS Foundation Trust. Accessed on 11 August 2017 at www.salisbury.nhs.uk/AboutUs/media/Documents/Salisbury%20NHS%20Foundation%20Trust%20Jimmy%20Saville%20Investigation.pdf

Savile is believed to have visited Odstock Hospital, Salisbury, in the late 1980s but no allegations were made.

Corcoran, S. (2014) *Investigation into Allegations That Jimmy Savile Abused Two Patients on the Booth Hall Hospital Site circa 1959–1975*. Manchester: Central Manchester University Hospitals NHS Foundation Trust. Accessed on 11 August 2017 at www.cmft.nhs.uk/media/967688/jimmy%20savile%20report.pdf

Two alleged incidents of abuse in 1959 against a seven–eight-year-old girl and a nine–ten-year-old girl in 1974 at Booth Hall Children's Hospital, Manchester. No conclusive evidence was found that the events described by both alleged victims took place.

Draycott, C. and McAdam, M. (2014) *Report of an Investigation into an Allegation Relating to a Reported Incident Involving Jimmy Savile at the Former Saxondale Hospital, Nottingham, in or around 1971/72*. Nottinghamshire Healthcare Trust. Accessed on 11 August 2017 at www.nottinghamshirehealthcare.nhs.uk/independent-investigations

An alleged incident in 1971–1972 at a hospital disco at Saxondale Mental Health Hospital, Nottinghamshire, hosted by Savile. The alleged victim was a teenager who was a local resident, not a patient, who said that Savile had raised her skirt by a 'few inches' with a 'hockey stick'. The inquiry found her account credible.

Edge, W. (2014) *Investigation into a Visit Made by Jimmy Savile to Shotley Bridge Hospital and Information Received Concerning Jimmy Savile and Dryburn Hospital*. Darlington: County Durham and Darlington NHS Foundation Trust. Accessed on 11 August 2017 at www.cddft.nhs.uk/media/380213/dryburn%20and%20shotley%20bridge%20hospitals%20(final%20investigation%20report).pdf

A woman working at Dryburn Hospital, Durham, was said to have alleged that in the 1990s young girls and boys were lured to hotels on behalf of Savile. A visit by Savile to Shotley Bridge Hospital, Consett, in 1981 was also reviewed for possible impropriety. No evidence of abuse was found in relation to either, though other possible concerns were identified.

Firth, K. (2014) *Investigation into the Allegations Made Regarding Jimmy Savile in Relation to the Mid Yorkshire Hospitals NHS Trust*. Accessed on 11 August 2017 at www.midyorks.nhs.uk/jimmy-savile-report

Two allegations against Savile, both at Dewsbury and District Hospital. One was that in 1969 Savile sexually assaulted a 15-year-old patient by attempting to lay on top of her and 'French kissing' her. The investigators concluded that the alleged incident took place as she described. The other was that in 2010, when Savile was a member of the official visiting party at the official opening of a new facility, a member of staff overheard Savile make a lewd comment about a young woman who was an inpatient.

Gloster, J. (2014) *Investigation into an Allegation against Jimmy Savile at Digby Hospital, Exeter*. Totnes: Devon Partnership NHS Trust. Accessed on 11 August 2017 at www.theexeterdaily.co.uk/news/local-news/savile-exeter-rape-full-report

An allegation of rape by Savile in his motor home of a 25-year-old female patient in 1970 at the Russell Clinic, Digby Hospital, Exeter. The inquiry found no reason to doubt the veracity of her account.

Henderson, A., Rae, M. and Morgan, S. (2014) *Internal Investigation into Allegations Made by Four People Relating to Jimmy Savile at Moss Side Hospital (Previously Part of Ashworth Hospital, Mersey Care NHS Trust)*. Liverpool: Mersey Care NHS Trust. Accessed on 11 August 2017 at www.merseycare.nhs.uk/media/1881/mersey-care-report-into-savile-investigation-26-june-2014.pdf

Three alleged incidents and a fourth allegation of periodic abuse between 1971 and 1985: in an allegation involving the sexual abuse of a female patient between 1971 and 1973, the alleged victim declined to be involved in the inquiry; an allegation

that in 1984–1985 a female patient was encouraged to sit on Savile's knee and he then put his hand on her thigh under her nightdress and moved it upwards towards her intimate area; a report by an ex-patient that whilst Savile was visiting the hospital in 1975 he saw him put his hand down the front of a female patient's clothing; and an ex-member of staff in the education department for 21 years from 1975 advised that there were many rumours at the time regarding Savile's visits. The inquiry concluded that there is a possibility that abuse did occur at Moss Side Hospital but that owing to the fact that Savile appears to have been escorted at all times while he was in the hospital it is likely that, if did occur, it was limited (though still distressing) in its nature.

Hogston, S. and Cheverton, S. (2014) *Investigation Report Following Allegations Made as Part of Operation Yewtree and Sue Ryder – Wheatfields Hospice: A Report for the Council of Trustees.* Sudbury: Sue Ryder. Accessed on 11 August 2017 at www.sueryder.org/~/media/files/about-us/wheatfields_%20investigation%20 report.pdf

One alleged incident in 1978 involving inappropriate touching and inappropriate comments to a 16-year-old girl visiting Wheatfields Hospice, Leeds. The inquiry concluded that the incident took place.

Jessop, S. (2014) *Investigation into Allegations about Jimmy Savile at De La Pole Hospital, Hull.* Hull and East Yorkshire NHS Trust.

An allegation from a nurse that she had been told by another nurse that in 1969–1970 Savile had sexually assaulted a 14–16-year-old female patient while she was in orthopaedics traction. The patient was contacted and denied that any incident took place. See also the Hull and East Yorkshire Hospitals Trust (2015) entry below.

Kirkup, B. and Marshall, P. (2014) *Jimmy Savile Investigation. Broadmoor Hospital: Report to the West London Mental Health NHS Trust and the Department of Health.* London: West London Mental Health NHS Trust. Accessed on 11 August 2017 at www.gov.uk/government/publications/jimmy-savile-investigation-broadmoor-hospital

Eleven allegations of sexual abuse, six of them involving patients, two staff and three children, at Broadmoor Psychiatric Hospital, Berkshire. The report said the number of cases of abuse it found was likely to be an underestimate.

Laban, A. and Gilby, S. (2014) *Investigation into an Allegation against Jimmy Savile by a Patient at the Former St Catherine's Hospital, Birkenhead.* Birkenhead: Wirral Community NHS Trust.

An allegation that Savile came to the ward in which a 14-year-old was an inpatient at St Catherine's Hospital, Birkenhead, in 1964. It was alleged that, while accompanied by the hospital matron and some other people, he pulled back the covers of her bed, jumped into bed with her and touched both the top of her thigh and her bottom. He quickly got off the bed and moved on. The inquiry considered the allegation both credible and convincing.

Lampard, K. (2014) *Independent Oversight of NHS and Department of Health Investigations into Matters Relating to Jimmy Savile: An Assurance Report for the Secretary of State for Health*. London: Department of Health. Accessed on 11 August 2017 at www.gov.uk/government/uploads/system/uploads/attachment_data/file/323488/Assurance_report.pdf

The quality assurance report ordered by the Health Secretary to confirm the quality and robustness of the various NHS-related investigations undertaken.

Maloney, A., Clancy, K. and Backhouse, R. (2014) *Investigation into Allegations Related to Jimmy Saville* [sic] *and Prestwich Psychiatric Hospital, Manchester*. Greater Manchester West Mental Health NHS Foundation Trust. Accessed on 11 August 2017 at www.gmmh.nhs.uk/download.cfm?doc=docm93jijm4n988.pdf&ver=1907

One allegation that a female member of the public was brought onto the Prestwich Psychiatric Hospital, Manchester, site around 1960 and sexually abused by Savile. The inquiry concluded there was nothing in the witness's statements that would cause them to question the veracity of her account of what happened.

Mellor, P. (2014) *Report Regarding an Alleged Incident at The Royal Hospital, Portsmouth Involving Jimmy Savile*. Portsmouth Hospitals NHS Trust. Accessed on 11 August 2017 at www.porthosp.nhs.uk/Downloads/Publications/Public-Interest/JS%20Portsmouth%20Report%20May%202014%20v7.pdf

The complainant had been informed by a cleaner at the Portsmouth Royal Hospital when he attended a follow-up outpatient clinic in 1968 when he was 16 years old that when he was an inpatient at the hospital, as a result of a road traffic accident, she had seen him being sexually assaulted by Savile when the complainant was unconscious. The inquiry concluded that it is highly unlikely that the alleged incident took place.

Miller, E. (2014) *Investigation into the Potential Involvement of Jimmy Savile with Whitby Hospital*. York Teaching Hospital NHS Foundation Trust. Accessed on 11 August 2017 at www.yorkhospitals.nhs.uk/about_us/reports_and_publications/investigation_into_the_potential_involvement_of_jimmy_savile_with_whitby_hospital

One alleged incident of Savile inappropriately touching a female member of staff at Whitby Hospital between 1964 and 1968. The inquiry concluded that the incident took place.

Parker, A. (2014) *Investigation into the Role Jimmy Savile played at Queen Victoria Hospital NHS Foundation Trust, East Grinstead*. Queen Victoria Hospital NHS Foundation Trust.

One allegation of a female patient in her 20s being groped by Savile at Queen Victoria Hospital NHS Foundation Trust, East Grinstead, in 1954.

Parkyn, S. and Baker, J. (2014) *Investigation Report into an Allegation of Abuse by Jimmy Savile at Great Ormond Street Hospital for Children NHS Foundation Trust.* London: Great Ormond Street Hospital for Children NHS Foundation Trust. Accessed on 11 August 2017 at www.gosh.nhs.uk/news/press-releases/2014-press-release-archive/savile-report-press-statement

A former patient claimed Savile sexually abused another inpatient in 1971 at Great Ormond Street Hospital, London. The inquiry concluded that it was not possible to say for certain if the alleged incident on the premises of Great Ormond Street Hospital took place.

Plumridge, C. (2014) *Investigation into the Possible Association of Jimmy Savile with Hammersmith Hospital, London.* Imperial College Healthcare NHS Trust (ICHT).

Two alleged incidents involving Savile and a friend of his making inappropriate comments to a 13-year-old girl. No evidence was found that Savile had a relationship of any sort with the hospital that enabled him to abuse his position as a celebrity.

Proctor, S., Galloway, R., Chaloner, R., Jones, C. and Thompson, D. (2014) *The Report of the Investigation into Matters Relating to Savile at Leeds Teaching Hospitals NHS Trust.* Leeds Teaching Hospitals NHS Trust. Accessed on 11 August 2017 at www.leedsth.nhs.uk/assets/Uploads/40482-2901955-Libra-Executive-SUMMARY-accessible2.pdf

Sixty people came forward to say they had been abused between 1962 and 2009 at Leeds General Infirmary. They were aged between 5 and 75. Thirty-three of the 60 were patients and 19 were children. The inquiry indicated that it had received genuine and serious allegations of sexual abuse, of unwelcome contact and of inappropriate behaviour perpetrated by Savile. It was also alleged he posed for photographs and performed sex acts on corpses in the Leeds hospital mortuary. Whilst no evidence of this was found, the inquiry concluded that Savile's interest in the mortuary was 'not within accepted boundaries' (p.98).

Rayani, M. and Williams, S. (2014) *Investigation into an Allegation Concerning Jimmy Savile at Cardiff Royal Infirmary, New Years Day 1963/1965.* Cardiff and Vale University Health Board. Accessed on 11 August 2017 at www.cardiffandvaleuhb.wales.nhs.uk/js-report

One allegation involving inappropriate touching of a patient in her early 20s that occurred between 1963 and 1965 at Cardiff Royal Infirmary. The inquiry was unable to reach a conclusion about whether the incident took place.

Smith, F. (2014) *Investigation into the Role Jimmy Savile Played at Barnet and Chase Farm NHS Trust.* Accessed on 11 August 2017 at http://s3-eu-west-1.amazonaws.com/files.royalfree.nhs.uk/News/Final_version_BCF_JS_confidential_inquiry_110614-1.pdf

One alleged incident of Savile having sex with a corpse in 1985 at Barnet General Hospital, Hertfordshire. No evidence was found that Savile was ever involved with Barnet General Hospital.

Thompson, H. and Trewin, J. (2014) *Investigation into the Possible Involvement of Jimmy Savile with Wythenshawe Hospital (University Hospital of South Manchester NHS Foundation Trust): A Report for the University Hospital of South Manchester NHS Foundation Trust.* Wythenshawe University Hospital of South Manchester NHS Foundation Trust. Accessed on 27 August 2017 at www.infotextmanuscripts.org/djetc/rolf-v-report-2.pdf

A patient raised a concern about a conversation with another patient at Wythenshawe Hospital, Manchester, in 1962–1963 that suggested Savile's behaviour at his home was possibly abusive. No evidence was identified by the investigation team to suggest that Jimmy Savile was ever present on the Wythenshawe Hospital site.

Walters, S. (2014) *Investigation into an Allegation That Jimmy Savile Abused Children at Roecliffe Manor in the Village of Woodhouse Eaves, Leicester in the Late 1950s/1960s.* University Hospitals of Leicester NHS Trust. Accessed on 11 August 2017 at www.leicestershospitals.nhs.uk/aboutus/performance/publications-and-reports/roecliffe-manor-jimmy-savile-investigation

An allegation of Savile sexually abusing a child at Roecliffe Manor children's convalescent home in the late 1950s or early 1960s. No evidence was found of abuse.

Walters, S. (2014) *Investigation into an Allegation of Attempted Unsupervised Access by Jimmy Savile and Three Associates at Queen Mary's Hospital, Carshalton.* Carshalton: Epsom and St Helier University Hospital. Accessed on 11 August 2017 at www.infotextmanuscripts.org/djetc/rolf-v-report-1.pdf

A claim that Savile and three associates were denied access to a hospital ward at Queen Mary's Hospital, Carshalton, by a nurse in the 1970s. The inquiry found no evidence that Savile ever attended St Mary's Hospital.

Wilcox, S. (2014) *An Investigation into an Allegation of Two Incidents Involving Jimmy Savile at High Royds Hospital, Leeds.* Leeds and York Partnership NHS Trust.

Two alleged incidents of abuse at a hospital gala at High Royds Hospital, Leeds, in 1988. A 44-year-old patient alleged that Savile put his hand up her skirt and rubbed her bottom and that she also observed him doing the same to a nurse. A 20-year-old member of staff described him being 'free with his hands', putting them round females' waists and then upwards, cupping under breasts and up skirts. The inquiry concluded that the allegations were true.

NO REPORTS PUBLISHED

An investigation by the Newcastle upon Tyne Hospitals NHS Foundation Trust found that Savile visited the children's wards of the Royal Victoria Infirmary in 1986/1987 and 1991, as well as Newcastle General Hospital in the early 1990s. It concluded that nothing untoward occurred and that Savile was continually supervised. No report was published.

Investigations at two hospitals, the Royal Free Hospital, London, and Pennine Acute NHS Hospitals Trust, found nothing to report.

26 February 2015 reports

Seventeen NHS reports were published on 26 February 2015. They addressed 74 new allegations of abuse, of which 66 were at Stoke Mandeville Hospital. A 'lessons learnt' report by Kate Lampard and Ed Marsden, based on all the investigations, was also published.

Allen, R. and Bull, P. (2015) *Investigation into the Role and Actions of Johnny Savile at Springfield Hospital.* South West London & St George's Mental Health NHS Trust.

No evidence of Savile visiting the hospital, but the report investigated seven allegations of sexual assault by his brother, Johnny, who worked there as a recreation officer in the late 1970s.

Barlow, J. and Scott, S. (2015) *A Further Investigation into the Allegations of Abuse by Jimmy Savile at Leeds General Infirmary.* Leeds Teaching Hospitals NHS Trust. Accessed on 12 August 2017 at www.leedsth.nhs.uk/assets/Uploads/A-Further-Investigation-into-the-Allegations-of-Abuse-by-Jimmy-Savile-at-Leeds-General-Infirmary-A-Report-by-Leeds-Teaching-Hospitals-NHS-Trust.pdf

An update to the original report published in 2014. The original report identified 60 alleged victims and the update identified a further six, though not all allegations were considered to be substantive.

Britton, L. (2015) *Report of an Investigation into an Allegation Concerning Jimmy Savile.* Leeds and York Partnership NHS Foundation Trust.

An investigation into the background of a statement made by a former student nurse on a month's placement in a MENCAP nursery in Leeds in 1981–1982 that advised her not to let Savile near the children. The inquiry concluded that it was likely that the warning was issued based on a perception that Savile was a 'disruptive nuisance' as opposed to a sexual threat.

Brown, M. and Harte, R. (2015) *Investigation into the Allegation of Assault by Jimmy Savile at St Martin's Hospital, Canterbury in 1969.* Maidstone: Kent and Medway NHS and Social Care Partnership Trust. Accessed on 12 August 2017 at www.kmpt.nhs.uk/downloads/News/JS%20report-Final.pdf

Concluded that on the balance of probability it is unlikely Savile visited St Martin's Hospital, Canterbury.

Department of Health (2015) *Jimmy Savile NHS Investigations: Update on the Themes and Lessons Learnt from NHS Investigations into Matters Relating to Jimmy Savile.* London: Department of Health. Accessed on 24 October 2017 at https://www.basw.co.uk/resource/?id=4806

Collated responses from all NHS Trusts and NHS Foundation Trusts on progress in meeting the Lampard and Marsden (2015) report recommendations (see below).

Fidler, I., Landreth, L. and Noble, P. (2015) *An Investigation into the Association and Activities of Jimmy Savile with Rampton Hospital, Its Patients, Staff and Services.* Nottinghamshire Healthcare NHS Trust. Accessed on 12 August 2017 at www.nottinghamshirehealthcare.nhs.uk/independent-investigations

Four separate allegations of sexually inappropriate behaviour at Rampton Psychiatric Hospital, Nottingham, with individuals who were not patients; one was a young child at the time. No evidence was found of such inappropriate conduct with patients. The report also describes 'patient outings' led by Savile to Scarborough, where they had tea with mayor Peter Jaconelli (see Operation Hibiscus entry, above).

Harris, E. and Fenwick, L. (2015) *Investigation into Jimmy Savile and Any Association with the Newcastle upon Tyne Hospitals NHS Foundation Trust – Response to a Specific Allegation Received in October 2014.* Newcastle upon Tyne Hospitals NHS Foundation Trust. Accessed on 12 August 2017 at www.newcastle-hospitals.org.uk/downloads/file6162939401.pdf

One allegation relating to a former child day patient at Royal Victoria Hospital, Newcastle, in 1998 that could not be substantiated as the person did not wish to be interviewed.

Johnstone, A. and Dent, C. (2015) *Investigation into the Association of Jimmy Savile with Stoke Mandeville Hospital.* Aylesbury: Buckinghamshire Healthcare NHS Trust. Accessed on 12 August 2017 at www.speakingoutinvestigation.com/Downloads/Speaking%20out%20investigation/2902210_Investigation%20into%20the%20Association%20of%20Jimmy%20Savile%20with%20Stoke%20Mandeville%20Hospital.pdf

The inquiry found that Savile abused 63 people – patients, staff, visitors, volunteers and charity fundraisers – almost half of whom were aged under 16 and ten under the age of 12. Just over 90 per cent of the victims were female.

Lampard, K. and Marsden, E. (2015) *Themes and Lessons Learnt from NHS Investigations into Matters Relating to Jimmy Savile: Independent Report for the Secretary of State for Health.* London: Department of Health. Accessed on 12 August 2017 at www.gov.uk/government/uploads/system/uploads/attachment_data/file/407209/KL_lessons_learned_report_FINAL.pdf

A summary and consideration of the themes and lessons learnt from the various NHS investigations.

Linley, C. and Owen, J. (2015) *Investigation into Matters Relating to Jimmy Savile at Birch Hill Hospital.* Manchester: Pennine Acute Hospitals NHS Trust Board. Accessed on 12 August 2017 at www.pat.nhs.uk/homepage/FINAL%20REPORT%2014%20%20JANUARY%202015%20v%20x%2025%20PDF.pdf

No evidence Savile had any association with Birch Hill Hospital, Rochdale, but it is possible abuse was carried out by an unidentified male.

Lloyd, H., Stead, R., Jones, K. and Coleman, J. (2015) *Investigation into a Visit Made by Jimmy Savile to Bensham Hospital.* Gateshead Health NHS Foundation Trust. Accessed on 12 August 2017 at www.qegateshead.nhs.uk/jsbh

No specific allegations but suggestions of inappropriate behaviour towards staff at Bensham Hospital, Gateshead, including 'hand licking'.

Mattin, A. and Sheridan, A. (2015) *Investigation into an Allegation against Jimmy Savile at Shenley Hospital, London.* Central and North West London NHS Foundation Trust. Accessed on 12 August 2017 at www.cnwl.nhs.uk/wp-content/uploads/Savile_Report.pdf

One incident that could not be confirmed at Shenley Hospital, London, but the alleged victim's account was considered credible.

Proctor, S., Jones, C. and Galloway, R. (2015) *NHS Savile Legacy Unit: Oversight Report. An Assurance Report for the Secretary of State for Health.* London: Department of Health. Accessed on 11 August 2017 at www.gov.uk/government/uploads/system/uploads/attachment_data/file/407192/Savile_Legacy_Unit_final_report.pdf

The NHS Savile Legacy Unit (SLU) was established by the Department of Health in July 2014 to provide assurance and oversight of NHS investigations arising from new allegations of abuse concerning Jimmy Savile in the NHS.

Reid, J. (2015) *Investigation into an Allegation that Jimmy Savile Visited Crawley Hospital during the 1970s and 1980s.* Brighton: Sussex Community NHS Trust. Accessed on 12 August 2017 at www.sussexcommunity.nhs.uk/downloads/about-us/trust-reports/sct-jimmysavile-report.pdf

No specific allegation of an assault, but concern about Savile's presence at the Crawley Hospital site.

Tynan, J. and O'Hear, S. (2015) *Investigation into Matters Relating to Jimmy Savile and the Rochdale Children's Hospital (Scott House) (now a Part of Calderstones Partnership NHS Foundation Trust).* Accessed on 12 August 2017 at www.calderstones.nhs.uk/media/files/Safeguarding/savile%20legacy%20unit%20report%20calderstones.pdf

No specific allegation of an assault but concern that Savile had taken children out in his car from Rochdale Children's Hospital (Scott House). No evidence of a visit by Savile and no allegation of abuse.

Vize, C. and Klinck, B. (2015) *Legacy Report – Further Investigation into the Association of Jimmy Savile with Stoke Mandeville Hospital.* Aylesbury. Buckinghamshire Healthcare NHS Trust. Accessed on 12 August 2017 at www.speakingoutinvestigation.com/Downloads/Speaking%20out%20investigation/2903580_Legacy%20Report%20Accessible%20v2.pdf

Following the preparation of the substantive report into Savile and his contact with Stoke Mandeville Hospital, but prior to its publication, information was received from six other people alleging abuse at Stoke Mandeville. This investigation therefore considered these additional matters.

Warner, K. and Page, S. (2015) *The Report of the Investigation into Matters Relating to Savile's Association with the Ambulance Services in Yorkshire.* Wakefield: Yorkshire Ambulance Service NHS Trust. Accessed on 12 August 2017 at www.yas.nhs.uk/Publications/Savile_Report_29_01_.pdf

No allegations of sexual abuse by Savile, but his relationship with Yorkshire ambulance services that gave him access to staff and patients was considered entirely inappropriate.

Williams, H. (2015) *Report of the Investigation of an Incident of Concerning Savile During His Visit to the Opening of the Interim Medium Secure Unit (on Tyson West 1 Ward) at the Bethlem Royal Hospital on 18th September 1980.* South London and Maudsley NHS Foundation Trust. Accessed on 12 August 2017 at www.slam.nhs.uk/media/341184/savile_investigation_-_february_2015.pdf

An inconclusive investigation as it was not possible to substantiate a claim of abuse at Bethlem Royal Hospital, London, by Savile.

Subsequent reports

Hull and East Yorkshire NHS Trust (2015) *Investigation into Allegations about Jimmy Savile at De La Pole Hospital, Hull.* Hull and East Yorkshire NHS Trust. Accessed on 28 September 2017 at www.humber.nhs.uk/news/Investigation-into-allegations-about-Jimmy-Saville-at-De-La-Pole-Hospital.htm

Unpublished report into an allegation involving Jimmy Savile and a patient and a second allegation from a former student nurse about an event in the 1970s. The conclusion by Humberside Police and the report author was that the event involving the patient took place, and the author further concluded that the event involving the former student nurse is likely to have taken place.

Saunders, D. (2016) *Investigation into Information about Jimmy Savile in Relation to Guy's and St Thomas' NHS Trust.* London: Guy's and St Thomas' NHS Foundation Trust. Accessed on 27 August 2017 at www.guysandstthomas.nhs.uk/resources/about-us/board-minutes/2016-board-papers/january/[9]%20GSTT%20Savile%20Report%202016.pdf

Two reported visits by Jimmy Savile to Guy's Hospital: one in 1980 when he is said to have visited a children's ward unaccompanied at night time, and a second visit when he opened the private unit at the hospital in 1990. During this second visit the report found that two staff recalled accounts of inappropriate behaviours toward them, including being over-familiar, touching and kissing them.

Relating to the Department for Education

Published on 26 February 2015 (at the same time as the second group of Department of Health reports) were 14 reports ordered by the Department for Education and an independent oversight report commissioned by the Department for Education from mental health and human rights lawyer Lucy Scott-Moncrieff.

Summary

In her report, Ms Scott-Moncrieff (2015) states that 19 separate pieces of information were investigated, resulting in 13 reports and one executive summary (listed below). Six were allegations of sexual assault and three of sexual abuse. The remaining ten pieces of information were about sightings of Savile or reports of visits by him to schools and children's homes, but contain no specific allegation of abuse. They came from former residents of children's homes, former pupils and former local authority employees, and others are from members of the public. They ranged from an informant who had witnessed Savile with a girl sitting on his leg (but had not witnessed any impropriety) to an informant reporting that Savile visited a school.

Specific allegations about abuse or assault were said to have occurred at a fundraising visit at a school, at a party at a children's home, on an outing to a park from a children's home, and on an outing to a television studio.

None of the investigations were able to reach firm conclusions about whether the alleged abuse took place, although many of them considered the informant credible. It was the lack of corroborating evidence that prevented any definitive conclusion. In view of this individual report, descriptions are not given below.

Links to all the reports are listed on the Department for Education website, although not all are still 'live'. Where possible, alternative links have been provided. Accessed on 15 August 2017 at www.gov.uk/government/speeches/investigations-into-abuse-in-childrens-homes-and-schools

Avis, M., Ward, F., Harrison, W. and Ferguson, L. (2015) *Investigation into an Allegation about Jimmy Savile Concerning Henshaws School: A Report for Henshaws Society for Blind People.* Manchester: Henshaws Society for Blind People.

Bradley, J. (2015) *An Investigation into Reported Contact by Jimmy Savile with Bassetlaw Special School.* Nottinghamshire County Council.

Clarke, S. (2015) *The Report of the Investigation into Matters Relating to the Late Jimmy Savile and Barnardo's Children's Homes in Ilford.* Accessed on 15 August 2017 at www.barnardos.org.uk/jsinvestigationfinalreport.pdf

Cooper, B. (2015) *Investigation by Nottingham City Council into Matters Relating to Jimmy Savile's Involvement with Aspley Wood School, Nottingham (Now Closed).* Nottingham City Council.

Hamilton, C. and Hewitt, P. (2015) *Investigation into an Allegation about Jimmy Savile at the 'Little Ride' Children's Home, Brentford, London Borough of Hounslow.* London Borough of Hounslow.

Kelly, S. (2015) *Investigation into an Allegation about Jimmy Savile at Penhurst School.* Watford: Action for Children. Accessed on 15 August 2017 at www.actionforchildren.org.uk/media/3242/action-for-children-savile-investigation-penhurst-school.pdf

Liddicott, S. (2015) *Report of an Investigation into an Allegation about Jimmy Savile and St Leonards Children's Home.* Tower Hamlets Council. Accessed on 15 August 2017 at www.childrenandfamiliestrust.co.uk/wp-content/uploads/2015/02/St-Leonards-Report-V10-1-2-published-26.02.152.pdf

Noble, M. (2015) *Investigation into Allegations about Jimmy Savile at Broome House Children's Home (Broome House), The Sarah Laski Children's Home (Sarah Laski), and the Manchester Taxi Drivers Organisation for Handicapped Children (MTDOHC).* Manchester City Council. Accessed on 15 August 2017 at www.manchester.gov.uk/download/downloads/id/22814/jimmy_savile

Quin, A. (2015) *Investigation into an Allegation about Jimmy Savile at The Hollies Children's Home: A Report for Southwark Council.* Southwark. Accessed 24 October 2017 at www.2.southwark.gov.uk/holliesreport

Scott-Moncrieff, L. (2015) *Independent Oversight of Investigations into Matters Relating to Jimmy Savile at Schools and Children's Homes.* London: Department for Education. Accessed on 15 August 2017 at www.gov.uk/government/uploads/system/uploads/attachment_data/file/407429/Independent_oversight_report_relating_to_JS_at_schools_and_childrens_homes_26_feb_2015.pdf

Shadbolt, J., Channon, N., Morris, A., Morris, K., *et al.* (2015) *Investigation into an Allegation about Jimmy Savile at Colleton Lodge, Colleton Crescent, Exeter, EX2 4DG.* Exeter: Devon County Council. Accessed on 15 August 2017 at www.devon.gov.uk/js-colleton-lodge-report.pdf

Stewart, J. (2015) *Report of an Investigation into Allegations and Information Raised about the Association of Savile with Beechwood Home, Northways School and Notre Dame Grammar School and Any Knowledge of Concerns or Allegations about Savile by Leeds City Council's Children's Social Work Service.* Leeds City Council. Accessed on 15 August 2017 at www.leeds.gov.uk/docs/Savile%20investigation%20report.pdf

White, J. (2015) *Investigation into an Allegation about Jimmy Savile at an Unnamed Children's Home in Bournemouth.* Bournemouth Borough Council. Accessed on 15 August 2017 at www.bournemouth.gov.uk/childreneducation/ChildrensSocialCare/Documents/Bournemouth-Final-Yewtree-Report-03-10-2014.pdf

SUBJECT INDEX

AUTHOR INDEX